THE AGE OF ENTERPRISE:

The Emergence and Evolution of Entrepreneurial Management

Patricia Carr

SCHOOL OF BUSINESS AND MANAGEMENT,
BRUNEL UNIVERSITY

BLACKHALL
Publishing

This book was typeset by Gough Typesetting Services for
Blackhall Publishing
26 Eustace Street
Dublin 2
Ireland

e-mail: blackhall@eircom.net
www.blackhallpublishing.com

ISBN: 1 901657 83 3

A catalogue record for this book is
available from the British Library.

Printed in Ireland by
Betaprint

Contents

Acknowledgements

The author and publisher gratefully acknowledge the following for permission to reproduce copyright material in this book.

Chapter 1, 4, 12: Approach taken to the place of the customer in enterprise culture and excerpts from Du Gay, P. & Salaman, G. 1992: 'The Cult[ure] of the Customer', *Journal of Management Studies,* 29: 5, pp.615-633, Oxford: Blackwell Publishers.

Chapter 2, 3, 4, 7, 11, 12: Approach taken to the exercise of political power in advanced liberal societies and excerpts from: Miller, P. & Rose, N. 1990: 'Governing economic life', *Economy and Society,* 19:1, pp. 1-31, London: Routledge, a member of the Taylor & Francis Group, 11 New Fetter Lane, London EC4P 4EE.

Chapter 5: Framework on entrepreneurship developed by Cunningham, J.B. & Lischeron, J. 'Defining Entrepreneurship', *Journal of Small Business Management,* 25: 1, pp. 45-61, West Virginia University: Bureau of Business and Economic Research.

Chapter 6: Approach taken to the evaluation of government policies and excerpts from Dean, M. 1995: 'Governing the unemployed self in an active society', *Economic and Society,* 24: 4, pp. 559-583, London: Routledge, a member of the Taylor & Francis Group, 11 New Fetter Lane, London EC4P 4EE.

Chapters 6, 7, 8: Discussion on political power in advanced liberal societies and excerpts from Rose, N. & Miller, P. 1992: 'Political power beyond the state: problematics of government', *British Journal of Sociology,* 43: 2, pp. 173-205, London: Routledge, a member of the Taylor & Francis Group, 11 New Fetter Lane, London EC4P 4EE. Grateful acknowledgement is also made to the London School of Economics.

Chapter 7: The research presented in this chapter first appeared in Carr, P. 1998: 'The Cultural Production of Enterprise: Understanding Selectivity as Cultural Policy', *Economic and Social Review,* 29: 1, pp. 27-49, Dublin: Economics and Social Studies.

The development of the argument in this book owes much to a distance learning module entitled *Entrepreneurial Management* written by the author for the Brunel MBA, and a module entitled *Enterprise Culture and Entrepreneurialism* taught by the author on the full-time management degree in Brunel University.

For Paul, with love

Introduction

'For the future, after the enterprise culture. . . .'

(Burrows & Ford, 1998:97)

'Blair starts up enterprise era'

(The Times, March 1999)

'The discourse of enterprise deserves much more serious attention than it has tended to receive . . . especially when reports of its death are so exaggerated'

(*Du Gay & Salaman*, 1992:631)

Conceptual Confusion

Enterprise culture, entrepreneurship and small business have become key topics in management writing over the past 15 years. Despite much academic work there is little agreement among researchers as to the exact meaning of each of these terms. 'Enterprise culture' as many commentators have pointed out is a slippery and devious concept which even its most staunch advocates have great difficulty in defining. Similarly 'entrepreneurship' and the 'entrepreneur' are concepts which are almost as baffling, though more attention has been paid to these, then to their 'enterprise culture' counterpart. This lack of conceptual clarity has had various effects on writing in the area including the tendency to use the terms enterprise culture, entrepreneurship and small business interchangeably, thus treating them synonymously. Alternatively where attempts are made to look at the three concepts separately, the difficulties attached to giving concepts such as 'enterprise culture' and 'entrepreneurship' some solidity, have led to a privileging of small business as an analytical category.

The confusion surrounding the essence and status of the 'enterprise culture' concept has led some commentators such as Burrows (1991:5) to suggest that enterprise culture '...possesses only a small residual explanatory status in accounts of the materiality of (the) restructuring...' of Western economies. From Burrows' points of view enterprise culture has had no independent effect on the material reality of recent economic life in Britain and other countries, save to act as a justificatory discourse for the massive restructuring changes which many countries have experienced. Further this function is now obsolete, as according to Burrows & Ford (1998) we live in a post enterprise culture era. Though certainly contemporary economic restructuring cannot solely be attributed to the political reforms put in place to create an enterprise culture, neither can such reforms be understood in simple 'justification' terms. Thus this book will argue that 'enterprise culture' is much more than a justificatory discourse which has now served its purpose. In doing this it will explore the concepts of 'enterprise culture', 'the entrepreneur' and 'small business individually, while at the same time analysing the tightly interwoven links between them. One overall purpose of such explication is to highlight the emergence of an entrepreneurial management discourse which has had a significant impact on the day-to-day management practices of a range of organisations, including small business, large business and public sector organisations. In addition themes which are at the core of contemporary management writing such as co-operation, feminization, globalization, and their impact on enterprise, entrepreneurship and small business will be examined.

Structure of the book

The book is divided into three sections. The first section will delineate the dimensions of enterprise culture, outlining how these have contributed to the creation of an entrepreneurial management discourse. *Chapter one* focuses on developing an understanding of the concept of 'enterprise culture viewing this as the overarching 'glue' which draws the various strands of the entrepreneurial management subject area together. In doing this it will introduce the notion of an entrepreneurial management discourse, examining the different dimensions of this contemporary form of management style. *Chapter two* explores the changing nature of the state-economy relationship in enterprise culture, focusing on the opposition between the passive and the active state. This classic opposition will be examined within the context of a theme raised in chapter one, namely the privileging of the private sector as the site of enterprise and the most efficient location for the delivery of products and services. In particular, attention will be paid to the process of privatization and its impact on management practice and the business world. *Chapter three* is further involved in exploring the privileging of the private sector as the site of enterprise through an examination of the insertion of private sector management practices into the public sector. Following on from this, *chapter four* examines the shift from a bureaucratic management style to an entrepreneurial management style within large organisations in the private sector. In particular this chapter focuses on the issue of the cultural reconstruction of large organisations, and the similarities between the concepts of corporate culture and enterprise culture.

Section two takes the notion of the entrepreneurial management discourse developed in section one and explores how this discourse impacts on our understanding of the characters of enterprise culture, specifically the entrepreneur, the small business owner and the enterprise advisor. *Chapter five* analyses understandings of the entrepreneur and the activity of entrepreneurship, with the aim of demonstrating how such understandings attempt to influence, shape and regulate the conduct of management. In *chapter six* the rebirth of the small business sector and the special position it occupies within enterprise culture is assessed. Picking up a theme raised in chapter four, this chapter will demonstrate how enterprise culture as a concept does alot more than just provide a rationale for this renaissance, rather it actively impacts on the business activity of small firms. Following on from this (and picking up a theme from chapter two), *chapter seven* will explore the contribution of government policy to the creation of an enterprise culture. In particular it will highlight how government policy, implemented by government enterprise advisors, attempts to mould the behaviour of small business as a way of making it "fully enterprising". In *chapter eight* the relationship between enterprise and growth within the British context is explored by highlighting the growth orientation of small business policies. It will demonstrate how growth policies attempt to mould the behaviour of small businesses. In addition it will contrast the UK ethos of supporting small business to *grow large*, with the Italian ethos of encouraging small business to *stay small*, as a means of demonstrating how different policy approaches impact on small firm activity.

Section three focuses on the evolution of the entrepreneurial management discourse relating this to contemporary issues in the management of enterprise. In *chapter nine* the gender of enterprise is explored, contrasting the 1980s "macho" image of the entrepreneur with the perceived 1990s feminization of enterprise and entrepreneurship. Following on from this and picking up a theme raised earlier, *chapter ten* will explore the issue of co-operation and networking between small firms. In particular the background to- and various forms of inter-establishment co-operative practices, both formal and informal, engaged in by small businesses, will be explored. *Chapter eleven* will explore the changing nature of the world economy and the impact of this on small firm activity and the entrepreneurial management discourse. In particular it will assess how we should understand such change through an exploration of the concepts of internationalisation and globalisation. Finally in *chapter twelve* the book concludes with an assessment of the future of enterprise and entrepreneurial management as a management ethic.

Understanding Enterprise and Enterprise Culture

CHAPTER 1

Enterprise Culture and the Emergence of the Entrepreneurial Management Discourse

Task : Dissertation or treatise on an academic subject.

> I used to have a nightmare for the first six years in office that, when I got the finances right, when I had got the law right, the deregulation etc., that the British sense of enterprise and initiative would have been killed by socialism. I was really afraid that when I had got it all ready to spring back, it would no longer be there and it would not come back...But then it came. The face began to smile, the spirits began to lift, the pride returned.

(Margaret Thatcher, *Sunday Times*, 8 May 1988)

 ## CONCEPTUAL UNCERTAINTY

The creation of an enterprise culture has been a key aim of the UK government over the past two decades. The pursuit of this objective has been used to justify a range of government policies, as well as providing a template for the kind of society that government wants to see emerge.[1] The commitment to the creation of an enterprise culture in the UK was reiterated by Tony Blair in his first Labour Party Conference speech as Prime Minister, when he stated that he wanted Britain "to be a country of enterprise and ambition, where small businesses grow, manufacturing and engineering revive".[2] Nevertheless despite the fact that 'enterprise culture' is a popular and powerful term, and one which is referred to often, it is a difficult and cunning concept which many commentators have great difficulty in defining. It is a term which is heavily loaded with emotion of both a favourable and unfavourable nature, and as with the terms 'entrepreneur' and 'small business' is swathed in con-

---

1. Gamble, A, *The Free Economy and the Strong State* (London: The Macmillan Press) 2nd edn, 1994.
2. Gavron, R, M Cowling, G Holtham & A Westall, *The Entrepreneurial Society* (London: Institute for Public Policy Research) 1998, p. i.

fusion.[3] The ill-defined nature of the enterprise culture concept is clear in the following statement:

> How should enterprise culture be regarded?
>
> Just like some handy little slogan? A simple shorthand way for describing developing small business activity? Some proverbial wisdom about such? Small businesses' new guiding spirit? Or just some well-promoted party political trademark? Maybe the latest populist catchphrase? A carefully sanitized euphemism which glosses over something else?
>
> (Ritchie 1987 quoted in Burrows, 1991: 18)

[handwritten margin note: a mild or vague expression substituted for i thought to be too harsh]

1.1 The Vagueness of Enterprise Culture – should it surprise us?

Such conceptual ambiguity should not necessarily surprise us. The concept of enterprise culture was not clearly defined in policy terms when the British Conservative Party first came to power in 1979,[4] a lack of definition which has not substantially diminished. Research conducted by Pratt (1990) failed to elicit a clear elucidation of the term 'enterprise culture' from Conservative Central Office or the Department of Trade and Industry. Up to the late-1980s and early-1990s, the enterprise culture concept received attention almost exclusively from researchers interested in the education for enterprise movement, with researchers in other areas only entering the field at this time.[5] In addition, management researchers exploring the area of entrepreneurship and small business appear reluctant to focus on enterprise culture judging by the small amount of research on this concept.[6] Difficulties attached to trying to 'pin down' something like enterprise culture has often meant that it has been sidelined in favour of the more accessible concept of small business, with the latter being privileged as an analytical category.

[handwritten margin note: True by definition]

However, given the fact that enterprise culture has been in existence for nearly two decades, and that the current British government has committed itself to making Britain "a country of enterprise",[7] it is important that we

---

3. Marquand, D, "The enterprise culture: old wine in new bottles?" in P Heelas & P Morris (eds), *The Values of the Enterprise Culture* (London: Routledge) 1992.
4. Du Gay, P, *Consumption and Identity at Work* (London: Sage) 1996.
5. Rees, T, *Women and the Labour Market* (London: Routledge) 1992.
6. Blackburn, R, J Curran & A Woods, "Exploring Enterprises Cultures: Small Service Sector Enterprise Owners and their Views" in M Robertson, E Chell & C Mason (eds), *Towards the Twenty-First Century: The Challenge for Small Business* (Cheshire: Nadamal Books) 1992.
7. Gavron, R, M Cowling, G Holtham & A Westall, (1998) *op. cit.*, p.i.

investigate what the notion of an enterprise culture means, and its relationship with other entities such as the entrepreneur and small business.

1.2   An Exploration of Enterprise Culture ε_c

Why is it necessary?

① • Such an analysis will allow us to understand 'enterprise culture' in and
of itself and its impact on business life and life in general over the past
two decades. ε^R

② • It can help us understand other concepts such as the entrepreneur and
thus act as a lead-in to the general area of enterprise and entrepreneurship. ε^P ε^{RP}

③ • An understanding of enterprise culture will allow us to assess its lon-
gevity and that of the management style it promotes.

The following discussion of enterprise culture is largely located within the
British context. The main reason for this is that the creation of the phenomenon of enterprise culture has a strong affinity with the politico-ethical objectives of Thatcherism,[8] and the current New Labour government. Nevertheless despite this close relationship:

> . . . the development of an 'enterprise culture' must be lo-
> cated within the context of increasing globalization. In other
> words, the project of reconstruction that the notion of an
> 'enterprise culture' signifies and encapsulates may be seen
> as one that has its roots in developments outside the will
> and control of any one national government . . . this also
> suggests that the decline of Margaret Thatcher herself in
> no way heralds an end to the project of enterprise. . . . In-
> deed it can be persuasively argued that the 'entrepreneurial
> revolution' to which Thatcherism contributed with such pas-
> sionate brutality is still working its way through the system.
>
> (Du Gay & Salaman, 1992:627)

Therefore, though our discussion is centred largely around the UK, as a key
site for the creation and construction of enterprise culture, the shift that its
emergence signifies can be found in countries throughout the world, as can
the dimensions of enterprise culture which will be outlined below. Thus countries, such as Ireland, have set about creating an Irish enterprise culture which
though nationally specific to Ireland, has many characteristics in common

---

8.   Du Gay, P & G Salaman, "The Cult[ure] of the Customer" *Journal of Management Studies* (1992) 29:5, pp. 615-633.

with the UK enterprise culture project, such as promotion of the market, the private sector (particularly small businesses), and the enterprising individual.

1.3 Exploring Enterprise Culture – what will be found?

An exploration of enterprise culture will suggest that the creation and evolution of this phenomenon has led to the emergence of an entrepreneurial management discourse, which has had a significant impact on the day to day management practices of small businesses in particular, but also other economic entities such as large businesses and public sector organisations. In what follows, it will be suggested that understanding enterprise culture, the position of the entrepreneur, small business, large business, etc. within it, and the activity of entrepreneurship, also implies understanding a way of thinking about the practice of management. Throughout the 20th century, different writers have presented different notions of what a manager does or should do, most with the aim of looking for a better way to manage. Examples of such management writing include Fayol's classic analysis of management, Taylor's scientific management or Mayo's human relations. Such treatises on management have attempted to influence, shape and regulate the conduct of management.[9]

Management discourse of the 1980s and 1990s has placed an emphasis on flexible, dynamic managers and organisations which can respond quickly, innovatively, and decisively to the constant presence of change. These developments are seen as a move away from the bureaucratic structures and practices of the past, a form of management and organisation which has come under much criticism. Bureaucracies are believed to be inappropriate for the future of management, whether in the large or small organisation.[10] These developments can be understood as a response to general post-fordist economic restructuring within Britain and elsewhere. However, enterprise culture and the discourse of enterprise and entrepreneurship which it gives rise to, can also be seen as a fundamental structuring element of these transformations. In this context, the entrepreneur is assigned a privileged position. According to Kanter (1989), the entrepreneur has become the new culture hero of the Western world since the early-1980s, with managers being expected to behave entrepreneurially – in effect to be entrepreneurs. Within this management discourse therefore a number of themes emerge including marketisation, debureaucratisation and the reconditioning of the moral fabric of a variety of organisations. All of these elements and more are present in

---

9.   Du Gay, P (1996a), "Making Up Managers: Enterprise and the Ethos of Bureaucracy" in S Clegg & G Palmer (eds), *The Politics of Management Knowledge* (London: Sage) 1992.

10. Wood, S J, "New Wave Management?" *Work, Employment & Society* (1989) 3:3, pp. 379-402.

the entrepreneurial management discourse of enterprise culture as we will see below.

EXPLORING THE CONCEPT OF ENTERPRISE CULTURE

'Culture' is one of those concepts which burst on to the intellectual land-scape in the 1980s and since then has exerted considerable influence in a variety of spheres including the academic world, the business world and the world of formal politics. Within organisational discourse, the pre-eminence of 'culture' is obvious, clearly revealed by the importance attached to it in governing contemporary organisational life.[11] However despite the pivotal role assigned to culture, what is meant by this concept is by no means clear,[12] and is according to Wallerstein (1990:31) "probably the broadest concept of all those used in the historical and social sciences".

The ambiguous nature of the culture concept, allied to the ambiguous nature of enterprise, is illustrative of the difficulties attached to developing an understanding of the notion of enterprise culture. Nevertheless, despite the difficulties involved in giving enterprise culture any kind of analytic solidity, some attempts have been made to understand this concept.[13] Discussions about enterprise culture largely tend to manifest themselves in terms of an 'inside-outside' dichotomy – you are either part of this culture through your own dynamic initiative, or you are cut off from it through your own inertia. Many discussions about the promotion of an enterprise culture tend to frame themselves in terms of how we get more 'outsiders' to become 'insiders', with an emphasis being placed on institutional and psychological reform.

Sharp paradoxical contrast

2.1 Creating Enterprise Culture   *External Structural Changes*

The creation of the enterprise culture first centred on the establishment of a 'culture for enterprise', a culture which would emerge through external structural changes.[14] The aim was to enhance the competitive and productive per-

---

11. Green, S, "Organisational Culture, Strategic Change and Symbolism" in B Leavy & J S Walsh (eds), *Strategy and General Management* (Dublin: Oaktree Press) 1995; P Du Gay, (1996) *op. cit.*
12. Hebdige, D, *Subculture: The Meaning of Style* (London: Routledge) 1979.
13. Burrows, R & J Curran, "Not Such a Small Business: Reflections on the Rhetoric, the Reality and the Future of the Enterprise Culture" in M Cross & G Payne (eds), *Work and Enterprise Culture* (Basingstoke: The Falmer Press) 1991; R Blackburn, J Curran & A Woods, (1992) *op. cit.*
14. Morris, P, "Freeing the Spirit of Enterprise: The Genesis and Development of the Concept of Enterprise Culture" in R Keat & N Abercrombie (eds), *Enterprise Culture* (London: Routledge) 1991.

formance of the British economy, so that Britain could challenge countries
such as Germany, Japan and America effectively. In general a retreat from
government intervention, and the reinstatement of the market mechanism as
the fundamental determinant of the economy, was emphasised.[15] Such structural changes which began during the 'culture for enterprise' phase, and continued into later stages of the creation and evolution of enterprise culture
include the following.

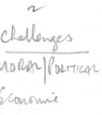

2.2   Structural Changes in Enterprise Culture

- dismantling the welfare state;
- reducing the power of trade unions;
- deregulation;
- marketisation;
- privatisation;
- cuts in taxation;
- reducing the state's role and enlarging that of the individual;
- reducing the public sector borrowing requirement;
- introducing firm monetary and fiscal discipline thus bringing inflation under control;
- promoting self-employment.

However it was soon recognised in the early stages of the enterprise culture
construction, that structural reform was not enough. Though this structural
reform was continued, increasingly a recognition emerged that the success of
a market order was heavily dependent on the individuals who populate it.
This was acknowledged very early on and articulated at the Conservative
Party conference in 1975 when Mrs Thatcher stated:

> Serious as the economic challenge is, the political and moral
> challenge is just as grave, and perhaps more so, because
> economic problems never start with economics. They have
> much deeper roots in human nature, and roots in politics,
> and they do not finish at economics. . . .These are the two
> great challenges of our time – the moral and political chal-
> lenge, and the economic challenge. They have to be faced
> together and we have to master them both.

> (quoted in Hall 1988:85)

---

15. Morris, P, (1991) *op. cit.*; J Wigley & C Lipman, *The Enterprise Economy* (Lon-
    don: The Macmillan Pres) 1992.

Thus the creation of an enterprise culture was increasingly represented in cultural terms and believed to be concerned with the self-understanding, values and attitudes located in individual and institutional activities.[16] This was a recognition that structural change alone could not bring about the required cultural metamorphosis.[17] Such an acknowledgement led into a phase of 'cultural engineering', where a conscious attempt is made to initiate the economic and moral revival of Britain through a programme of cultural change, which would release or create an enterprising spirit.[18] Education was identified as the prime location for the required cultural engineering with unprecedented government intervention at all educational levels, an issue we will come back to later.

2.3 Enterprise Culture: A Source of Change?

Definitions of enterprise culture often tend to be broad and universalist in nature casting little light on how such a culture is actually produced. This has led various authors to suggest that government efforts to create it, have had little real *material* impact on the restructuring of the British economy. Enterprise culture from this perspective is only contingent to the many material changes which have occurred in the business world over the past two decades. For example, from this point of view, enterprise culture has had little or no independent effect on the material reality of small business in terms of its rebirth, development, or day to day experience of business, save to act as a justificatory discourse, or means of interpretation, of the massive restructuring which Britain has experienced.[19] From this perspective, therefore, enterprise culture is an entity which exists *outside* government, but is used by government as a means to counteract the dependency culture of the late-20th century, as well as providing a justification for a range of government policies. However despite this government use, it is suggested that it has had little impact on, or consequence for, business in general and small business in particular. A conceptual separation exists between the entity of enterprise culture, government use of it, and those supposedly subject to it.

---

16. Keat, R, "Introduction" in R Keat & N Abercrombie (eds), *Enterprise Culture* (London: Routledge) 1991.
17. Morris, P (1991) *op. cit.*
18. Morris, P (1991) *op. cit.*; P Du Gay, "Enterprise Culture and the Ideology of Excellence" *New Formations* (1991) 13, pp. 45-61.
19. For example, R Burrows, "The discourse of the enterprise culture and the restructuring of Britain: A polemical contribution" in J Curran & R Blackburn (eds), *Paths of Enterprise: The Future of Small Business* (London: Routledge) 1991; R Burrows, (1991a) "Introduction: entrepreneurship, petty capitalism and the restructuring of Britain" in R Burrows (ed.), *Deciphering the Enterprise Culture* (London: Routledge) 1991; R Burrows & J Curran, (1991) *op. cit.*; D Goss, *Small Business and Society* (London: Routledge) 1991.

A somewhat similar understanding of enterprise culture and its relation-ship with government and small business is offered by Ritchie (1991). Ritchie identifies several positions on enterprise culture, each of which constitutes enterprise culture differently, leading him to suggest that there are several enterprise cultures. Government and small business in this understanding of enterprise culture are separated by suggesting that they hold different stand-points and assumptions in relation to enterprise culture. From Ritchie's per-spective, government is located in a *revivalist-believer* version of enterprise culture, which suggests that enterprise (embodied in the small business) is the key to the revival of the British economy. This emphasis on enterprise works at a national, regional and local level, with all areas of government keen to demonstrate their enterprise credentials.

In contrast, small business owners are located in a lived *experience-sub-ject* version of enterprise culture and constitute the enterprise culture differ-ently, drawing their understanding of it from their experience. From Ritchie's perspective 'making do', 'getting by' and 'doing the business' characterises the enterprise culture of the small business owner, illustrating their survivalist instinct. In Ritchie's account we again observe a reification of enterprise cul-ture as something which exists *outside*, with government and small business having a different relationship to it. In addition the two constructions of en-terprise culture stand in opposition to each other, with the small business version short-circuiting government claims, concerning the transformational role of the small business sector.

Research on small business owners and their understanding of the term 'enterprise culture' would appear to suggest something similar. In explora-tory research on small business owners' views of enterprise culture, doubts that government attempts to create an enterprise culture had much to do with what SMEs were doing on an everyday basis, were frequently expressed by respondents in all types of enterprises.[20] It appeared that enterprise culture had become reified in the minds of most of the small business respondents, taking on a concrete reality as something 'out there' but having very little to do with their business experiences or views. In addition, a belief that enter-prise culture was something which was connected to political activities em-bodied in government aid schemes, and not connected to the everyday expe-rience of small business, was expressed. From Blackburn *et al.*'s (1992) re-search it seems that small business owners are unable to make a connection between public notions of the enterprise culture, as expressed by government and politicians, and their own everyday experience. Separation between gov-ernment and individuals in enterprise culture appears to be expressed here.

Two characteristics of these explorations of enterprise culture can there-fore be identified. Firstly, these considerations of the impact of enterprise culture tend to centre on the small business, ignoring other organisations,

---

20. Blackburn, R, J Curran & A Woods, (1992) *op. cit.*

such as large businesses and the public sector. Though the small business sector has a privileged position within enterprise culture, the creation of the latter has influenced other forms of organisation. Secondly, the notion that government and small business are pitted against one another clearly emerges. Such an understanding of the relationship between government and small business is problematic, as the former's attempts to create an enterprise culture successfully, relies heavily on the latter. In other words, it is clear that enterprise culture will not succeed unless individuals and businesses behave in a manner which is conducive to the market order. Therefore, it is crucial that a conceptualisation of enterprise culture be constructed which can highlight how the aptitude of individuals (in small business and elsewhere) as subjects, as citizens, as selves, is a central target and resource for the government, in attempts to create an enterprise culture, and not in opposition to it.[21]

THE CULTURAL PRODUCTION OF ENTERPRISE

To change the way we think about the relationship between business and government in enterprise culture, we need firstly to outline in more detail its dimensions. Gibb (1987) associates enterprise culture with a range of enterprising traits and activities. From Gibb's perspective, some individuals may possess innately more of these enterprising attributes than others. However, leaving the question of innate abilities aside, he suggests that it is likely that each individual will have a different mix and strength of these attributes. In addition how these attributes will be used and developed will depend on the institutional circumstances within which an individual is located, allied to the freedom and motivation allowed within the situation, which will impact on their use and cultivation.

3.1 Enterprising Traits and Activities

- initiative;
- risk-taking;
- flexibility;
- creativity;
- independence;
- leadership;
- strong work ethic;
- daring spirit;
- responsibility.

---

21. N Rose, "Governing the enterprising self" in P Heelas & P Morris (eds), *The*

Gibb argues that these enterprising attributes can be exercised within a range of organisations, large and small. However, these characteristics are *more likely* to be developed within the context of independent business ownership. Thus small business ownership contributes to the generation of enterprise by:

- providing positive role models of successful small business ownership;
- familiarising people with the phenomenon of independent business ownership;
- encouraging networking with other business owners thus providing a variety of market opportunities;
- providing knowledge of the independent business process;
- massaging the range of entrepreneurial attributes outlined above. (Gibb, 1987)

From Gibb's perspective the combination of the above 5 components on a sufficient scale contributes to and supports the existence of an enterprise culture.

3.2   Broad Conceptualisation of Enterprise Culture

This understanding of enterprise culture concentrates on the broad range of values, attitudes and beliefs which support independent entrepreneurial behaviour in a business context.

(Gibb, 1987:11).

An equally broad understanding of enterprise culture drawn from right-wing think tank policy documents is outlined by Morris (1991:23) as:

. . . the full set of conditions that promote high and rising levels of achievement in a country's economic activity, politics and government, arts and sciences, and also the distinctively private lives of the inhabitants.

Overall, therefore, Gibb and others in presenting a broad definition of enterprise culture, argue that the potential for entrepreneurship is spread among the population. This enterprising potential may be cultivated through a proc-

---

Values of the Enterprise Culture (London: Routledge) 1992; P Carr, "Reconceptualising Enterprise Culture" *The Conference of the British Sociological Association* (University of Reading) 1996.

Dimensions

ess of 'social engineering', i.e. through education and training. Like many other commentators, Gibb suggests that the existing formal education system is inimical to the development of enterprise as described above, and needs radical reform to allow the appropriate psychological transformation to take place. Thus for Gibb, psychological reform requires the promotion of the enterprising attributes listed above within the context of the education system (which itself needs reform), whilst institutional reform centres on the promotion of the small business within which enterprising attributes will flourish.

Keat's (1991) explanation of enterprise culture also centres on two interwoven strands of the concept, i.e. institutional and ethical (psychological). The first strand of enterprise culture privileges the private commercial enterprise as the form of organisation in which the provision of goods and services is best facilitated:

> Thus 'the commercial enterprise' takes on a paradigmatic status, the preferred model for any form of institutional organization and provision of goods and services; and this is at least one of the primary senses to be given to the concept of an 'enterprise culture.
>
> (Keat, 1991:3)

The privileging of the commercial enterprise has meant that a range of different organisations, e.g. hospitals, banks, government departments, schools and charities, have been required to reconstruct themselves along the lines of a private sector business functioning in a free market economy. Such reconstruction usually leads to the introduction of new managerial structures, performance review, the setting of targets and flexible employment contracts.[22] Associated with these changes is the emergence of a 'language of economy' illustrated by such phrases as 'letting the market decide', 'levelling the playing field', 'living in a competitive world', 'market niche', 'satisfying the consumer', allied to the progressive enlargement of the market.[23]

The second dimension of enterprise culture centres on ethical reform which focuses on the forms of conduct and practices, of both individuals and organisations, which display 'enterprising' qualities. From Keat's (1991) perspective the picture of the enterprising individual which emerges is as follows.

---

22. Keat, R, (1991) *op. cit.*
23. Keat, R, (1991) *op. cit.*; P Du Gay, (1996a) *op. cit.*; J K Gibson-Graham, *The End of Capitalism (as we know it): A Feminist Critique of Political Economy* (Cambridge MA: Blackwell Publishers) 1996.

3.3   **The Enterprising Individual**

1. **Self-reliant and independent**, the enterprising individual makes his/ her own decisions, taking responsibility for their own lives, accepting blame when necessary, and not expecting someone or something else to put things right when they go wrong.

2. The activities of the enterprising individual are **achievement oriented** with clear goals and objectives being set. Progress towards these goals is monitored, and any skills or resources needed to help achieve the set objectives are acquired.

3. The enterprising individual is **optimistic and energetic** and works on his/her own initiative. Enterprising individuals view the world as full of opportunities which they are only too happy to avail of. Problems which emerge are there to be solved and are never allowed to act as a barrier to the accomplishment of goals.

4. The material rewards which result from success in a competitive world are keenly **pursued** by enterprising individuals.

                                                              (Keat, 1991)

The extensive acquisition and practice of qualities, such as a willingness to engage in activities which involve risk-taking, demonstrating initiative and a daring spirit, being self-reliant and energetic and accepting responsibility, are highly valued. Individuals and commercial entities are strongly encouraged, to involve themselves in activities which display these enterprising attributes.[24] The aim of such 'cultural engineering' is not only to make individuals less passive and dependent, but to equip them with the virtues of enterprise to enable them to contribute to an enterprising free market economy.[25]

Within the language of economy and enterprise these two strands are intricately entwined. This is demonstrated by the strong belief that it is within the institutional context of the commercial enterprise (as a business entity), that individuals are likely to demonstrate the ethic of enterprise (as an activity), i.e. display enterprising qualities such as risk-taking, etc.[26] In particular the small business as a commercial enterprise has been identified as the home of enterprise with it being argued that:

---

24. Keat, R, (1991) *op. cit.*; P Du Gay, (1996) *op. cit.*; J McGuigan,*Culture and the Public Sphere* (London: Routledge) 1996.
25. Keat, R. 1991: *op. cit.*
26. *Ibid.*

> . . . this same entrepreneurship would contribute to a culture emphasising self-reliance and personal responsibility such that governments could increasingly withdraw from economic management and the provision of a wide range of personal, social and welfare services. For many then the example set by entrepreneurs offers a solution to the institutional, attitudinal and cultural ills of present day Western society. Thus it is necessary to return to the core values of Western capitalism, represented as they are by these people.
>
> (Scase & Goffe 1980, quoted in Rainnie 1985:146)

The suggestion is that small business will contribute in significant ways to a culture which values self-reliance and personal responsibility.

However, a significant qualification needs to be made here. Despite the linkage that exists between the institutional and ethical strands of enterprise, there would seem to be a suggestion that *commercial enterprises, in particular small businesses as commercial enterprises, are not always completely enterprising.* Therefore they must be encouraged to thoroughly express enterprising qualities. Such attributes are given an instrumental value in relation to the performance of a market economy.[27] Thus, for commentators such as Keat, the creation of an enterprise culture is twofold. Firstly a wide variety of organisations will have to remodel themselves along the lines of a commercial enterprise, and secondly individuals and organisations will have to acquire and exercise enterprising qualities.

3.4 Reflecting on the Dimensions of Enterprise Culture

Though there are differences between Gibb's (1986) and Keat's (1991) analysis of the dimensions of enterprise culture, strong similarities are also evident. Both commentators place an emphasis on economic and cultural reconstruction, identifying institutional and ethical (psychological) strands within the enterprise culture entity. Looking at the institutional strand first, Gibb and Keat differ in that the former focuses on the institution of small business, while the latter concentrates on commercial enterprises in general. With regard to the ethical strand they both place an emphasis on enterprising attributes such as risk-taking, self-reliance, independence, etc., recognising that a market order is possible only if the moral values suitable to it prevail. Cultural values, such as risk-taking and self-reliance, ensure that the world is

---

27. *Ibid.*

comprised of individuals with a self-understanding and psyche congenial to enterprise.[28]

Both commentators link the two strands of enterprise culture. Gibb suggests that it is within the context of the small business that enterprising attributes are nurtured, while Keat states that within the commercial enterprise in general individuals are more likely to display enterprising characteristics. However, despite the linkage which both commentators make between the institutional and ethical strands of enterprise culture they identify, there is a suggestion that this link is often severed. Both commentators recognise that small business and commercial enterprises in general are not always *fully enterprising*, and therefore need encouragement to express enterprising qualities. Finally both commentators identify the requirement for an explicit enterprise strategy in which a 'cultural engineering' through education takes place.

From Gibb's perspective, enterprise education would encourage the development of enterprising attributes and align educational experience with the world of the entrepreneur and business. This alignment, he suggests, would entice more individuals to experience independent business ownership. Similarly Keat suggests that education is used in enterprise culture, in an attempt to ensure, that individuals are trained in the virtues of enterprise. Such training would ensure that individuals are equipped with enterprising qualities so that they are able to make the right choices and respond positively to the enterprise environment which is held out to them. For example a Technical and Vocational Education Initiative (TVEI) was set up during the 1980s with the aim of developing initiative, motivation, problem-solving skills and appropriate enterprising attributes in students.[29] Thus they would be equipped with the ability to make a contribution to the success of an enterprising free market economy.

Commentators, such as Gibb and Keat, present a broad account of the dimensions of enterprise culture, highlighting an enterprise strategy of 'cultural engineering' through education, so that individuals and businesses are equipped with the right enterprising qualities. Inherent to their account of enterprise culture is a recognition that the desired market order will not be achieved unless the moral values necessary to it prevail. Nevertheless, even with such recognition insufficient attention is paid to the link between culture and government, despite the fact that to enable such a cultural transformation to take place, the active intervention of the state is required.[30] This lack of attention may be due to the fact that a declared element of the enterprise culture project is limiting the role of the state. However the paradox

28. Heelas, P, "Reforming the Self: Enterprise and the Characters of Thatcherism" in R Keat & N Abercrombie (eds), *Enterprise Culture* (London: Routledge) 1991.
29. Morris, P, (1991) *op. cit.*
30. Marquand, D, (1992) *op. cit.*

here is that the cultural revolution called for can only be achieved through the actions of a strong and intrusive state. To guarantee the desired market order, the state has been forced to engage in a project of social engineering as invasive as any past state activity.[31] Given this we need to move away from broad, static accounts of enterprise culture which only identify its various facets, and shed little light on the actual mechanics of enterprise culture production. To do this we need to include a notion of 'government' within our understanding of enterprise culture. This can be done by conceiving of enterprise culture in terms of norms, practices and techniques of conduct, which in partnership with government, individuals and companies are encouraged to adopt, particularly if they want to access state resources. Thus it would appear that essential to any understanding of the phenomenon of enterprise culture, is a focus on the link between culture and government.[32]

3.5

Incorporating Government into Enterprise Culture

From our discussion it is clear that enterprise culture will not succeed unless individuals behave in a manner conducive to the market order. However, the accounts of enterprise culture outlined above shed little light on the links between individual (business) activity, government, and the wider enterprise culture environment. Changing the way we think about the relationship between business (e.g. small business) and government in enterprise culture, will allow us to expose these links and make visible the impact of enterprise culture. Such exposure will emerge by paying attention to the institutional systems and moral techniques which *produce* enterprise culture. In other words, the relationship between culture and government is highlighted, through a focus on the cultural technology (i.e. institutional and organisational structures and policies) which produces enterprise culture.

One area where the cultural technology of enterprise culture has been explored extensively is that of education. It is suggested that an education system which is enterprising in nature, would contribute significantly to making the UK a more entrepreneurial society. As stated above, the aim of enterprise education is to promote independence, flexibility, autonomy, and self-motivation among students, as well as encouraging them to enter into independent business ownership.[33] Nevertheless, this is not the only form of en-

31. Marquand, D, "The Paradoxes of Thatcherism" in R Skidelsky (ed.), *Thatcherism.* (Oxford: Basil Blackwell) 1988; D Marquand, (1992) *op. cit.*; A H Halsey, "A Sociologist's View of Thatcherism" in R Skidelsky (ed.), *Thatcherism* (Oxford: Basil Blackwell) 1988.

32. Carr, P, "The Cultural Production of Enterprise: Understanding Selectivity as Cultural Policy" *Economic and Social Review* (1998) 29:2, pp. 27-49.

33. Gibb, A, "Enterprise Culture – Its Meaning and Implications for Education and Training', *Journal of European Industrial Training* (1987) 11:2, pp. 3-38; R

terprise cultural technology. Increasingly, an emphasis has been placed on what individuals do once they are in business. For example the *quality* of small business has been identified as important, with a range of policies and initiatives put in place by government to promote this. According to Gavron *et al.* (1998), government policies have shifted towards advice and guidance and not just financial subsidies to improve the calibre of new and existing business.

What is being expressed here is a desire to make our understanding of enterprise culture more useful in a practical sense, by putting 'policy' into enterprise culture theoretically, practically and institutionally.[34] From this perspective therefore enterprise culture is treated "as a historically specific set of institutionally embedded relations of government in which the forms of thought and conduct of extended populations are targeted for transformation".[35] Here the population being targeted is existing and potential businesses, with the aim of shaping and regulating their conduct through the growing 'advisory' role of government. The necessary corollary of this orientation to enterprise culture is that it can be suggested that policies, as instruments of government, have a cultural dimension in the sense of influencing the way in which enterprise culture is produced. Thus we are moving away from the broad definitions of enterprise culture outlined above, to an "aesthetically narrower"[36] understanding of this phenomenon.

3.6   Narrow Conceptualisation of Enterprise Culture

This conceptualisation of enterprise culture concentrates on the links between the activities of government and the activities of the individual. This linkage can be understood in terms of the strategies and policies drawn upon by government, for the direction of the behaviour of individuals and business in enterprise culture. In other words the focus is on the range of policies and initiatives which aim to mould and shape entrepreneurial behaviour in business, both large and small, and the response of individuals and business to this.

What is being suggested is that, to truly understand the essence of enterprise culture, we should focus on how attempts are made to align the sense of purpose of businesses, with the values that are designed into state and government activities.[37] For example, this process of alignment can be facilitated

---

Keat, (1991) *op. cit.*; T Rees, (1992) *op. cit.*; R Gavron, M Cowling, G Holtham & A Westall, (1998) *op. cit.*

34. Bennett, T, "Putting Policy into Cultural Studies" in L Crossberg, C Nelson & P Treichler (eds), *Cultural Studies* (London: Routledge) 1992.

35. *Ibid.*, p. 26.

36. *Ibid.*

37. Carr, P, (1996) *op. cit.*; P Carr, (1998) *op. cit.*

through the relationship between personnel in government agencies such as TECs and Business Links, (which are the centrepiece of the public support infrastructure of small business in the UK), and individuals in business. The agents of the TECs and Business Links can be conceptualised as "cultural specialists"[38] who within the context of enterprise culture implement its cultural techniques. These agents are actively involved in the creation of enterprise culture through the implementation of a range of enterprise policies, which encourage individuals and businesses to be fully enterprising. Similar support edifices are present in other countries, for example Ireland, where a range of national and European-funded enterprise support initiatives have developed in recent years.

3.2
Entrepreneurial Management Discourse

The understanding of enterprise culture which is presented here, is one which focuses on the range of policies, strategies, and initiatives, which are used to shape and regulate entrepreneurial behaviour. Such a conceptualisation of enterprise culture is commensurate with the growth in enterprise initiatives over the past decade. Currently, in the UK, there are 200 central government business support initiatives, sponsored by five departments, which cost £632 million in 1995/1996.[39] In Ireland in 1994, nearly £100 million in grants was paid out to multinational companies and Irish firms, and by 1996, grant figures had increased to £160 million.[40] In addition an understanding of enterprise culture which incorporates government initiatives and policies within it, allows us to assess its impact on a sector such as that of small business, in a way that previous research[41] could not. However, it is important to recognise that the production of enterprise culture, through the implementation of enterprise policies and initiatives, has led to the emergence of an entrepreneurial management discourse. This entrepreneurial management discourse encourages the adoption of an enterprising management style within a range of organisations.

A starting point for understanding what this management discourse looks like is the new wave management theory of the 1980s which called for flatter, leaner, decentralised organisations. This management theory places an emphasis on loosely defined roles, a proactive stance, entrepreneurship, and the forging of a work-based identity which centres on the individual achieving fulfilment through work.[42] It emphasises the replacement of bureaucracy

---

38. Featherstone, M, *Undoing Culture* (London: Sage) 1995.
39. Gavron, R, M Cowling, G Holtham & A Westall, (1998) *op. cit.*
40. Carey, B, "Riding the Celtic Tiger comes easily to IDA's Magnet for Industrial Investors" *The Sunday Business Post* 9 March 1997.
41. For example, R Blackburn, J Curran & A Woods, (1992) *op. cit.*
42. Wood, S J, (1989) *op. cit.*; P Du Gay, (1991) *op. cit.*

and bureaucratic culture with entrepreneurship, creativity, action, initiative, risk-taking and flexibility. All of these traits are given a premium value within enterprise culture as outlined above. Thus the first dimension of the entrepreneurial management discourse, which emerges out of government attempts to shape and regulate entrepreneurial activity, promotes the extensive procurement of such qualities. Individuals are encouraged to involve themselves in activities, (e.g. independent business ownership, or entrepreneurial activity within a large firm) which require these qualities.

The second dimension of the entrepreneurial management discourse is one which focuses on the manager and management activities. This emphasis on management is linked to the reconstruction of a range of organisations along the lines of a commercial enterprise, the institutional dimension of enterprise culture. According to Woods (1989), during the 1960s and early-1970s managers and business people were often mocked. However this view of management changed with commentators suggesting that:

> . . . it is managers and management that make institutions perform. Performing responsible management is the alternative to tyranny and our only protection against it...For management is the organ, the life-giving, acting, dynamic organ of the institution it manages.

> (Drucker cited in Pollitt, 1993:3)

From this statement, the assumption that better management will solve a range of economic and social ills is evident.[43] Kenneth Clarke, a member of the Conservative government in 1992, stated in a radio interview that one of the achievements of the Thatcherite revolution was the restoration of "management to its proper place in society".[44]

Thus during the 1980s two powerful figures emerged: the entrepreneur and the manager with both located in the commercial enterprise, the preferred organisation for the provision of goods and services within enterprise culture. However the relationship between these two figures has been widely contested. Three accounts of this relationship can be identified as follows:

- The entrepreneur is conceived of as a 'failed' manager, i.e. unable to work within the management boundaries of a large organisation.

- The differences between the entrepreneur and the manager have been extensively explored, usually with the suggestion that the entrepreneur is a superior business figure to the manager.

---

43. Pollitt, C, *Managerialism and the Public Services* (Oxford: Blackwell Publishers) 2nd edn, 1993.
44. Cited in J Clarke & J Newman, "The Right to Manage: A Second Managerial Revolution?" *Cultural Studies* (1993) 7: 3, pp. 427-441.

- Adopting a life cycle or developmental approach, it has been suggested that the entrepreneur progresses from entrepreneurship to management within the mature organisation, leaving behind his or her entrepreneurial attributes.

However, one difficulty with these considerations of the relationship between the entrepreneur and the manager, is that entrepreneurship and management are presented as discrete entities, and a very clear 'either/or' relationship is posited. However, this understanding of the relationship as one of mutual exclusivity is problematic. For an individual to succeed in the marketplace of today and tomorrow, he/she needs to be an entrepreneur *and* a manager. The notion of a 'both/and' relationship is posited, with a dialectic co-existence prevailing between entrepreneurship and management. This type of co-existence mirrors the new wave management theory mentioned above, which not only promotes enterprising qualities, but also articulates "a highly rationalistic discourse of enhanced managerial control".[45] As we will see such managerial control often takes a calculative form based on procedures such as performance reviews and efficiency checks.

A good empirical example of this entrepreneurial co-existence is Richard Branson and his Virgin organisation. Though the public image of Virgin is of a one-man-band, i.e. Richard Branson, the reality is quite different. Virgin employs 15,000 people, has a turnover of £2.4 billion and operates in 24 countries. To enable Branson to run such an organisation, he has appointed a number of high-calibre senior managers.[46] Branson's success is not only based on a flair for marketing, but also on the ability to pick senior managers successfully. It is usually the case that Branson will be heavily involved in the idea for a new venue. However once the business is launched, with Branson being centre-stage at its inauguration, he will step back and leave the running of the business to a "hand-picked deputy".[47] The co-existence of entrepreneurship and management in Virgin is clear, with entrepreneurship being located in Branson, and management being located in the layer of senior management he has appointed. The enterprising Branson has brought management into his business through the appointment of a management team. However in a smaller business, entrepreneurship and management capabilities can be located in the individual owner.

As we shall see in later chapters, the range of policies, strategies, techniques of conduct, which are used to shape and mould entrepreneurial behaviour, are characterised by these two dimensions of the entrepreneurial

---

45. Harris, M, "Rethinking the Virtual Organisation" in P Jackson & J M Van der Wielen (eds), *Teleworking: International Perspectives* (London: Routledge) 1998.
46. Blackhurst, C, "At the Court of King Richard" *Management Today* (April 1998) pp. 39-44.
47. Blackhurst, C, (1998) *op. cit.*, p. 42.

management discourse, which is produced by attempts to create and nurture an enterprise culture. Individuals and businesses are encouraged to display 'enterprising' qualities', such as risk-taking, etc., and are also expected to perform competently a range of managerial skills including planning, organising, budgeting, staffing, controlling, co-ordinating.[48] However, it should be noted that the way in which this entrepreneurial management discourse manifests itself, particularly in terms of the relationship between its two dimensions, will vary across a large business, a small business and a public-sector organisation. This combination of enterprising and management qualities is believed to enhance the strength of a business (no matter what size) and allow it to exist successfully in a period of uncertainty, rapid change and innovation. Thus attempts to make individuals and businesses 'fully enterprising' through a range of enterprising initiatives, all of which are built around the dialectic co-existence of entrepreneurship and management, is the means by which enterprise culture is produced.

What is being exposed here is that the promotion of enterprising qualities does not just entail encouraging individuals and organisations to be risk-takers, etc., it also entails encouraging individuals and organisations to adopt better business practices, e.g. planning, marketing and financial controls. This illustrates the essential paradox that exists at the heart of enterprise culture, which is that whilst individuals and organisations are expected to be daring risk-takers, they are also expected to adopt this persona in a planned, rational manner, so that a significant material gain (profits, value-added, employment, etc.) will emerge from their dynamic, daring, bold, risk-taking initiatives. Thus the dialectic contradiction at the heart of enterprise culture reveals itself as follows.

3.8   The dialectic contradiction at the heart of enterprise culture

The free unfolding of desire for capitalist accumulation and the need for a rational ordering of this.

(Carr, 1996a)

This contradiction exists both within and outside a business. Within a business there is the co-existence of the enterprising and management attributes of its owner(s). Outside the business, this contradiction can be understood as an attempt on the part of government, to align the enterprising abilities of individuals and businesses with the aims and objectives of the enterprise economy within which they are located. The essence of enterprise culture, therefore, is to nurture individuals' desire for self-fulfilment and profit by encouraging them to be enterprising, whilst at the same time promoting the

---

48. Carr, P, (1998) *op. cit.*

need for a rational, professional, managed approach to giving these desires a material reality. This essence manifests itself in an entrepreneurial management discourse which is operationalised through the enormous range of enterprise initiatives put in place by government.

SUMMARY OF KEY IDEAS

- The creation of an enterprise culture has been a key aim of government for the past two decades.

- Despite the popularity and power of enterprise culture, it is a notoriously difficult concept to understand.

- As a concept enterprise culture has often been sidelined in favour of the more accessible concept of small business. In addition it has also been suggested that it has had no effect on the development and evolution of the small business sector.

- Where enterprise culture as a concept has been explored, broad and universal understandings which focus on (often undefined) the values and attitudes which support entrepreneurship have been presented.

- Within these broad conceptualisations, the role of government in producing enterprise culture is often ignored or down-played, despite recognition that the cultural transformation called for can only come about with strong and intrusive government intervention.

- It is suggested that to truly understand the enterprise culture phenomenon and its impact, we should concentrate on developing an understanding of the way in which the subjectivity and activity of individuals and business is directed and rationalised by government inspired enterprise initiatives, policies and strategies.

- Further it is suggested that out of this rationalisation and direction, an entrepreneurial management discourse emerges which is built around the dialectic co-existence of entrepreneurship and management.

- The manifestation of this entrepreneurial management discourse and its impact will vary depending on whether an organisation is large, small or part of the public sector.

CHAPTER 2

The Enterprising State

Thatcherism . . . signalled the reversal of the trend towards paternalistic collectivism. . . . Thatcherism's mission . . . was to force the middle class to become independent and self-reliant again and to abandon collectivism . . . a bad dream which the British people had to endure and from which Margaret Thatcher bade them wake.

(Gamble, 1994:157)

THE RELATIONSHIP BETWEEN THE STATE AND ECONOMY

Different conceptualisations of the relationship between state and economy can generally be allocated to one of two categories. On the political 'left' are those who argue for an active state which is heavily involved in the economy both in terms of ownership and control.

The 'Left' Perspective on the State

- Collective ownership of the economy for the benefit of the majority of working people. There is a concern that all citizens have access to the benefits of economic growth.

- Such collective ownership manifests itself through state proprietorship of all large-scale property, which it is suggested will lead to the most effective and just use of productive resources.

- Extensive involvement of the state in the economy as:

  - an owner;
  - a welfare provider;
  - an employer;
  - a regulator;
  - a re-distributor;
  - an economic policy maker.

- A key aim of the 'left' state post-1945 was to secure full employment through demand-side management, adjusting demand to the needs of Fordist mass production.
- Overall the state aims to modify the excesses and extremes of the logic of the market, while at the same time grafting alternative goals, such as needs, as well as profits, on to the system.

(Hall, 1988; Jessop, 1994; Pierson, 1994)

From the 'left' perspective therefore, the state is understood as a vital agent which is actively involved in directing and intervening in the process of economic development.

In contrast on the political 'right' are those who argue for a minimal state, and the greatest freedom, space, and autonomy for private ownership and entrepreneurship within an economy.[1] From this perspective it is suggested that the best economic outcomes can be guaranteed for individuals, and for society as a whole, by placing trust in the workings of the free market. This view of the state can be summarised as follows:

The 'Right' Perspective on the State

- Private ownership and self-interest will lead to the most efficient use of resources.
- The highest levels of individual freedom possible should be promoted to facilitate the efficient use of productive resources.
- Social policy is subordinated to the needs of labour market flexibility and the pressures of international competition.
- State activities should be limited to getting the environment right, i.e. providing a 'neutral' framework which should ensure:
  - law and order;
  - the working of the free market;
  - the provision of a small number of public goods, which are essential to overall well being, and which the private sector could not reasonably be expected to provide.
- Overall the 'right' state aims to promote innovation in products, processes, organisations and markets, with a view to strengthening the structural competitiveness of the economy through supply-side interventions.

(Pierson, 1994; Jessop, 1994)

---

1. Pierson, C, *The Modern State* (London: Routledge) 1996.

Thus from the 'right' perspective, the state should not intervene but merely facilitate entrepreneurial activity, and implement policies which are designed to foster an enterprise culture. Therefore, we have what Hall (1988:225) refers to as "two opposed 'continents' – the domain of capital and the market versus the domain of the logic of social needs, imposed through the state".

This right-left dichotomy has been the single most important political cleavage of the past 200 years.[2] However from 1917 up to the 1970s, the liberalism of the right was believed to be more and more irrelevant, and was overshadowed by the collectivist doctrines of the left. The latter presented a formidable justification for a strong and extensive state role. This promotion of collectivism came not only from totalitarian doctrines such as communism, but also from state programmes for social amelioration implemented by the 'centre right' and 'centre left'.[3] During the first half of the 20th century, commentators (whether in mourning or rejoicing) suggested that industrial society in the future would be collectivist, organised and regulated, with the state having strong control over the economy, as well as owning substantial economic assets.[4] Between the end of World War II and the 1970s, the state became the largest single employer of labour, as well as becoming more and more interventionist and regulatory, in all areas of social life leading to a situation where:

> . . . instead of progressively withering away, the state has become a gigantic, swollen, bureaucratic and directive force, swallowing up almost the whole of civil society, and imposing itself (sometimes with tanks), in the name of the people, on the backs of the people.

(Hall, 1988:221)

The state-owned industry sector in Britain was largely created during the 1950s. By 1979 the proportion of British industry owned and controlled by the state was at its highest ever level, with nationalised industries and public corporations accounting for over 11 per cent of gross domestic product. They employed 2 million workers (8 per cent of the total workforce), and made up 13 per cent of total investment in the economy.[5] Some public sector organisations, such as the BBC and Post Office, were originally set-up by the government, whereas others, such as gas, coal, electricity, iron and steel, and the railways, were taken over by the government from the private sector.[6] Na-

---

2. *Ibid.*
3. Gamble, A, *Hayek: The Iron Cage of Liberty* (Cambridge: Polity Press) 1996.
4. *Ibid.*
5. Saunders, P & C Harris, *Privatization and Popular Capitalism* (Buckingham: Open University Press) 1994.
6. *Ibid.*

tionalisation in general was pursued as a matter of principle. There was a strong belief that bringing industries into state ownership would instil both management and workers, with a sense of the public good. Productivity and efficiency would increase and wage demands and price increases would be moderated. Unfortunately, this faith was not justified, with trade unions constantly seeking to acquire higher wages while resisting attempts to modernise industry. In addition, management within nationalised industries more often than not, opted for the path of least resistance.[7]

Ungovernability

The immense expansion of the state, and the increase in its interventionist and regulatory roles within modern capitalism, particularly in Western Europe, was not without its problems. Government spending expanded rapidly, and large-scale organisations, which were producer-dominated, unresponsive and inefficient, providing low-quality services, predominated. These problems were recognised by both the right and the left, with a number of structural similarities existing between 'right' theories of the ungovernability of the state, and 'left' critiques of advanced capitalism, though both sides were loath to acknowledge this comparability.[8] The concept of ungovernability which became a standard topic in international political science and political journalism from 1974 onwards, outlines the urgent threat ". . . of a chronic or even acute failure of the state".[9] Focusing on the disparity between the volume of claims and demands put on the state and the government's steering capacity it is suggested that:

> The level and volume of articulated demands increase, just as the action capacities of the besieged state decrease. Thus in essence the prognosis implies that the basic discrepancy between claim level and performance capacity unleashes a dynamic ensuring that this discrepancy is reproduced in intensified form: an ungovernable system always becomes more ungovernable.

> (Offe, 1984:71)

Writers, such as Habermas (1976), suggested that economic management and public administration difficulties led to a "legitimation crisis" of the state, and were reinforced by a motivational crisis, which produced individuals

---

7. *Ibid.*
8. Offe, C, "Ungovernability: On the Renaissance of Conservative Theories of Crisis" in J Habermas (ed.), *Observations on the Spiritual Situation of the Age* (Cambridge: MIT Press) 1984.
9. *Ibid.*

with values and attitudes that were harmful to the system. Continuously rising expectations were matched by an aversion to work, discipline and achievement.[10]

This discourse of crisis expressed in terms of 'political overload', 'fiscal crisis', the 'crowding out' of private investment by public expenditure, has led to a shift in government priorities from stable economic growth to the control of inflation, and the suppression of re-distributive pressures in society.[11] Though the left recognised problems with the gigantic expansion of the state, it was the right who capitalised on them, building the foundations for the shift from state to market regulation of economic and social life.[12]

THE 'ROLLING BACK' OF THE STATE

The creation of a "new (enterprise) common sense"[13] which swept aside many of the taken-for-granted assumptions of the social welfare state, to be replaced with "pervasive market reasoning", can be dated from the ascendancy to power of politicians such as Margaret Thatcher in the UK and Ronald Reagan in the USA. Though the enterprise culture project is traditionally located in Britain and America, policy makers in other countries, such as Ireland, have explicitly embraced the aim of establishing an enterprise culture. From the late-1970s, the discourse of enterprise and the market took hold, reflected in numerous OECD and national government publications advocating the freeing of market forces.[14] For example within the Irish context such publications include the "Culliton Report" (1992), "Employment through Enterprise" (1993) and "Shaping our Future" (1996). These reports, particularly the "Culliton Report", represent "the culmination of a decade of discontent about the role of state intervention in general and the efficiency of public sector industry in particular".[15] It appeared that the dominance of collectivist doctrines was no more, and countries, such as the UK and Ireland, had interpreted the existence of economic problems, as stemming from excessive state intervention and a failure to promote an enterprise culture.

10. McGuigan, J, *Culture and the Public Sphere* (London: Routledge) 1996.
11. Rustin, M, "Unfinished Business: From Thatcherite Modernisation to Incomplete Modernity" in M Perryman (ed.), *From Altered States: Post-Modernism, Politics, Culture* (London: Lawrence & Wishart) 1994.
12. Hall, S. 1988: *The Hard Road to Renewal.* London: Verso.
13. McGuigan, J, (1996) *op. cit.*
14. Rustin, M, (1994) *op. cit.*
15. Taylor, G, "In Search of the Elusive Entrepreneur" *Irish Political Studies* (1993) 8, pp. 89-103.

Selling Off the Family Silver

The implementation of market reasoning into every sphere of life required a profound reversal of state intervention into the economy. Privatisation formed part of the policy response in the restructuring of the relationship between state, market and society.[16] In countries such as the UK, its contribution to this restructuring was dramatic and radical. Though examples of privatisation in the 1960s and 1970s can be found in a variety of countries (e.g. in Ireland with the sale of the assets of the Dairy Disposal Company in 1972 or the sale of shares in British Petroleum by Labour in 1977), this was a limited and sporadic phenomenon. Privatisation in the 1980s and 1990s became widespread, frequent and routine.[17] For many commentators privatisation represented a new and formidable policy development, one of the most profound policy transformations implemented in the UK during the 20th century, which negated what appeared to be a relentless historical trend of collectivism and regulation[18] as the following suggests.

> Privatisation is at the vanguard of a worldwide movement in thinking and politics about the legitimate role of the state in an industrial society in the 1980s. Socialism, in whatever form, has both lost the battle of ideas and has been forsaken as a practical solution to the immediate industrial problems that most economies are now confronting. The intellectual currents throughout the world are moving strongly in the opposite direction and have in practical policy been led by the Conservative government of Mrs Thatcher. . . . Privatisation redefines the role of the state and constrains it to a supporter of the market, which is a social organisation where there is freedom to choose within the rule of law. It is this more than anything else which represents the radical character of privatisation and it is this which is perhaps the most poorly understood.
>
> (Veljanovski, 1987:205-206)

Though Drucker (1985) states that the term 'privatisation' was coined by him in 1969 in his book *The Age of Discontinuity*, it did not appear in dictionaries in 1979. Neither did it rate a mention in the Conservative Party manifesto for the 1979 election, though it did appear in the 1983 and 1987 mani-

---

16. Wright, V, "Industrial Privatization in Western Europe: Pressures, Problems and Paradoxes" in V Wright (ed.), *Privatization in Western Europe: Pressures, Problems and Paradoxes* (London: Pinter Publishers) 1994.
17. *Ibid.*
18. Sweeney, P, *The Politics of Public Enterprise and Privatisation* (Dublin: Tomar Publishing Ltd) 1990; G Taylor, (1993) *op. cit.*

festos. However, no matter what the origins of the term, the privatisation programme was the single biggest cause of the growth in individual shareholders in the UK during the 1980s.[19]

Defining Privatisation

Privatisation, or denationalisation, can broadly be understood as the transfer of activities and responsibilities, from the public sector to the private sector, through the sale of publicly owned assets, which include industry, housing and the contracting out of services. Broadly this means that the financing and provision of goods and services shifts away from the public sector due to a withdrawal of the state. This includes the following:

- Sale of nationalised industries or parts of them to the public. In Britain a state-owned firm is privatised when over 50 per cent of its equity is sold.
- The sale of government held shares in private companies.
- Sale of government shares to a private company where a relationship between the government and that company already exists.
- The sale of public assets, such as land and council housing.
- Competitive tendering and the contracting out of goods and services which the state provided in the past. This was legislated as a mandatory procedure for local government and health services in 1987 in the UK, e.g. rubbish collection and cleaning previously carried out by local authority employees.
- The elimination of certain state functions and deregulation.

The reasons given for the public to private switch are competition, efficiency, self-determination, consumer choice, cost-effectiveness, all within an enterprise culture.

However, though privatisation means that the balance of service provision and production is tilted towards the private sector, this should not be taken to imply, that the state has completely withdrawn from all involvement in industry. A state presence in industry is maintained through:

- regulatory agencies which oversee the activities of privatised organisations;
- ensuring the environment is right for business;
- maintaining 'golden shares', i.e. having an interest in a number of privatised companies.

(Veljanovski, 1987; Sweeney, 1990; Mitchell, 1990;
Taylor, 1993; Samson, 1994; Richardson, 1994)

---

19. Sweeney, P, (1990) *op. cit.*; J Mitchell, "Britain: Privatisation as Myth?" in J

The UK was the pioneer in implementing a vigorous privatisation programme, the most extensive outside Eastern Europe, which generated much interest in a number of countries. The UK accounted for nearly a third of the total assets privatised in the world between 1984 and 1991.[20] Though privatisation is retrospectively presented as a systematic and reasoned plan of action, evidence would appear to suggest that the Thatcher government, the vanguard of privatisation in Western Europe, staggered and stumbled towards it, with the reasons following rather than preceding the programme.[21]

The Phases of Privatisation in the UK

In 1958, 7 per cent of the adult population in the UK owned shares. By 1979 this had fallen to 4.5 per cent which is approximately 2.5 million people. However by 1992 there were at least 11 million individual shareholders in Britain representing a quarter of the adult population.[22] In considering the implementation of the privatisation policy, three phases can be identified as follows.

Phase One

Starting slowly and cautiously, this phase of the privatisation programme lasted from 1979 to the end of 1983. Little excitement in the process of privatisation was sparked among the general public, and the proceeds were less than 4 per cent of the privatisation revenue collected between 1984 and 1992. The main objective of privatisation in this phase was to raise revenues and reduce the public sector borrowing requirement.[23]

Phase Two

1984, the beginning of phase two, has been identified as a watershed year in the privatisation process. In this year, the first large and strategic state enterprise was sold off with British Telecom moving out of public ownership. The sale of British Telecom, representing at the time the biggest flotation ever in the world, was an enormous success, raising £3.9 billion and attracting an exceptional 2.3 million applications for shares. The sale of the Trustee Savings Bank and British Gas followed. The latter replaced British Telecom as

Richardson (ed.), *Privatisation and Deregulation in Canada and Britain* (Aldershot: Dartmouth Publishing) 1990; P Saunders & C Harris, (1994) *op. cit.*

20. Wright, V, (1994) *op. cit.*
21. Mitchell, J, (1990) *op. cit.*; G Thompson, *The Political Economy of the New Right* (London: Pinter Publishers)1990; P Saunders & C Harris, (1994) *op. cit.*; V Wright, (1994) *op. cit.*; J Richardson, "The politics and practice of privatization in Britain" in V Wright (ed.), (1994) *op. cit.*
22. Saunders, P & C Harris, (1994) *op. cit.*
23. *Ibid.*

the biggest flotation ever. A huge advertising campaign which encouraged small investors was put in place and 4.6 million applications were received.[24] By the end of 1986, there were 9 million shareholders in Britain. In 1987 further privatisations took place including British Airways, Rolls Royce and the British Airports Authority (owner of 7 national airports in Britain), which were all oversubscribed. The success of this second phase of privatisation led to the emergence of a cultural objective, i.e. the creation of popular capitalism.[25]

Phase Three
From 1989 onwards, privatisation reached its climax with the government moving to sell off virtually every public sector industry possible, even where there was widespread opposition, e.g. the privatisation of water. Thoughts of privatisation were extended to areas such as immigration control, the prison service and the computerisation of police records. The UK government also sought legal advice on the implications of privatising the tax system and the tax assessment of 34 million people.[26] The privatisation of water marked the beginning of the third phase and despite disapproval, over two and a half million people subscribed for shares, attracting more buyers than any other privatisation except British Gas.[27]

However, this British Gas record was broken by the privatisation of electricity, which was broken up into twelve English and Welsh regional supply companies, three power generating companies, a national grid company and two Scottish generation and supply companies. The twelve English and Welsh regional supply companies were the first to be sold, and with a combined value of over £5 billion were hugely oversubscribed.[28]

By the 1992 general election, the Conservatives had succeeded in selling off practically the entire public sector with virtually all of the nationalised industries being transferred into private ownership. The privatisation programme involved 46 large companies and dozens of smaller ones, with nearly a million jobs being transferred from the public to the private sector. By 1993, nationalised industries accounted for barely 3 per cent of GDP compared to 9 per cent in 1979.[29] Utilisation of the privatisation option continued into the 1990s, with the privatisation of the rail network and train services taking place between 1993 and 1997. British Rail was broken up into 25 companies each of which would run a passenger train service, and three rolling stock

---

24. *Ibid.*
25. *Ibid.*
26. Wright, V, (1994) *op. cit.*
27. Saunders, P & C Harris, (1994) *op. cit.*
28. *Ibid.*
29. Saunders, P & C Harris, (1994) *op. cit.*; V Wright, (1994) *op. cit.*; J Richardson, (1994) *op. cit.*

companies, which would lease coaches and locomotives to the train companies. In addition the track, signalling and major stations were grouped into a company called Railtrack. Other parts of British Rail, such as freight, were also privatised. Consideration has also been given to the privatisation of the London Underground and the postal services.

Privatisation around the World

Since the 1980s, many countries have experienced an "intellectual disenchantment"[30] with collectivism and high levels of state intervention. High taxation, soaring inflation and significant public indebtedness have contributed to the rise of neo-liberalism within a number of European countries. As part of this turn to the right, many countries have considered and embarked on the implementation of a policy of privatisation. The success of the British privatisation policy led to:

> . . . the emergence and diffusion of a pro-privatisation model based on the experience of the UK. The apparent success of the privatisation model – one of Britain's few successful exporting industries – was diffused with remarkable success across Europe (both Western and Eastern), feeding the ideological aspirations of the neo-liberals, whetting the appetite of revenue-hungry governments of all political colours, and pressuring the sceptics and critics into apologetic and defensive postures. The British model also influenced the mechanics of other European privatisation programmes: selling by tranches; spreading the payments period; reserving a share of the privatised stock for employees or the public at below market prices.
>
> (Wright, 1994:5)

Though many countries have followed the British lead, the UK has embraced the widest possible approach to privatisation, with few countries embarking on a programme of privatisation as extensive as that in the UK. Nevertheless it has been suggested by some commentators that the privatisation programme in France, which first took place between 1986 and 1988, was in some ways more extreme than that of the British.[31]

During this period the privatisation of 66 *grandes entreprises* (if subsidi-

30. Wright, V, (1994) *op. cit.* p. 2
31. Sweeney, P, (1990) *op. cit.*; V Wright, (1994) *op. cit.*; H Dumex & A Jeunemaitre, "Privatization in France: 1983-1993" in V Wright (ed.) *Privatization in Western Europe: Pressures, Problems and Paradoxes* (London: Pinter Publishers) 1994.

aries are included this figure rises to 1,454) which encompassed 42 in the banking sector, thirteen in insurance, nine in the industrial sector, and two in communications, was proposed. This privatisation programme affected 750,000 employees and about a third of the programme was completed in less than two years.[32] The financial crash of October 1987 halted the programme which was abandoned when Francois Mitterand became President in 1988. Though privatisation was supposed to be officially discarded, it did continue throughout Mitterand's reign, and was officially endorsed again with the election of a right-wing government in 1993.[33]

It is clear that, whilst the pursuit of privatisation has been ideologically inspired at times in countries including the UK, the Netherlands, Portugal, Greece and Sweden, for some other countries it is viewed as a managerial adjustment to changing economic and financial situations.[34] Within the Irish context, public ownership often acted as a barrier to the development and expansion of an organisation. For example, the Irish Life Assurance Company was prevented from expanding overseas, particularly into the American market, because of American regulations against state involvement in financial businesses such as insurance. Reasons such as these along with financial concerns accounted for the move towards privatisation within the Irish context, with ideology having little to do with this shift.

PRIVATISATION AND ENTERPRISE CULTURE

Privatisation: Promoting the Private Sector Commercial Enterprise

The reversal of state intervention in the economy through a radical privatisation programme is reflective of the institutional and ethical strands of the enterprise culture discussed in Chapter 1. Taking the institutional strand first, which assigns paradigmatic status to the private sector commercial enterprise,[35] it is clear how privatisation as a policy embodies this dimension of the enterprise culture entity. It is also clear how privatisation represents the enterprise culture aim of 'rolling back the state'. The withdrawal of the state from the production of goods and services means that in many areas private sector business becomes the key location for the provision of a wide range of products and services. In addition, the privileging of the commercial enter-

---

32. Wright, V, (1994) *op. cit.*
33. *Ibid.*
34. *Ibid.*
35. Keat, R, "Introduction" in R Keat & N Abercrombie (eds), *Enterprise Culture* (London: Routledge) 1991;

prise as an economic entity, denotes a disavowal of social partnership in favour of managerial authority and market forces.[36]

The key justification given for this process of "de-differentiation of previously distinct modes of organization"[37] is that the private commercial business is a more efficient entity than the public sector organisation.[38] This privileging of the private sector enterprise, one of the primary interpretations to be given to the concept of enterprise culture, gives prime position to a range of objectives, which the general promotion and creation of an enterprise culture hoped to accomplish. These include achieving value for money, reducing government involvement in the economy, satisfying the demands of consumers, promoting competition and efficiency and marketising social relations. The objectives of privatisation clearly mirror some of the general aims of enterprise culture outlined here. The key aims of the policy of privatisation were firstly to act as a source of revenue for the government; secondly to encourage competition and efficiency; thirdly to curb the power of public sector trade unions; and finally a cultural objective which seeks to create a more entrepreneurial society.

Privatisation: A Source of Revenue for the Government?

The implementation of the privatisation programme created a significant source of revenue for the British government, even though this aspect of privatisation was not originally emphasised.[39] Between 1979 and 1992, the British government disposed of £41.5 billion worth of state assets,[40] no mean feat given the supposed "staggering and stumbling" nature of the process. However, despite the original unacknowledged revenue generating aspects of privatisation, the Treasury was not unimpressed by the benefits to the Exchequer of this programme.[41] Proceeds from the programme of privatisation became critical to government budgets presented by the UK Conservatives after 1983, with many government financial targets being met because of it.[42]

Across many countries (e.g. Spain, Italy, Norway, Portugal, Ireland) the selling off of state assets raised money for both public sector managers and

36. Vickers, J & G Yarrow, *Privatization: An Economic Analysis* (London: MIT Press) 1988; B Jessop, "The transition to post-Fordism and the Schumpeterian workfare state" in R Burrows & B Loader (eds), *Towards a Post-Fordist Welfare State?* (London: Routledge) 1994.
37. Keat, R, (1991) *op. cit.*
38. Veljanovski, C, *Selling the State: Privatisation in Britain* (London: Weidenfeld & Nicolson) 1987; V Wright, (1994) *op. cit.*
39. Sweeney, P, (1990) *op. cit.*
40. Saunders, P & C Harris, (1994) *op. cit.*
41. Mitchell, J, (1990) *op. cit.*
42. Mitchell, J, (1990) *op. cit.*; P Sweeney, (1990) *op. cit.*

government facing huge budgetary pressure. In fact many supporters of privatisation were disappointed that raising revenue became a more significant feature of privatisation, than increasing competition and creating a competitive free market. In effect the short-term benefits of placing industries in the private sector and getting the revenue from this exercise into the Exchequer, became more important than the longer term aims of increasing competition and efficiency.[43]

Throughout the 1980s, the Conservatives emphasised the need to reduce public expenditure as one means of 'rolling back the state'. Pressure in the form of rising levels of unemployment made this aim difficult to achieve. Taking public expenditure as a percentage of gross domestic product (GDP), total government expenditure under Mrs Thatcher rose from 41 per cent of GDP in 1979, to 46 per cent in the mid-1980s, averaging 42 per cent throughout the decade, falling to only 37 per cent in 1990.[44] Revenue generated through the privatisation programme, which was presented as "negative expenditure" in public accounts, allowed the appearance of a reduction in public expenditure to manifest itself. In practical terms this form of accounting had no effect. However, politically speaking it was highly symbolic, masking the fact that the Conservative government was failing significantly in its aim of reducing public expenditure. This led some commentators to suggest that privatisation resulted largely from the failure of government to reduce public expenditure. Therefore the impact of privatisation revenue on public expenditure was highly attractive during the 1980s, and it was felt that its importance as a revenue earner would continue into the 1990s.[45]

Nevertheless, despite the considerable amount of revenue which the privatisation programme generated, the notion that the privatisation objective of raising revenue was achieved unproblematically, needs to be qualified somewhat. Though it is clear that privatisation had a major impact on fiscal policy, it did not, as seen above, reduce the public sector borrowing requirement significantly, which would have been far higher without privatisation receipts.[46] In addition it can be persuasively asserted, that those companies which did not generate significant returns prior to privatisation but did so after, achieved such results because of the financial and manpower restructuring initiated by the government *before* privatisation. Thus by selling off these companies before the benefits of such restructuring manifested themselves, the government relinquished a potentially lucrative revenue source by cutting off a future income stream. The sale of many public assets represented a once-off

43. Wright, V, (1994) *op. cit.*; J Mitchell, (1990) *op. cit.*; J Richardson, (1994) *op. cit.*
44. Sweeney, P, (1990) *op. cit.*
45. Mitchell, J, (1990) *op. cit.*; P Sweeney, (1990) *op. cit.*; P Saunders & C Harris, (1994) *op. cit.*
46. Sweeney, P, (1990) *op. cit.*

financial gain for the government, but did not enhance the government's long-term net worth.[47]

Secondly, though it is clear that privatisation raised revenue for the government, the amount of revenue received was certainly less than could have been expected, largely due to the fact that most public assets were sold off below market value. Profitable state assets sold off too cheaply can also contribute to the deterioration of a government's long-term net worth.[48] In addition, in some cases of privatisation, e.g. water in the UK, it cost the government more to dispose of this industry than it received in return, largely through the writing off of debt, the provision of money for investment to upgrade the industry and advertising costs.[49]

The fact that the UK government also ignored the existence of extensive opposition to the privatisation of water, which emerged from a range of groups including the European Commission, farmers' organisations, the Confederation of British Industry, water industry chiefs, unions and the environmental lobby, begins to indicate the ideological nature of the privatisation programme. Such insights into the mechanics surrounding the privatisation process, demonstrate how ideology often rode rough shod over economic common sense, as well as illustrating the resolve of the Conservative government in pursuit of its ideological project.[50] As one commentator who explored one of the most expensive advertising campaigns ever to be launched observed:

> Anyone who predicted 10 years ago that, by 1989, expenditure on water advertising would be running at a rate of £1 million per month would have been laughed out of court. Margaret Thatcher herself, committed to eliminating wasteful expenditure, would have had apoplexy.
>
> (quoted in Mitchell, 1990:31)

Privatisation: Enhancing Competition and Efficiency?

John Moore, the minister who had responsibility for privatisation in 1983, suggested that the *raison d'être* for privatisation was to promote competition thereby increasing efficiency as follows:

> The long-term success of the privatisation programme will stand or fall by the extent to which it maximises competi-

---

47. Sweeney, P, (1990) *op. cit.*; J Mitchell, (1990) *op. cit.*; V Wright, (1994) *op. cit.*
48. Sweeney, P, (1990) *op. cit.*; V Wright, (1994) *op. cit.*
49. Saunders, P & C Harris, (1994) *op. cit.*
50. Carr, P, Book review of *Privatization and Popular Capitalism* 1994 by P Saunders & C Harris *Sociology,* (1995) 29: 4, pp. 755-756.

tion. If competition cannot be achieved, an historic opportunity will have been lost.

(quoted in Saunders & Harris, 1994:20)

Privatisation is clearly associated with the ideological belief that private ownership is inherently superior to public ownership. Deriving from this belief is the notion that private enterprise is *more competitive* than public enterprise, and that the former *excels* at providing better goods and services to the consumer at a lower cost. Throughout the 1980s, the Thatcher governments loudly applauded the private sector for being a naturally efficient and productive source for the satisfaction of consumer needs.[51] However, no *decisive* evidence exists which supports these suggestions. Empirical research, which explores whether private firms are more efficient than state-owned firms, is not definitive. Some studies suggest that privately owned firms are more efficient, others that publicly owned firms are better, and still other research claims that there is no difference between public and private sector efficiency.[52]

This situation has led some commentators to argue that the claim that private property per se is a more efficient form of ownership than public property is vacuous. Further it is suggested that, on balance, levels of competition rather than ownership has the biggest effect on efficiency.[53] Nevertheless, the strong belief that the Conservative governments of the 1980s had in the private sector, manifested itself in the transformation of public sector monopolies, such as British Telecom, British Gas and British Airways, into private sector monopolies. A serious encouragement of competition would have required the breaking up of these state monopolies prior to being sold.[54]

However, instead of promoting competition, public monopolies were privatised intact and new regulatory agencies which would monitor pricing policies were established.[55] In addition, research suggests that those companies which performed well and grew most *after* privatisation, were the ones which performed well *prior* to privatisation. Companies such as British Coal, British Steel and electricity which were all still nationalised in 1988, performed just as well in terms of productivity gains, as the privatised British Gas. Other companies, such as British Telecom, did not perform particularly well after privatisation.[56] The privatisation of British Rail has also not led to a significant improvement in performance.

51. Sweeney, P, (1990) *op. cit.*; C Samson, "The Three Faces of Privatisation" *Sociology* (1994) 28: 1, pp. 79-97.
52. Saunders, P & C Harris, (1994) *op. cit.*
53. Veljanovski, C, (1987) *op. cit.*; P Sweeney, (1990) *op. cit.*; P Saunders & C Harris, (1994) *op. cit.*
54. *Ibid.*
55. Saunders, P & C Harris, (1994) *op. cit.*
56. Sweeney, P, (1990) *op. cit.*

At the Labour Party Conference in September 1998, John Prescott, Minister for Transport, stated that since privatisation there has been a reduction in trains and an increase in fares, culminating in a general failure of the train service. He concluded that the performance of the privatised trains was a "national disgrace". This is despite the fact that privatised train companies received twice the level of subsidy that British Rail as a public company received. Richard Branson, owner of Virgin Rail, which was singled out for criticism by Prescott, stated that the 40 years of neglect that the train service experienced in public ownership could not be rectified overnight. Thus Branson echoed the sentiments of a 1986 OECD report which argued that it is the impact of *government practices* not *government ownership* which is crucial. The elimination of negative government practices could arguably have achieved the same results as it was hoped privatisation would achieve.[57]

Looking at privatisation, the general consensus seems to be that it is *competition **not** ownership* which is a key factor in generating improved performance in companies. Ownership per se has no direct connection to economic performance, no matter how such performance is judged. The radical programme of privatisation implemented by the Conservative governments failed to achieve the most important of its aims, i.e. increased levels of competition, leading to greater efficiency, lower prices and better services.[58] Though re-nationalisation as a solution to the problems surrounding the privatised companies was rejected at the Labour Party Conference in September 1998, a refusal to accept continued inefficiency and bad service was signalled by John Prescott, for example, when he stated "we will call time on the trains if they can't run to time".

The commitment behind this statement was demonstrated when he said that the existing rail regulatory bodies were going to be replaced. Perhaps Labour's contribution to privatisation in the United Kingdom will not be to re-nationalise or simply continue to privatise, rather it might be to set about getting the appropriate competitive and regulatory structures in place, which are recognised by most commentators as more important determinants of performance than ownership. In addition, the Labour government may involve itself in the business of ensuring that privatised companies are "fully enterprising". As suggested in Chapter 1, it is recognised that private commercial enterprises, despite their paradigmatic status, are not always as enterprising as they should be. Therefore:

> . . . commercial organisations must continually struggle to become ever more enterprising. Thus the discourse of enterprise also envisages a new type of rule and imagines new ways for people to conduct themselves within the pri-

---

57. *Ibid.*
58. *Ibid.*

vate business enterprise, as well as in public sector institutions.

(Du Gay & Salaman, 1992:623)

The demand to be "ever more enterprising" could become further inscribed into the range of mechanisms which Labour puts in place to ensure privatised companies:

. . . satisfy the needs and desires of the enterprising sovereign consumer and thus ensure business success.

(Du Gay & Salaman, 1992:624)

Nevertheless despite the failure of the privatisation programme to achieve its objective of increased competition from the beginning, it did establish new management aims for the managers of public and private companies, namely the rejection of social objectives in favour of profit.[59] Privatisation is said to have:

. . . symbolised the government's determination to take seriously the need to instil a competitive spirit in the public sector...They created an expectation of change which made effective management easier . . . engendering a more commercial and more abrasive management style.

(Sweeney, 1990:145)

Within the context of the programme of privatisation (a policy which as with other enterprise initiatives and strategies is involved in the production of enterprise culture), we can observe the emergence of an entrepreneurial management discourse, as discussed in Chapter 1. Here the aspects of this discourse which are prominent are, firstly, the emphasis which is placed on commercial success in the form of profit, and, secondly, the focus on strong management. Within the context of the privatisation programme, a clear preference emerged for market-oriented, profit-seeking entrepreneurs as opposed to budget-maximising bureaucrats and vote-maximising politicians.[60] This shift began prior to privatisation and continued post-privatisation with the increasing adoption of private sector management practices and attitudes, illustrated by the emergence of a strong orientation to the customer.[61] This

---

59. *Ibid.*
60. Wright, V, (1994) *op. cit.*
61. Du Gay, P & G Salaman, "The Cult[ure] of the Customer" *Journal of Management Studies* (1992) 29: 5, pp. 615-633; J Richardson, (1994) *op. cit.*

shift has been summarised by Pitt (1990) through his observations of the impact of privatisation in BT.

> *First management style is changing with the appointment of managers at the commanding heights who are acting as the carriers or 'champions' of an entrepreneurial risk-taking culture at variance with its predecessor the Post Office – bureaucratic and risk averse. Secondly marketing style is becoming more aggressive with 'new look' sales promotions, advertising and the recognition of discrete marketing niches requiring service from 'dedicated' account managers. Thirdly, the organisation has become more 'result-orientated'. Devolution and decentralisation have been accompanied by improvements in management information systems. The quality of information provided for effective management in a fast changing, competitive and commercial environment has improved. . . .The introduction of profit centres has done much to make staff aware of 'profit' as a* sine qua non *of organisation viability in an open market situation.*

(Pitt 1990, cited in Richardson, 1994:74)

Privatisation: Restricting the Powers of Public Sector Trade Unions

On achieving power in 1979, a major ambition of Margaret Thatcher was to restrict the power of public sector trade unions. Though privatisation has often been understood as one of the means by which public sector trade unions were tackled, it was not the major one. The critical weapon used against the unions was strong anti-union legislation introduced in 1980, 1982 and 1984, which significantly reduced trade union power. At most privatisation bolstered the legislative strategy adopted by the government, but it was not essential to it. Where privatisation may have played a role is that the forceful, enterprising management style which it promoted, centring around the notion of *a manager's right to manage,* may have obliged unions to be more flexible.[62] From the government's perspective, private management was more likely to challenge unions which attempted to protect inefficient work practices and employment levels.[63]

---

62. Mitchell, J, (1990) *op. cit.*; P Sweeney, (1990) *op. cit.*
63. Wright, V, (1994) *op. cit.*

Privatisation: Promoting an Ethic of Enterprise

The fourth and final objective of the privatisation programme (reflective of the ethical strand of enterprise culture itself) is one which seeks to promote a highly distinctive cultural agenda which contributes "towards the internalisation of a particular world view among segments of the public".[64] According to Veljanovski (1987) there was a strong belief that an anti-enterprise culture had contributed in no small way to Britain's economic decline. Within the canopy of enterprise initiatives which were put into place to promote an enterprise culture, privatisation was viewed as one means, along with others, such as education, by which the attitudes and values of the population could be significantly altered, a sentiment expressed by John Moore, minister for privatisation.

> Our aim is to build upon our property-owning democracy and to establish a people's capital market, to bring capitalism to the place of work, to the high street, and even to the home. As we dispose of state-owned assets, so more and more people have the opportunity to become owners. . . . [T]hese policies also increase personal independence and freedom, and by establishing a new breed of owner, have an important effect on attitudes.
>
> (quoted in Saunders & Harris, 1994:26)

The intention is clear here, i.e. that more people would become enterprising, in the sense outlined in Chapter 1 (self-reliant, optimistic, energetic, dynamic etc.), through experience of – and participation in – the free enterprise system by purchasing shares. As also stated in Chapter 1, it was believed that it is within the institutional context of the private commercial enterprise that individuals are likely to demonstrate an ethic of enterprise. Therefore within this context, privatisation was understood as the means by which attitudes would be transformed, through a transferral of ownership.[65]

In judging whether privatisation has achieved its cultural objective of changing attitudes and values, most commentators have focused on the impact of widespread share ownership. With regard to the issue of increasing the numbers of shareholders, privatisation had a measure of success. In 1984 only 6 per cent of the population held shares, a figure which increased to 20 per cent by the beginning of 1988.[66] Where it was less successful was in introducing the 'ordinary person on the street' into the boardroom. In this

64. Samson, C, (1994) *op. cit.*
65. Saunders, P & C Harris, (1994) *op. cit.*
66. Thompson, G, (1990) *op. cit.*

area it clearly failed largely due to a rapid sell off of shares by most 'ordinary' investors.

To illustrate this we can look at the situation of British Airways, British Telecom, British Gas and Rolls Royce. On privatisation the number of shareholders in British Airways was 1,100,000 which fell to 347,897 by March 1990. In British Telecom the number of shareholders fell from 2,051,373 to 1,236,870. In British Gas shareholders fell from 4,407,079 to 2,780,813, while in Rolls Royce share ownership dropped from 2,000,000 to 924,970 shareholders.[67] These shares were taken up by institutional investors who ended up holding more than 90 per cent of the shares in most of the privatised companies.[68] Arguably then no cultural change occurred because of this, though commentators such as Sweeney (1990) and Mitchell (1990) do not extrapolate from their discussion of share ownership to consider its cultural impact.

In contrast Saunders and Harris (1994) explicitly state that they are going to explore whether privatisation led to a change in cultural norms and values, through their analysis of the impact of share ownership on British culture. They do this by looking at the issue of share ownership across three dimensions. Firstly, they examined whether people who purchased shares demonstrated an increased interest in the organisations in which they invested. Secondly, they considered how important an individual's shareholding was to them. Finally, they assessed whether purchasing shares made individuals more self-reliant, achievement oriented, and more likely to pursue material rewards. On all three dimensions the authors judged "that the spread of share ownership has been irrelevant and inconsequential in the government's desire to foster an enterprise culture".[69]

However, given the very narrow approach which Saunders and Harris adopted to this issue of cultural change, it is not in the least bit surprising that they reached this conclusion.[70] Though certainly the Thatcher governments took a similarly narrow approach to the issue of cultural change attached to privatisation, as illustrated by John Moore's comments above, and this in itself is arguably problematic, whether or not a measurable cultural change emerged is not the only thing that is important here. Rather what is also important for our purposes, in terms of understanding the relationship between policy and the production of enterprise culture, is that within the context of the privatisation policy, the two strands of the enterprise culture concept identified in Chapter 1, are clearly evident. From this perspective what needs to be recognised is that the 'will to govern' through a range of policies, programmes, initiatives, etc. should be understood less in terms of their success,

---

67. Richardson, J, (1994) *op. cit.*
68. Sweeney, P, (1990) *op. cit.*; J Mitchell, (1990) *op. cit.*
69. Saunders, P & C Harris, (1994) *op. cit.*
70. Carr, P, (1995) *op. cit.*

and more in terms of the difficulties attached to operationalising policy choices and achieving the desired ends.[71] In addition, it is also clear that the "rolling back of the state" structurally, in the form of privileging the private sector over the public sector, is not enough if an ethic of enterprise is to be promoted and an enterprise culture is to be created.

Government at a Distance

As stated earlier, discussions of the role of the state and its relationship with economic activity tend to be constructed around the dichotomy of the passive and active state, with a manifest component of the enterprise culture project being the limiting of the role of the state. The post World War II period was characterised by an expansion of the boundaries of state and government action, with regard to intervention in the economy, through subsidisation, economic regulation and nationalisation, an expansion which was interrupted decisively in the late-1970s and early-1980s with the rise of the right.[72] However the apparent "rolling back of the state", which is said to characterise the enterprise culture and lead to the emergence of an enterprise ethic, through programmes such as privatisation, should be viewed cautiously.

Such caution can be attributed to the existence of a significant paradox highlighted in Chapter 1, that attempts to limit the scope of government, while promoting autonomy and individual freedom, require a complex array of government technologies, initiatives and strategies for success in this endeavour.[73] The conventional dichotomies of state versus society, public versus private, active versus passive, right versus left, etc., which conventionally surround the way we think about the role of government and state in our economic and social life, are of little use in understanding this apparent contradiction. Therefore rather than understanding programmes such as privatisation "as a simple 'withdrawal' from intervention to allow the market a freer hand",[74] they are perhaps best understood as a *change in the form of intervention*.

From Thompson's (1990) perspective, the *relatively extensive* regime of intervention characteristic of the post World War II era, has been replaced with a *relatively intensive* interventionary system which has four main characteristics. Firstly this new regime of intervention has a narrower field of operation than its predecessor while at the same time there is a "widening of its scope and a deepening of its character".[75] This leads into its second char-

---

71. Miller, P & N Rose, "Governing economic life" *Economy and Society* (1990) 19: 1, pp. 1-31.
72. Thompson, G, (1990) *op. cit.*
73. Miller, P & N Rose, (1990) *op. cit.*
74. Thompson, G, (1990) *op. cit.*
75. *Ibid.* p. 140.

acteristic where the narrowing of the field of intervention is offset by "a more intensive gaze"[76] directed at the economic activity under scrutiny. Sectors, companies and individuals are likely to be subject to a more detailed scrutiny of their affairs than in the traditional interventive system. Thirdly this new regime of intervention has what Thompson (1990) calls a "layered" character, where mechanisms of intervention purposefully overlap and overlayer, rather than complimenting each other. Instead of there being just one layer of regulatory mechanisms, there are now a number of layers. Finally the level of discretion exercised by the interventionary and regulatory structures and those involved with them, has increased significantly. This increase in discretion arises out of the high levels of autonomy granted to these structures in the performance of their business. However it should be noted that this is tempered by the general rules laid down by government, guiding the formation of regulatory bodies.

The new regulatory agencies (e.g. OFTEL for the telecommunications industry, OFGAS for the gas industry, OFWAT for the water industry, etc.), set up alongside the privatised companies to monitor and control their activity can be understood in these terms. The existence of such agencies indicates the move towards a *re-regulation* of large parts of the economy. This re-regulation can be understood in terms of a regulation of structure and a regulation of conduct. The former refers to the way the market is organised, while the latter refers to behaviour within that market. The existence of such regulation indicates that the state has not withdrawn in any simple sense from intervention in the economy. The issue, therefore, is not whether intervention exists or not – it does – rather it is the form that such regulation or intervention takes.[77]

Understanding privatisation as firstly a *change* in state regulation, as opposed to a *withdrawal* of state direction, and secondly as one of the means by which enterprise is produced, takes us back to our suggestion in Chapter 1 that we need to include a notion of 'government' within our understanding of enterprise culture. Such a conceptualisation directs our attention to the technological dimensions of government which have sought to enable what Thompson (1990) and Miller and Rose (1990) term "intervention/government at a distance". Understanding the role of the state in enterprise culture in these terms can also highlight how government may involve itself in the business of ensuring that companies and individuals are "fully enterprising".

This conceptualisation of state activity in enterprise culture can be understood in terms of Foucault's concept of *governmentality,* a concept which allows us to assess how a state acts at a distance, on the action of individuals, either together or individually, with the aim of shaping, guiding, correcting and modifying the ways in which they conduct themselves. Governmentali-

---

76. *Ibid.* p. 139.
77. *Ibid.*

sation refers to the numerous diverse techniques of government which are not necessarily inherent to the state, or operationalised in an intentional fashion. It is an array of technologies, i.e. strategies, methods and procedures, which different administrations use to set in train government programmes in a variety of areas. It should be understood as the complex of institutions, procedures, analyses, reflections, calculations and strategies which have sought to act upon the lives and behaviour of individuals in order to achieve such goals as health, wealth and tranquillity within a state.[78]

Nevertheless, we need to be clear that though such government strategies may lead to the efficient management of individuals, one cannot assume that there is by definition a causal link between these strategies and a centralised state power.[79] The notion of state activity and government which Foucault presents is one which accentuates the multiplicity of strategies, techniques, knowledges and powers involved in opening up areas to intervention, but state control remains incomplete, confused and contradictory.[80] This approach allows us to understand state activity not as:

> . . . the direct imposition of a form of conduct by force, but through a delicate affiliation . . . [which] involves alliances formed not only because one agent is dependent upon another for funds, legitimacy or some other resource which can be used for persuasion or compulsion, but also because one actor comes to convince another that their problems or goals are intrinsically linked . . . that each can . . . achieve their ends by joining forces or working along the same lines . . . [where] one actor or force (e.g. the state) is able to require or count upon a particular way of thinking and acting from another (e.g. individuals or individual businesses), hence assembling them together into a network not because of legal or institutional ties or dependencies, but because they have come to construe their problems in allied ways and their fate as in some way bound up with one another.
>
> (Miller & Rose, 1990:10)

Therefore within the context of incorporating a notion of government into our understanding of enterprise culture, enterprise policies, initiatives and

---

78. Foucault, M, "Governmentality" in G Burchell, C Gordon & P Miller (eds), *The Foucault Effect: Studies in Governmentality* (London: Harvester Wheatsheaf) 1991; N Rose, "Governing the enterprising self" in P Heelas & P Morris (eds), *The Values of the Enterprise Culture: The Moral Debate* (London: Routledge) 1992.
79. McNay, L, *Foucault: A Critical Introduction* (Cambridge: Polity Press) 1994.
80. Miller, P & N Rose, (1990) *op. cit.*

programmes can be understood as types of "governmental rationality" which aim "to develop those elements constitutive of individuals' lives in such a way that their development also fosters that of the strength of the state".[81] This understanding of government activity in enterprise culture will be further explored and expanded upon in the following chapters.

SUMMARY OF KEY IDEAS

- In any account of enterprise culture a crucial issue is the role of state and government in economic activity. From a 'right' perspective the state should not intervene in the economy, from a 'left' perspective the state should actively intervene in the process of economic development.

- Both the 'right' and the 'left' recognised problems with the gigantic expansion of the state during the 20th century. However only the 'right' capitalised on these problems, setting the scene for a shift from state to market regulation of economic and social life.

- As part of a wider policy approach, privatisation made a dramatic and radical contribution to the restructuring of the relationship between state, market and society. Privatisation can broadly be understood as the transfer of activities and responsibilities out of the public sector into the private sector.

- Though the UK was the pioneer in implementing extensive privatisation programmes, many European countries have followed the British example.

- Privatisation as a policy is reflective of the institutional and ethical dimensions of enterprise culture, firstly in its privileging of the private sector commercial enterprise, and secondly in its hope that privatisation would promote enterprising values.

- We need to be careful about interpreting policies such as privatisation as an uncomplicated withdrawal of state intervention, rather it is best understood as a *change* in the form of state intervention.

- Understanding privatisation as a *change* in state regulation, and one of the means by which enterprise culture is produced, brings us back to the suggestion in Chapter 1, that we should include a notion of government in our understanding of enterprise culture.

---

81. Foucault quoted in L McNay, (1994) *op. cit.*

CHAPTER 3

Entrepreneurial Management in Public Sector Organisations

Public services of all kinds have been subjected to a penetrating process of marketisation requiring their managers to change themselves from public service bureaucrats or professionals into new kinds of public service entrepreneurs.

(Rustin, 1994:76)

MANAGING THE PUBLIC SECTOR

Earlier we suggested that a key aim of the enterprise culture project was the "rolling back of the state", and the privileging of market activity and market forces. This restructuring of the relationship between state, market and society was facilitated by policies such as privatisation, which centred on the transfer of activities and responsibilities out of the public sector into the private sector. However this reshaping of the public/private divide is highly complex, and privatisation is not the only means by which the relationship between 'public' and 'private' has been reconfigured.[1] In certain areas of the public sector, it has proved very difficult to transfer activities such as welfare services into the private sector, despite the fact that aspects of welfare services have been privatised through the introduction of subcontracting relationships.[2] This led to a recognition that there are core public services which cannot be privatised and must be funded by the Exchequer.[3]

However, where the public sector has not easily been transferred into the private sector, the private sector has been brought into the public sector through the introduction of private sector management practices, which place an emphasis on managerial efficiency and a market orientation. Calls for public

1. Clarke, J & J Newman, *The Managerial State* (London: Sage) 1997.
2. Kelly, A, "The enterprise culture and the welfare state: restructuring the management of health and social services" in R Burrows (ed.), *Deciphering the Enterprise Culture.* (London: Routledge) 1991.
3. Kirkpatrick, I & Lucio M Martinez, "The use of 'quality' in the British government's reform of the public sector" in I Kirkpatrick & M Martinez Lucio (eds), *The Politics of Quality in the Public Sector* (London: Routledge) 1995.

sector organisations to become more 'business-like' in their behaviour have contributed to a blurring of the boundaries between the public and private sectors.[4] Within the context of this blurring of boundaries, the enterprise culture technologies of privatisation and the 'businessing up' of the public sector, are significantly linked to each other. As suggested in Chapter 2 privatisation contributed to the increasing adoption of commercial management practices and attitudes, and public sector business reforms have been judged against the reference point of privatised companies.[5]

This shift in management within the public sector, from a model which is administrative to one which is performance oriented, traverses all state-related institutions and activities within the UK, including health, education, general welfare provision, the criminal justice system, local government and the civil service. Similarly, as with privatisation, this reorganisation of public services can also be found in a number of European countries, such as Ireland, and in other countries around the world, such as the USA and New Zealand. A commitment to this shift is also evident within the New Labour government of Tony Blair. For example, in the area of education, David Blunkett, the Education Secretary, is said to have done more than any previous Secretary of State, regarding the introduction of business values into schools.[6] Reforms in this area have included Education Action Zones, superheads, compulsory literacy and numeracy hours, and national performance targets. He is also keen to further the introduction of private sector business values into education by injecting ". . . a business-style philosophy of competition into the staff room as well as the classroom".[7] This will be achieved through performance-related pay and the fast-tracking of individuals demonstrating high performance teaching, thus guaranteeing them quick promotion and higher rates of classroom pay. Such developments, set in train in the UK context by Conservative governments, and continued by the New Labour government, have led some commentators to suggest that one of the:

> . . . most profound accomplishment(s) of . . . government in Britain may not be that it literally rolled back the state in order to release the full blast of market forces but, rather, that it inserted the new managerialism and market reasoning into the state and state-related agencies of the public sector, in effect calling upon organisations that are not themselves private businesses to think and function as though they were.
>
> (McGuigan, 1996:62)

---

4.   Clarke, J & J Newman, (1997) *op. cit.*
5.   *Ibid.*
6.   Bright, M & P Wintour, "I'm going to teach them my three R's" *The Observer* 29 November 1998.
7.   *Ibid.* p. 12.

NEW MANAGERIALISM: WHAT IT WANTS TO MOVE FROM

As discussed in Chapter 2, the impetus for reform of the public sector strongly emerged from the belief that the state had grown too big, too expensive and too inhibiting of the free market and individual enterprise. In addition a further stimulus for reform was rooted in popular discontent with bureaucracy, with commentators such as Peters (1987) suggesting that everyone should have a public and passionate hatred of it.

The Characteristics of Bureaucracy

Bureaucracies are characterised by *rules*, laws and administrative regulations which operate in officially designated districts and provinces. The bureaucracy is a *hierarchically ordered* system with lower offices being supervised by higher ones. Bureaucratic management is characterised by general learned rules which are stable and exhaustive. A key feature of bureaucracy is the emphasis that is placed upon *written documents* which are maintained in the form of files. Within the bureaucracy there is a strict *separation* between the official activity of the bureaucracy and the private life of the bureaucrats who work within it. Office holding is not considered a source to be exploited for personal gain. In return for a secure existence, office holders are expected to be *loyal* and faithful to the *impersonal* and functional purposes of the bureaucracy. The 'pure' type of bureaucratic official is usually appointed by a superior authority and normally the position is held for life. By way of compensation the bureaucrat receives a *regular* fixed salary and old age pension. *Salary* level is not determined by the amount of work done, rather it is determined by the *status*, i.e. rank, function and length of service of the official. It is usually the case that the bureaucrat follows a career path within the hierarchical order of the bureaucracy, starting at the lower paid and less important ranks and moving up to a higher position over time. The reason for the increased prominence and advance of the bureaucracy was its purely *technical superiority* over any other form of organisation. Such superiority was said to manifest itself in precision, speed, clarity, knowledge, continuity, discretion, unity and strict subordination. All of these factors are said to be raised to the optimum point in the strictly bureaucratic administration. Bureaucratisation ensures the performance of specialised administrative functions according to purely *objective* considerations, that is, the discharge of business according to calculable rules *'without regard for persons'*. As a form of organisation, the benefits of bureaucracy are heightened the more it is 'dehumanised', i.e. the more it eliminates from official business love, hatred and all purely personal, irrational and emotional elements which escape calculation.

(Gerth & Mills, 1970)

According to Jacques (1990) bureaucracy became a dirty word even among bureaucrats, and in the business world there emerged the widespread view that hierarchy kills initiative and crushes creativity. Thus a convergence occurred between those on the right who characterised state bureaucracies as inefficient and paternalistic, and general public concern about the quality and effectiveness of state welfare services.

This coincidence of interest laid the groundwork for the promotion of a market solution to the perceived ills of the public sector.[8] Such criticism of public sector bureaucracy is in direct contrast to the original value that was placed on bureaucracy as a form of organisation. Within the context of a post-war state, which placed an emphasis on the centralised and uniform administration of government programmes, the advantages of bureaucratic organisation (such as consistency, reliability, and the detailed control of subordinate staff within a hierarchical structure), provided a means by which large public organisations, could carry out their functions in accordance with the requirements of public accountability.[9] Allied to this the emphasis on the depersonalisation of administration implied that the recipients of a bureaucracy's service, particularly a public sector bureaucracy, were subject to a formal equality of treatment. However the case *against* bureaucracy emerges out of the dysfunctions of bureaucratic organisation which are said to be exacerbated by the external environment of the late-20th century.

These dysfunctions include an *overemphasis* on rules and regulations thus losing sight of general organisational objectives; the possible existence of a *clash* between the objectives of the bureaucratic organisation and the aspirations of individual bureaucrats and that the possibility that non-adherence to rules may *increase* the efficiency of the organisation.[10] An external environment characterised by massive uncertainty, the increasing deployment of information technology, the competitive pressures resulting from global trading systems, and the general intensification of global interconnectedness, creates a situation where these dysfunctions are magnified.[11] In such an environment, bureaucracies, particularly public-sector bureaucracies, are said to fail us. Government critiques of public services, particularly within the UK, focused heavily on the possibility of a clash existing between bureaucratic objectives and individual bureaucrats' aspirations and interests. It was suggested that state bureaucracies very often put their own producer interests

---

8. Reed, M, "Managing quality and organizational politics: TQM as a governmental technology" in I Kirkpatrick & M Martinez Lucio (eds), (1995) *op. cit.*

9. Greenwood, J & D Wilson, *Public Administration in Britain Today* (London: Unwin Hyman) 1989.

10. Lawton, A & A Rose, *Organisation and Management in the Public Sector* (London: Pitman Publishing) 1992.

11. Reed, M, (1995) *op. cit.*; P Du Gay, *Consumption and Identity at Work* (London: Sage) 1996.

before that of the consumer, with the former being characterised as self-serving, inefficient and ineffective.[12]

As well as being highly critical of bureaucrats and bureaucracy, government reviews of the public sector were also highly censorious of professionals, reinforced by public opinion which demonstrated a high level of disenchantment with 'professionalised' welfare.[13] According to Wilding (quoted in Kirkpatrick & Martinez Lucio (1995:8)) "Thatcherism has questioned and substantially damaged the credibility of two basic instruments of collectivist welfare policy – bureaucracy and professionals". The British welfare state has been characterised by a regime of 'bureau-professionalism', based on a compromise between centralised bureaucratic control and decentralised professional syndicalism.[14] A complex of bureaucratic (defined as 'inflexible' bureaucrats), professional (defined as 'arrogant' professionals) and political (defined as 'interfering' politicians) power, was identified as a major barrier to the transformation of the state.[15]

However from the mid-1980s onwards, a challenge to this hegemony was posed through the introduction of private sector business practices into the public sector. These practices of commercialisation and marketisation "...challenged the hegemony of an institutional culture and organisational practice based on the morality of 'public service' and the politics of bureaucratic compromise".[16] Calls were therefore made for a new kind of market oriented organisation, which it was argued was more efficient than bureaucratic forms of organisation.[17] The aim was to engineer:

> . . . a paradigm shift in social values and managerial forms
> such that the principles and practices of bureaucratic ra-
> tionality were to be replaced by those constitutive of market
> rationality.

(Reed, 1995:44)

THE EVOLUTION OF NEW MANAGERIALISM

The past two decades have been characterised by a rejuvenation of the role of

---

12. Kirkpatrick, I & Lucio M Martinez, (1995) *op. cit.*
13. Kelly, A, (1991) *op. cit.*
14. Reed, M, (1995) *op. cit.*
15. Newman, J & J Clarke, "Going About Our Business? The Managerialization of Public Services" in J Clarke, A Cochrane & E McLaughlin (eds), *Managing Social Policy* (London: Sage) 1994.
16. Reed, M, (1995) *op. cit.*, p. 56.
17. Jacques, E, "In Praise of Hierarchy" *Harvard Business Review* (Jan-Feb 1990); D Osborne & T Gaebler, *Reinventing Government.* (Reading MA: Addison-Wesley) 1992; I Kirkpatrick & Lucio M Martinez, (1995) *op. cit.*

the manager. Post-1945, the role of the manager was proscribed by agreements between capital and labour. However the recessionary conditions of the 1970s formed the backdrop to a reassertion of managerial power,[18] with calls for the restoration of a manager's 'right to manage' as expressed in the following:

> Managers for twenty years have had a buffeting and beating from government and unions and we have been put in a can't win situation. We have an opportunity now that will last for two or three years. . . . Then the unions will get themselves together again; and the government, like all governments will run out of steam. So grab it now. We have had a pounding and we are all fed up with it. I think it would be fair to say that it's almost vengeance.
>
> (Collinson, *The Financial Times* (1981)
> cited in Newman & Clarke, 1994:17)

Managerialism, understood as the re-emergence of the manager as a significant and powerful individual in the economy,[19] is characterised by a range of specific beliefs identified by Pollitt (1993) as follows:

- Continued increases in productivity (defined economically) are identified as the key to social progress.
- The efficient and effective use of new technologies (information organisational 'hardware') will contribute to productivity increases.
- To make effective use of these new technologies the labour force must adopt a disciplined productivity ethic.
- Managers as individuals, and management as an activity, are identified as the key ingredient for business success, and crucial for the achievement of improved productivity.
- To perform their central role managers must be given the 'right to manage'.

Embedded in these beliefs is the notion that there is no more important area of human activity than managing and taken together they can be said to constitute an ideology.[20] According to Pollitt (1993) as an ideology managerialism

---

18. Clarke, J & J Newman, "The Right to Manage: A Second Managerial Revolution?" *Cultural Studies* (1993) 7 (3), pp. 427-441.
19. Wood, S J, "New Wave Management?" *Work, Employment & Society* (1989) 3, 3: pp. 379-402.
20. Pollitt, C, *Managerialism and the Public Services* (Oxford: Blackwell Publishers) 2nd edn, 1993.

has a range of attributes as follows:

- It consists of a range of ideas and values, with one of its main principles being the esteem in which management is held. This suggests that management is the key to economic revival and performance because it can eliminate waste, make effective use of resources, and be accountable for money spent.

- Managerialism should be recognised as a systematically structured set of beliefs. In particular there is a strong belief that the corporate sector has performed better over the past 50 years than the state.

- Managerialism privileges managers as heroes who are often requested to comment on a range of social issues, such as education as well as business affairs. In contrast, other groups, such as trade unions, are negatively valued because they are seen as an impediment to increased productivity.

- Managerialism as an ideology is actively disseminated and reinforced by certain individuals. In particular, managers themselves highlight their special contribution as a justification for their privileged position (and high salaries). However other groups, such as government, or even trade unions, may find it convenient to adopt elements of managerialism on occasion.

- Managerialism as an ideology can provide a justification for a certain course of action. For example a manager who acts without consulting other parties can justify this on the basis of the 'right to manage'.

Throughout the 1980s and 1990s the influence of managerialism as an ideology grew, with more and better management identified as the means by which Western economies could gain competitive advantage, in an increasingly uncertain business world.[21] However the image of the 'manager as saviour' which is promoted, is not that of the bureaucratic, time-serving organisational man who strictly adheres to procedure, rather it is of the dynamic leader who can act as an entrepreneurial, daring, inspirational change agent.[22] The revitalisation of management in the 1980s and 1990s presented managers:

> . . . as having a pivotal role in securing successful organisational change through fostering certain 'entrepreneurial' virtues, first within themselves and then among their subordinates. Thus, in opposition to the 'personally detached and strictly objective expert' deemed to characterise bureaucratic management the 'excellent' manager was represented as a 'charismatic' facilitator, teaching others to learn how to take responsibility for themselves and fostering an 'enter-

21. Clarke, J & J Newman, (1997) *op. cit.*
22. *Ibid.*

prising' sense of identification, commitment and involvement between employees and the organization for which they worked.

(Du Gay et al, 1996: 267)

Contained within this account of the contemporary manager is the notion of entrepreneurial management which is presented as *'calculatingly charismatic* (my emphasis) in essence',[23] a turn of phrase which reflects the management and enterprise dimensions of entrepreneurial management discussed in Chapter 1. As suggested in Chapter 1, these two dimensions of entrepreneurial management may be located in the one individual. Alternatively, managers may increasingly take on leadership tasks, such as creating a vision of the business (the enterprise dimension), while workers will increasingly perform tasks, such as planning or co-ordination (the management dimension).

Managerialism (Entrepreneurial Governance) in the Public Sector

New managerialism primarily developed within the private sector in the UK and USA. However it has had a marked impact on the British and American public sectors, with the exalted position given to the manager in the private sector, being carried over into the public sector.[24] Throughout the 1980s, the Conservative Party in the UK identified management as the means by which the public sector could be transformed ". . . from its staid bureaucratic paternalism . . . into a dynamic and effective series of organisations able to deliver 'value for money' services on a competitive basis".[25] Management was identified as efficient and outward-looking, and more concerned with providing an effective, customer-oriented service, than building and maintaining organisational 'empires'.[26] The organisational transformation brought about by this paradigm shift privileged market discipline and concern for the customer, over administrative regulation and professional autonomy.[27] Markets were introduced into the public sector through a range of policy mechanisms which as stated earlier included privatisation, the establishment of quasi-markets which facilitated the separation of the planning and purchase of services from their delivery, and the introduction of commercial norms and managerialist

23. Du Gay, P, G Salaman & B Rees, "The Conduct of Management and the Management of Conduct: Contemporary Managerial Discourse and the Constitution of the 'Competent' Manager" *Journal of Management Studies* (1996) 33: 3, pp. 263-282.
24. Newman, J & J Clarke, (1994) *op. cit.*
25. *Ibid.*, p. 15.
26. *Ibid.*
27. Reed, M, (1995) *op. cit.*; J Clarke & J Newman, (1997) *op. cit.*

management practices.[28] Thus the norms and values of conduct inscribed within the new managerialist discourse are articulated in explicit opposition to the norms and values of bureaucracy.[29]

Osborne and Gaebler's *Reinventing Government,* which coined the term 'entrepreneurial governance' to define the introduction of managerialism into the public sector, has become one of the major codifications of the theory and practice of managerialism in the public sector within the UK and USA. This was indicated by William Waldegrave, a former UK Minister for Public Service when he stated that *Reinventing Government* would become the 'bible' for British public sector managers in the 1990s, with many of its ideas underpinning public sector reform in many advanced economies.[30] According to Osborne and Gaebler (1992) within our contemporary environment, bureaucracy both public and private, continuously fails us. From their perspective what is required are flexible, adaptable, economic, efficient and effective organisations. Efficient and effective organisations are those which get more value for their money (as they phrase it "more bang out of every buck"), are responsive to customers by offering a wide range of non-standardised services and provide employees with a sense of ownership, meaning and control in their lives.

Defining Entrepreneurial Governance

Entrepreneurial governance (new managerialism) can be understood simply as the introduction of private sector management practices into the public sector. Conventionally it is presented as the panacea to the dysfunctions of public sector bureaucracy. There is an assumption that public sector organisations will 'work better', and all of their 'ills' will be eliminated, with the introduction of private sector commercial practices, which includes the following:

• A heavy emphasis is placed on the use of efficient and effective management practices, so that *'value for money'* and getting *'more for less'* can be delivered.

• Throughout the public sector organisations are divided into 'buyers' and 'sellers'. The effect of this is to redefine relationships in terms of an explicit *contract* between different parts of the public sector, or between the public and private or voluntary sectors. Alternatively a *pseudo-con-*

---

28. Kirkpatrick, I & Lucio M Martinez, (1995) *op. cit.*; M Reed, (1995) *op. cit.*; J Clarke & J Newman, (1995) *op. cit.*
29. Osborne, D & T Gaebler, (1992) *op. cit.*; P Du Gay, (1996) *op. cit.*
30. Du Gay, P, "Entrepreneurial Management in the Public Sector" *Work, Employment and Society* (1993) 7: 4, pp. 643-648; J McGuigan, *Culture and the Public Sphere* (London: Routledge) 1996; J Clarke & J Newman, (1997) *op. cit.*

tract is established between different parts of the public sector, which works like a contractual relationship, but no technical contract exists.

- *Competition* is promoted both internally and externally. Competition here can take a number of forms. For example, private sector firms may be asked to compete to provide a public service. Alternatively, different parts of the public sector are expected to compete with each other.

- Associated with competition is the *decentralisation* of responsibility and accountability but usually this is *not* aligned with a decentralisation of authority and control. Cost centres have been established to encourage an awareness of how resources are used at different levels of the organisation, as well as making visible the quality of services provided.

- An emphasis is placed on the establishment of a clear set of *strategic objectives* within all government departments. Divisions and sections within each department will also have their own objectives which will be unequivocally associated with the overall departmental strategy.

- Central pay bargaining has been replaced with individual, 'on-site' bargaining, thus providing managers within the public sector with another managerial tool. Individuals work to annually negotiated *personal targets* against which *performance* is judged. Decisions about promotion, training, pay increases, fringe benefits, etc. are heavily influenced by performance judged against these personal targets.

The principles of entrepreneurial governance can thus be summarised as competition, empowerment, performance, choice, decentralisation, and the market.

(Osborne & Gaebler, 1992; Pollitt, 1993; Newman & Clarke, 1994; Flynn, 1994; Burchell, 1996)

These principles were put in place through a range of management changes implemented in various parts of the public sector. These management changes were not just about facilitating a process of organisational restructuring, they were also concerned with inaugurating an era of cultural change.[31] Within current discussions of the transformation of the public sector it has been suggested that there are two varieties of entrepreneurial governance, which coincide with two phases of the restructuring of public services.[32] Though both varieties were concerned with ". . . shaking up public services management culture . . . ",[33] it is suggested that the variety of entrepreneurial governance identified with the second phase, is more strongly associated with attitudinal restructuring and cultural reconditioning along enterprise lines.[34]

31. Clarke, J & J Newman, (1997) *op. cit.*
32. Newman, J. & J Clarke, (1994) *op. cit.*
33. Clarke, J. & J Newman, (1997) *op. cit.*
34. Reed, M, (1995) *op. cit.*

The first phase, which can be dated from 1979 to 1987, focused on re-forming the public sector with a view to making it more accountable and more efficient in the provision of public services.[35] The style of entrepreneurial governance implemented during this phase was labelled as 'neo-Taylorist' by Pollitt (1993). This phase was characterised by a strong commitment to ensuring the 'three Es' of economy, efficiency and effectiveness, by way of a management approach, which concentrated on the rational analysis of organisational inputs and outputs.[36] Attention during this phase was directed at the reform of management structures through the appointment of managers with private sector experience, the delegation of the responsibility for budgets, and the development of performance targets and performance-related pay.[37] The overall objective was to provide 'value for money' services while increasing efficiency and productivity, through an intensification of control over resources, staff energy and staff endeavour.[38]

From 1987 onwards, the second phase emerged characterised by a thorough going market-based restructuring of the public sector. During this phase a fragmentation of public services occurred with the aim of setting up competing service providers. These radical market-based reforms of the public sector included initiatives such as the establishment of an internal market within the NHS, with, for example, the purchase of health care by GPs and health authorities being separated from the provision of health services by hospitals.[39] A second variety of entrepreneurial governance emerged characterised as 'people-centred', and concerned with releasing the 'enterprising spirit' of employees by loosening formal systems of control, though it was still concerned with providing 'value for money' and getting 'more for less'. An emphasis is placed on motivating individuals to be daring, dynamic and enterprising by getting close to the customer and valuing innovation.[40]

It has been argued by commentators that the first model has dominated and strongly influenced public sector reform, but Newman and Clarke (1994) suggest that by the end of the 1980s the second model was asserting itself. However, rather than understanding the relationship between these two varieties of entrepreneurial governance as one of succession, it would appear that both approaches have developed simultaneously within the public sec-

---

35. Bach, S & D Winchester, "Opting Out of Pay Devolution? The Prospects for Local Pay Bargaining in UK Public Services" *British Journal of Industrial Relations* (1994) 32: 2, pp. 263-282.
36. Newman, J & J Clarke, (1994) *op. cit.*
37. Bach, S & D Winchester, (1994) *op. cit.*
38. Newman, J & J Clarke, (1994) *op. cit.*; N Flynn, "Control, Commitment and Contracts" in J Clarke, A Cochrane & E McLaughlin (eds), *Managing Social Policy* (London: Sage) 1994; J Clarke & J Newman, (1997) *op. cit.*
39. Bach, S & D Winchester, (1994) *op. cit.*
40. Newman, J & J Clarke, (1994) *op. cit.*

tor.[41] Thus it has been suggested that the relationship between the two models should be viewed as one of co-existence and not one of succession or opposition.[42] This links to our discussion in Chapter 1, which suggested that the dimensions of management and entrepreneurship, within the entrepreneurial management discourse produced by enterprise culture, have a dialectic co-existence. Thus in looking at the way in which entrepreneurial governance has manifested itself within the public sector, we will see how it is reflective of the enterprising and management dimensions of the entrepreneurial management discourse, produced by attempts to create an enterprise culture.

ENTREPRENEURIAL GOVERNANCE AND ENTERPRISE CULTURE

Entrepreneurial Governance: Promoting Private Sector Management Practices and an Ethic of Enterprise in the Public Sector

To understand the significance and wider implications of the introduction of entrepreneurial governance within the public sector, we need to locate it within the wider ideological and political context of attempts to create an enterprise culture. Earlier we have emphasised the need to include a notion of 'government' within our understanding of enterprise culture by exploring the cultural technology (policies, initiatives, strategies, etc.) which actually *produces* it. Government here is understood as an activity and not just as an institution, contributing to an appreciation of enterprise culture as "...a rationally reflected way of doing things".[43] The suggestion here is that the policies and practices of entrepreneurial governance in the public sector, can be understood as one significant element of a broader range of technologies, policies, initiatives, strategies, etc., which make up an overriding rationality of government based on enterprise.[44] The most significant characteristic of enterprise culture as a rationality of government is its:

> ... generalisation of an 'enterprise form' to all forms of conduct – to the conduct of organisations hitherto seen as be-

41. *Ibid.*; N Flynn, (1994) *op. cit.*

42. Newman, J & J Clarke, (1994) *op. cit.*

43. Burchell, G, "Liberal government and techniques of the self" in A Barry, T Osborne & N Rose (eds), *Foucault and Political Reason* (London: UCL Press) 1996.

44. Reed, M, (1995) *op. cit.*; G Burchell, (1996) *op. cit.*; P Du Gay, "Organizing Identity: Making Up People at Work" in P Du Gay (ed.), *Production of Culture/ Cultures of Production* (London: Sage) 1997.

ing non-economic, to the conduct of government and to the conduct of individuals themselves – (which) constitutes the essential characteristic of this style of government: the promotion of an enterprise culture.

(Burchell, 1996:29)

Thus signalling that the way in which we can understand entrepreneurial governance is as part of a range of enterprise governmental techniques which *produce* enterprise culture. These techniques introduce an enterprise mode of action, that adheres to a competitive logic, into a range of public sector organisations which previously were seen as non-commercial.[45] Entrepreneurial governance can thus be understood in terms of a range of technologies and initiatives which operationalise the dimensions and values of enterprise culture, which in general include the privileging of the private sector commercial enterprise, private sector business practices and the promotion of an ethic of enterprise. In addition entrepreneurial governance, in the form of a range of policies, initiatives, etc., contributes to the production of an entrepreneurial management discourse in general, and within the public sector in particular. In looking at one key aspect of entrepreneurial governance, i.e. the implementation of performance indicators, we will see how they reflect and produce the key dimensions of enterprise culture. These include the marketisation of social relations, the privileging of commercial practices and the commercial enterprise, and the promotion of a range of enterprising qualities such as dynamism, self-reliance, responsibility, daring spirit, etc.

Performance Indicators

During the 1980s and 1990s performance indicators were introduced into a range of public sector activities. These indicators are conventionally understood as the means by which a series of organisational processes and outputs can be measured. The aim of such measurement is to evaluate the efficiency and effectiveness of service standards in the public sector, to ensure 'value for money', and to meet the needs and demands of consumers.[46] The introduction of performance indicators is associated with the establishment of an increased number of 'cost centres' and the decentralisation of activities into these autonomous sub-units.[47] Consumerism and an emphasis on the consumer (which will be explored in detail in Chapter 4) is part of the general

---

45. Burchell, G, (1996) *op. cit.*
46. Davies, A & I Kirkpatrick, "Performance indicators, bureaucratic control and the decline of professional autonomy: the case of academic librarians" in I Kirkpatrick & Lucio M Martinez (eds), (1995) *op. cit.*
47. Kelly, A, (1991) *op. cit.*

move towards decentralisation.[48] A key aim of decentralisation processes is the promotion of an ethic of enterprise. This is done by encouraging individuals within decentralised units to be active and dynamic in the performance of their duties, while at the same time undertaking a level of responsibility for their own management, self-co-ordination and organisational conduct, not previously available to them within a centralised system.

However, attempts to transform the public sector from an administrative system to one which is performance and enterprise oriented, would not be achieved by a simple structural decentralisation of activities. A structural change such as this is *by itself* an inadequate government strategy, if an ethic of enterprise is to be promoted and an enterprise culture is to be created. Government attempts to promote autonomy, initiative and individual freedom within the public sector require a complex array of government technologies and strategies, and not simply a structural 'rolling back of the state' through a process of decentralisation. Thus performance indicators are introduced as a government technology which can provide central government with the means to influence the activities of decentralised units. In particular, such indicators do not only measure the efficiency and effectiveness of public services, but also endeavour to promote a culture of performance and enterprise. What emerges therefore is a 'decentralised centralisation' where nominally autonomous agencies and the individuals within them, are empowered through a range of delegatory mechanisms, while at the same time being subjected to a range of regulation, surveillance and evaluation processes which aim to promote an ethic of enterprise.[49]

Clarke and Newman (1997) refer to this as a process of dispersal, a concept which is analogous to that of 'government at a distance' discussed in Chapter 2. The concepts of 'dispersal' and 'government at a distance' alert us to the fact that the emergence of an ethic of enterprise cannot simply be attributed to a straightforward withdrawal of the state, the terms within which policy programmes, such as privatisation and entrepreneurial governance, are conventionally understood. Integral to such policy programmes are a multiplicity of strategies and techniques which produce ". . . a more intensive gaze",[50] the purpose of which is to encourage individuals to adopt an enterprising (active, dynamic, disciplined, responsible, innovative, etc.) as opposed to a bureaucratic orientation to their work. 'Committed' employee behaviour as opposed to a simple adherence to formal procedures is the order of the day.[51] The extensive existence of such strategies which ". . . unobtrusively,

---

48. Thompson, A, "Customizing the public for health care: What's in a label?" in I Kirkpatrick & M Lucio Martinez (eds), (1995) *op. cit.*

49. Reed, M, (1995) *op. cit.*; J Clarke & J Newman, (1997) *op. cit.*

50. Thompson, G, *The Political Economy of the New Right* (London: Pinter Publishers) 1990 p. 139.

51. Storey, J, "Human resource management in the public sector" in G Salaman, S

monitor and correct the decisions and activities of nominally autonomous agencies",[52] confirm the need to include a notion of government in enterprise culture. This is largely because such government strategies are the means by which enterprise culture, entrepreneurial management and an enterprise orientation to work are produced.

Performance-Related Pay

A significant example of a performance indicator is performance-related pay which has long been a characteristic of managerial pay in the private sector, and was introduced and extensively implemented in the public sector during the 1980s.[53] Under a performance-related pay scheme, staff are systematically measured against a set of individual personal targets, and awarded pay increases according to whether they achieved these objectives or not. Appraisal systems are usually attached to performance related pay schemes. These appraisal systems often entail an annual discussion of proposed individual work targets for the coming year between a staff member and their immediate supervisor. At the end of this period the supervisor rates the performance of the staff member according to a range of criteria, and this rating will determine part or all of an employee's remuneration.[54]

Performance-related pay, therefore, involves the redefinition of the 'contractual' relationship that exists between individual staff members and the organisation for which they work. In contrast to the traditional bureaucratic 'contract' which exchanges security and long-term tenure for compliance and loyalty, employment contracts based on performance-related pay adopt a market-centred exchange. Here the continuous existence of the employment relationship is based on an ongoing assessment of employee performance, and the achievement of specified performance targets.[55] The achievement of a range of performance targets requires that an employee assumes personal ownership and responsibility for these targets, and the activities and functions that attach to them. Performance targets which employees are contracted to achieve can therefore be understood as a type of small business or 'enterprise form' which employees are expected to manage in an entrepreneurial manner.[56] Thus, performance reviews and performance-related pay signify

Cameron, H Hamblin, P Iles, C Mabey & K Thompson (eds), *Human Resource Strategies* (London: Sage) 1992.

52. Reed, M, (1995) *op. cit.* p. 49.
53. Marsden, D & R Richardson, "Performing for Pay? The Effects of 'Merit Pay' on Motivation in a Public Service *British Journal of Industrial Relations* (1994) 32: 2, pp. 243-261.
54. *Ibid.*; J Storey, (1992) *op. cit.*
55. Du Gay, P, G Salaman & B Rees, (1996) *op. cit.*
56. Du Gay, P, (1997) *op. cit.*

the importance of individual responsibility and individual enterprise, as well as challenging bureaucratic and professional modes of organisation.[57]

Careers and prospects within the public sector are no longer determined by seniority or previous job title. Rather they are largely dependent upon a range of personal attributes and skills which can be collectively designated as enterprising. This applies to staff at all levels, with for example, short-term contracts being introduced for senior personnel obligating them to reach performance targets or face non-renewal of their contract.[58] Senior staff, there-fore, who may feel that their commitment and performance is beyond dis-pute, have to prove themselves on a regular basis according to an increas-ingly changed set of criteria.[59] Nevertheless, despite the extensive implemen-tation of these enterprise technologies and strategies, we cannot assume that this leads to a systematic transformation of the public sector.[60] For example Marsden and Richardson (1994) report in their research of the Inland Rev-enue, that performance-related pay did appear to work in net financial terms but staff perceptions of the process had the potential to damage the work atmosphere, reduce staff confidence in the reporting system and depress motivation among senior and long-serving staff. In addition, it must be rec-ognised that some individuals might not wish to be empowered, and that some of those who do find the experience all too partial.[61] Such dissatisfac-tion may lead to an active resistance to entrepreneurial governance within the public sector, particularly on the part of old sites of bureau-professional power. However, it must also be recognised that not all groups within the public sector have opposed the reforms they are experiencing. A trend is emerging which demonstrates that within the public sector professional groups are subscribing to the new commercialised professionalism required of them, by prioritising profits, working to budgets and managing staff in an enter-prising manner.[62]

This differential acceptance of entrepreneurial governance as an enter-prise culture technology demonstrates that new strategies, initiatives and pro-grammes have to be negotiated. This negotiation very often takes place through processes which are highly political, and which have an enduring effect on the actual implementation of entrepreneurial governance programmes.[63]

---

57. Davies, A & I Kirkpatrick, (1995) *op. cit.*; M Reed, (1995) *op. cit.*
58. Halford, S & M Savage, "The Bureaucratic Career: Demise or Adaptation?" in T Butler & M Savage (eds), *Social Change and the Middle Classes* (London: UCL Press) 1995.
59. Hanlon, G, "Professionalism as Enterprise: Service Class Politics and the Re-definition of Professionalism" *Sociology* (1998) 32: 1, pp. 43-63.
60. Storey, J, (1992) *op. cit.*
61. Clarke, J & J Newman, (1997) *op. cit.*
62. Hanlon, G, (1998) *op. cit.*
63. Reed, M, (1995) *op. cit.*

Though enterprise culture technologies, such as the programme of entrepreneurial governance, anticipate and attempt to ensure a radical reconfiguration and transformation of attitudes and behaviour, it must be acknowledged that the implementation of such technologies must "...confront the everyday realities of shop-floor and office politics that sculpt the 'contested terrains' on which control struggles are fought and decided".[64]

Aspects of enterprise culture, which include the marketisation of social relations and the privileging of the consumer, are *practically* implemented by provider groups, who are well aware of the new commercial and enterprise ethos which characterises the wider political context. They are also aware of the weakening of the bureau-professional ethos which formerly characterised power struggles between conflicting interests.[65] Restructuring initiatives, such as entrepreneurial governance, lead to struggles among different groups within the public sector, with each trying to ensure that their position is legitimated and guaranteed through the adoption and adaptation of a commercial ethos.[66] What, therefore, needs to be recognised is that attempts at transforming the public sector through a range of enterprise technologies and strategies:

> . . . are rarely implanted unscathed, and are seldom adjudged to have achieved what they set out to do. Whilst 'governmentality' is eternally optimistic, 'government' is a congenitally failing operation. The world of programmes is heterogeneous and rivalrous, and the solutions for one programme tend to be the problems of another. 'Reality' always escapes the theories that inform programmes and the ambitions that underpin them; it is too unruly to be captured by any perfect knowledge. Technologies produce unexpected problems, are utilised for their own ends by those who are supposed to merely operate them, are hampered by underfunding, professional rivalries, and the impossibility of producing the technical conditions that would make them work.

> (Miller & Rose, 1990: 10-11)

Nevertheless, despite the fact that the organisational reality created by the enterprise technology of entrepreneurial governance, will fall short of the transformation which it desires, this does not negate its organisational significance or the contribution it makes to the creation of an enterprise culture

---

64. *Ibid.*, p. 53.
65. *Ibid.*
66. Hanlon, G, (1998) *op. cit.*

in general. Understanding entrepreneurial governance as an enterprise strategy which has the dimensions of enterprise culture 'written into' it as outlined above, allows us to demonstrate and appreciate how such technologies are used as the means by which an economy and society characterised by enterprise is produced. This again brings us back to the importance of including a notion of 'government' within our understanding of enterprise culture. As suggested in Chapter 1, incorporating a notion of government into enterprise culture allows us to treat this phenomenon as an historically embedded set of strategies, technologies, initiatives, etc., which aim to transform the thought and conduct of targeted populations.

Within the context of the transformation of the public sector, the population being targeted is that of public sector employees at all levels and of all kinds, with the aim of transforming and regulating their conduct along commercial enterprise lines, through the implementation of entrepreneurial governance strategies. Such strategies aim to replace hierarchically based control systems, characterised by a bureaucratic ethos, with contractual arrangements and practices, characterised by an enterprising ethos. The entrepreneurial governance programme, understood as an enterprise culture technology, has enacted in the public sector highly significant changes to that particular institutional landscape and organisational setting, despite its intrinsic contradictions and limitations.[67] Therefore, it should be understood as a vital enterprise technology, which attempts to align a broader commitment to the creation of an enterprise culture, with the complex realities of organisational life in the public sector, but often in a highly flawed and disputed manner.[68]

SUMMARY OF KEY IDEAS

- A key characteristic of attempts to create an enterprise culture is the reconfiguration of the public/private divide.

- Privatisation is one means by which the public/private divide has been reshaped. However, where privatisation has not been a viable option, the public/private divide has been reconfigured through the introduction of private sector management practices into the public sector.

- The commercialisation of the public sector has been put in place in explicit opposition to its traditional bureaucratic organisation. The promotion of a market solution is presented as the resolution of the perceived ills (e.g. inefficiency and rigidity) of the public sector.

---

67. Miller, P & N Rose, "Governing economic life" *Economy and Society* (1990) 19: 1, pp. 1-31; M Reed, (1995) *op. cit.*
68. Reed, M, (1995) *op. cit.*

- The introduction of private sector management practices into the public sector is associated with the re-emergence of the manager as a significant and powerful individual in the economy. However, the figure of the manager, which has been resurrected, is not the bureaucratic organisational man, rather it is the manager who can act as an entrepreneurial, dynamic change agent.

- 'Entrepreneurial governance' is the term coined to define the introduction of private sector management practices into the public sector.

- The strategies and initiatives (e.g. performance indicators) of entrepreneurial governance can be understood as a government technology, which is means by which central government can influence individuals in decentralised units, to perform their duties in an enterprising manner. This practice can be conceptualised as 'government at a distance'.

- Entrepreneurial governance in the public sector can thus be understood as one significant element of a broader range of policies, initiatives and strategies, which together are the means by which enterprise culture is produced.

- Entrepreneurial governance as a policy is thus reflective of the institutional and ethical dimensions of enterprise culture: firstly through its privileging of private sector commercial practices; and secondly in its hope that the marketisation and contractualisation of relations within the public sector will promote enterprising values.

- It must be remembered that a government technology such as entrepreneurial governance, which attempts to align the complex realities of organisational life with the wider goal of the creation of an enterprise culture, is likely to be contested and implemented in a decidedly inexact manner. Nevertheless, despite its inexactness, entrepreneurial governance has enacted highly significant changes along enterprise lines in the organisational life of the public sector, and thus contributes to the general production of an enterprise culture.

CHAPTER 4

Entreprise Culture and the Large Organisation

As more firms introduce market relations within their boundaries while blurring their boundaries by replacing market relations with organizational ones, it becomes much more difficult and perhaps much less useful to think in terms of activities taking place either inside or outside of firms, of decisions being made either by firms or by markets, or of assets being owned by one firm or another. At the extreme, firms become evanescent . . . little more than 'legal fictions' which serve as a nexus for a set of contracting relationships among individuals.

(Badaracco (1988) cited in Kanter 1991:85)

THE CULTURAL MANAGEMENT OF ENTERPRISE

Despite difficulties attached to understanding the notion of culture, a key starting point for developing an appreciation of it, is the idea that the concept of culture can be understood as 'a way of life'. Though this interpretation of culture is conventionally presented as an intrinsically even-handed one which accepts the value of all forms of culture, the reality is that different forms of culture are often antagonistic to one another (e.g. a national culture versus a regional culture), or culture in general is presented as opposed to something outside of itself, e.g. nature.[1] Such rivalries are hardly ever neutral, resulting in ". . . a hierarchical ordering of the relations between different components of the cultural field, one part of which is defined as a lack, an insufficiency, a problem, while the other is viewed as offering the means of overcoming that lack, meeting the insufficiency, resolving the problem".[2]

Given this inherent antipathy, it is therefore important that our understanding of culture reflects this and its reformist disposition, so that it is possible to illustrate how one cultural configuration shapes or moulds another.

---

1. Bennett, T, *Culture: A Reformer's Science* (London: Sage) 1998.
2. *Ibid.*, pp. 91.

Despite arguments to the contrary which claim that terms such as 'policy', 'management' and 'administration' are alien to notions of culture, they are in fact central to its formation, particularly in terms of understanding the impact of one (highly valued) cultural form on another (less valued) cultural form.[3] Thus it is argued that it is essential that a notion of 'government' and 'policy' is incorporated into our understanding of culture, if we are to comprehend the circumstances of such cultural change, and the means by which it comes about. Though culture and administration may be perceived as being opposites, they are also systematically entangled in historically exact patterns of interaction, with high levels of mutual dependency. However, this dependency is suffused with tension in the sense that culture is impaired when it is planned and administered, but equally the existence or possibility of effect may be lost if culture is completely left to itself.[4]

A key theme of this book is the contention that enterprise culture must be understood in similar terms. As suggested in Chapter 1, enterprise culture is conventionally understood as "a way of life" which encompasses all forms of activity, public and private, business and personal. As a way of life, it is believed to be superior to the collectivist culture, which, it is argued, has characterised social and economic life for a significant part of the 20th century, with social democratic institutions since 1945 promoting a permissive and anti-enterprise culture.[5] However, to enable us to make visible the means by which this collectivist, dependency culture was opened up to the reformist programmes of enterprise culture, we need to incorporate a notion of government into our understanding of this phenomenon. From this perspective what we are suggesting is that the formation of an enterprise culture is, as Bennett (1998) suggests about culture in general, a task of cultural management which can require a degree of governmental inventiveness, and diligent attention to questions of administrative detail. Such cultural management can be understood in terms of the range of programmes, initiatives and strategies, which are explicitly drawn upon to encourage the emergence and promotion of enterprise. The aim of such programmes is to ensure that individuals identify with and become subjects of the enterprise project.[6] Therefore what is being suggested is that 'being for enterprise' often means working through and by governmental means, despite the conventional notion that enterprise is explicitly set against government intervention.

In previous chapters we have illustrated this approach to understanding enterprise culture by exploring programmes such as privatisation and

3.   *Ibid.*
4.   *Ibid.*, pp. 196-197; T Bennett, (1992a), "Useful Culture" *Cultural Studies* (1992) 6: 3, pp. 395-408.
5.   Du Gay, P, "Enterprise Culture and the Ideology of Excellence" *New Formations* (1991)13, pp. 45-61.
6.   *Ibid.*

entrepreneurial governance in the public sector, assessing how they regulate and shape the capacities, along enterprise lines, of organisations and the individuals within. The overall aim of such an assessment was to attempt to show how programmes, such as privatisation and entrepreneurial governance, ". . . seek to act upon and instrumentalize the self-regulating propensities of individuals in order to ally them with socio-political objectives".[7] Where such programmes are implemented directly by the state, the link between them and attempts to achieve the socio-political objectives of the enterprise culture project are identifiable. However, in the case of organisations in the private sector (which though subject to general regulation by the state, are not subject to programmes of organisational change and reform such as those of privatisation and entrepreneurial governance), the link between their activities and the achievement of the socio-political objectives of the enterprise culture project are possibly not so direct. Nevertheless, the aim of this chapter will be to demonstrate the linkages between recent organisational reform programmes of large organisations, and the enterprise culture project. In doing this, it will be shown that the concerns and values implicit in the organisational reform programmes of the 1980s and 1990s, fitted well with, and mirrored those of, the wider undertaking of the construction of an enterprise culture.[8]

PROMOTING ENTERPRISE IN THE LARGE ORGANISATION

Reinventing the Private Sector Commercial Enterprise

Earlier we suggested that one significant dimension of enterprise culture is the privileging of the private sector commercial enterprise as the form of organisation in which the provision of goods and services is best facilitated, and where enterprising activity is most likely to be found. However, despite being granted this status, private sector businesses are not presented as being inherently enterprising. Instead it is argued that commercial enterprises must continually strive to become ever more enterprising.[9] Thus as well as public sector organisations having to become more enterprise minded, so must private sector organisations.[10] The suggestion is that being enterprising is some-

---

7. Miller, P & N Rose, "Governing economic life" *Economy and Society* (1990) 19: 1, pp. 1-31.
8. Legge, K, "Human resource management: a critical analysis" in J Storey (ed.), *New Perspectives in Human Resource Management* (London: Routledge) 1989; D Guest, "Human Resource Management and the American Dream" Journal of Management Studies, (1990) 27: 4, pp. 377-397; P Du Gay, (1991) *op. cit.*
9. Keat, R, "Introduction" in R Keat and N Abercrombie (eds), *Enterprise Culture* (London: Routledge) 1991.
10. Du Gay, P & G Salaman, "The Cult[ure] of the Customer" *Journal of Management Studies* (1992) 29: 5, pp. 615-633.

thing which cannot be taken for granted, but must be continually pursued.

Bureaucracy has been identified as the source of the lack of enterprise in large organisations, as the mechanism which is preventing private sector organisations from being fully enterprising. Throughout the 1980s discussions of large private sector organisations identified bureaucracy as a highly significant problem,[11] in much the same way as bureaucracy was identified as a problem in the public sector. It was, and still is, suggested that managerial hierarchy destroys initiative and creativity, and is inappropriate in the contemporary globalised business world.[12] The promotion of enterprise, therefore, led to an extraordinary transposition of management thinking, which suggested that, instead of thinking of bureaucracy as the means by which the inadequacies of the market can be dealt with, market co-ordination is presented as the instrument by which the deficiencies of bureaucracy can be taken care of.[13] Therefore two key concerns of management writing in the 1980s and the 1990s are increasing the entrepreneurial propensity of managers and employees and de-bureaucratizing organisations.[14] Organisations, it is argued, ". . . must either move away from bureaucratic guarantees to post-entrepreneurial flexibility or they stagnate".[15]

Kanter (1991) defines 'post-entrepreneurial' as the movement of established companies away from bureaucracy through the promotion of entrepreneurial activity. The latter has conventionally been associated with the creation of an independent business venture or ownership of a small business. From the perspective of the new right, owner-managed businesses of early capitalism and contemporary small businesses, are likely to be more entrepreneurial than large modern corporations.[16] However, it is argued that this understanding of entrepreneurial activity is too restrictive, and that it should be extended to include the application of entrepreneurial principles to the large organisation, ". . . creating a marriage between entrepreneurial creativity and corporate discipline, co-operation, and teamwork".[17]

The basic suggestion is that key characteristics of the small business (such as a flatter organisational structure, direct experience of capital and product market pressures, and an ownership stake in profits) should be introduced

---

11. Wood, S J, "New Wave Management?" *Work, Employment and Society* (1989) 3: 3, pp. 379-402.
12. Jacques, E, "In Praise of Hierarchy" *Harvard Business Review* (Jan-Feb 1990).
13. Du Gay, P & G Salaman, (1992) *op. cit.*
14. Hill, S, "How do you manage a flexible firm? The Total Quality Model" *Work, Employment and Society* (1991) 5: 3, pp. 397-415.
15. Kanter, R M, *When Giants Learn to Dance: Mastering the Challenges of Strategy, Management and Careers in the 1990s* (New York: Simon & Schuster) 1989 p. 356.
16. Hill. S, (1991) *op. cit.*
17. Kanter, R M, (1989) *op. cit.*, p. 10.

into large organisations so that various entrepreneurial virtues can be promoted. These include an ability to predict future requirements of the market, the competence to respond quickly to change, a strong profit orientation and a dynamic, energetic disposition.[18] Thus within the contemporary business world private sector organisations must strive to be completely enterprising, ensuring that they are ready and able to face ". . . a post-hierarchical entrepreneurial future where the old bureaucratic emphasis on order, uniformity, and repetition is gradually replaced by an entrepreneurial emphasis on creativity".[19] Enterprise, therefore, should not just be understood as the establishment of an independent business venture, rather it should be understood as the application of 'market forces' and entrepreneurial principles to every sphere of organisational life (large and small) and every sphere of human existence.[20]

The key to reinventing the large private sector organisation along enterprise lines is said to lie in the cultural transformation of these entities. Specifically what is required is the replacement of deteriorating bureaucracies with dynamic, organic, organisational cultures, in which individuals are expected to be entrepreneurs as well as managers.[21] Culture is identified as an area in which organisations can achieve significant competitive advantage, and as the solution to the many problems thrown up by an increasingly uncertain and turbulent business world.[22] The importance of culture lies in its perceived ability to structure the way people think, feel and act in organisations. This focus on changing the culture of an organisation, as the means by which its performance can be significantly improved, is broadly referred to as the 'corporate culture approach'.[23] Corporate culture, and its management, is concerned with changing people's values, norms and attitudes, so that their desires and needs are aligned with those of the organisation in which they work, thus ensuring that they make the type of choices which contribute to its success.[24]

---

18. Hill, S, (1991) *op. cit.*
19. Du Gay, P, (1991) *op. cit.*
20. Du Gay, P & G Salaman, (1992) *op. cit.*
21. Wood, S J, (1989) *op. cit.*; G Salaman, "Culturing Production" in P Du Gay (ed.), *Production of Culture/Cultures of Production* (London: Sage) 1997.
22. Willmott, H, "Strength is Ignorance; Slavery is Freedom: Managing Culture in Modern Organizations *Journal of Management Studies* (1993) 30: 4, pp. 515-552.
23. Salaman, G, (1997) *op. cit.*
24. Du Gay, P, *Consumption and Identity at Work* (London: Sage) 1996.

Defining Corporate Culture

A focus on the 'culture' of organisations emerged as a central theme in management and organisation studies during the 1980s and 1990s. Culture, from the perspective of the corporate culture approach, is understood as an internally consistent set of cultural signs, that generate organisation-wide consensus usually around a set of shared values. The abiding concern of the corporate culture school is to win the 'hearts and minds' of employees, by managing what they think and feel and not just how they behave. In general the corporate culture approach suggests the following.

- All organisations have cultures which have a significant impact on organisational performance. Organisations become more efficient and effective when they develop the right culture.

- Culture is made up of beliefs, ideologies, language, ritual and myth. It can be defined simply as 'the way we do things around here'.

- As a way of managing, the corporate culture approach appeals to the emotional, non-rational, affective elements within employees. It differs from conventional forms of management which focus on quantitative analysis, planning, formal rules and sanctions.

- It is argued that the right culture creates consensus and unity within an organisation, while also motivating staff. If a culture is not right, it should be changed.

- Strong cultures are created by effective cultural leaders, who build the culture around their own values. Senior managers propagate a transformative vision which is reinforced with formal policies, informal norms, stories and rituals.

- Proper implementation of the cultural vision will lead to the internalisation of the desired values and norms, followed by higher commitment and productivity, and ultimately more profits. It also means that constant surveillance of employees is unnecessary.

- Managers are encouraged to view the most 'effective' or 'excellent' organisations as those with strong cultures which encourage employees to identify with the aims and objectives of the company they work for.

(Peters & Waterman, 1982; Deal & Kennedy, 1982;
Ray, 1986; Du Gay, 1991, 1996; Wilmott, 1993;
Martin & Frost, 1996; Salaman, 1997)

Throughout the 1980s and 1990s, therefore, the commercial success of private sector enterprises was increasingly represented as a matter of culture.[25] This shift to 'culture' in management writing signalled an increased interest

---

25. Du Gay, P, (1991) *op. cit.*

in the management of the meaning of work, which is now viewed as a critical management priority and responsibility. According to Salaman (1997:240)

> The management of culture involves deliberate attempts to structure the meanings employees attribute to their employer, the organization, and their work, and this is presented . . . as the major method of achieving a new and necessary form of organization and control which will produce great benefits in organizational performance. Managers' attempts to define a culture of work for employees – to define what work and organizational membership really mean – thus represent an attempt to achieve an internalization of regulation. Corporate culture initiatives thus form a part – the most recent expression – of a long-term management interest in managing the meaning of work for employees . . . while management has always been concerned to ensure the 'morality' and discipline of the work force – to ensure that workers had the appropriate attitudes and values – corporate culture projects represent this interest in a particular energetic and self-conscious form.

This emphasis on culture is connected to what has been referred to as 'the search for excellence', a quest which is associated with Peters & Waterman (1982). It is argued that 'excellent' organisations are those that make meaning for people by encouraging employees to believe that they have control over their own futures, that no matter what their position, their contribution is vital to the success of the organisation as well as to the success of their own lives.[26] In general, excellence in management theory is about encouraging individuals to reconstruct themselves, to see themselves as 'winners', 'champions' and 'heroes'.[27] In other words, 'excellence', embodied in the promotion and creation of corporate cultures, advocates an entrepreneurial order, promoting 'enterprising' individuals who are autonomous, self-regulating, productive, and who display dynamism, energy, initiative and self-reliance. Thus, the concerns of the excellence school mirror the concerns of the general enterprise culture project, i.e. economic and moral renaissance through a programme of cultural change.[28] The promotion of an ethic of enterprise is central to both projects, leading Du Gay (1991:47) to argue that the emergence of enterprise culture cannot solely be attributed to political reforms, but is also due ". . . to wider processes of de-differentiation at work", which are not peculiar to the UK. Thus enterprise has entered the lives of individu-

---

26. Du Gay, P, (1996) *op. cit.*
27. Du Gay, P, (1991) *op. cit.*
28. *Ibid.*; K Legge, (1989) *op. cit.*; D Guest, (1990) *op. cit.*

als in a number of ways and from a number of sources, many of which are not directly related to the policy initiatives of successive governments, nor primarily a function of political interventions.[29]

UNDERSTANDING THE PROCESS OF "ENTERPRISE ALLIANCE"

In previous chapters, we identified what appeared to be a key paradox attached to attempts to create an enterprise culture. We stated that a crucial element of the enterprise culture project is a limiting of the role of the state. However, the cultural transformation which enterprise requires can, paradoxically, only be achieved through the actions of a strong and intrusive state. Thus we suggested that, rather than understanding the promotion of an enterprise culture through the implementation of programmes (such as privatisation) as a withdrawal of the state, it is best understood as a change in the form of intervention. Likewise, the promotion of enterprise within private sector organisations should not be interpreted as the active abandonment of control on the part of managers. Managers no long aim to discipline, instruct, moralise or 'bully' their employees into compliance. Rather they endeavour to align the aims and aspirations of individual employees with those of the organisation, thus "...channelling them into the search of the firm for excellence and success".[30] Just as enterprise culture attempts to engage the self-fulfilling impulses of individuals to secure the success of an economy, corporate culture also tries to captivate the self-fulfilling impulses of individual employees to procure business success.[31] Both the project of enterprise culture and the project of corporate culture take the subjectivity of the individuals within their ambit as their target. Enterprise culture which operates at the level of the national economy, and corporate culture which operates at the level of the organisation, demonstrate how the self-determining subjectivity of the dynamic and energetic individual has become a central economic resource, with both projects aiming to turn this self-governance into an ally of economic success.[32]

'Enterprising up' private sector organisations requires a significant change in the behaviour, values and attitudes of organisational members, with a culture change being required to achieve this. A key question, therefore, is how

---

29. Abercrombie, N, "The Privilege of the Producer" in R Keat & N Abercrombie (eds), *Enterprise Culture* (London: Routledge) 1991; P Du Gay & G Salaman, (1992) *op. cit.*
30. Rose, N, "Governing the enterprising self" in P Heelas & P Morris (eds), *The Values of the Enterprise Culture: The Moral Debate* (London: Routledge) 1992.
31. Du Gay, P, (1991) *op. cit.*
32. Miller, P & N Rose, (1990) *op. cit.*

do we understand how this change emerges? Earlier we have argued that in order for us to understand how a cultural transformation takes place, it is important that we inscribe a notion of government (understood in terms of policy and administration) into our understanding of culture. Thus to allow us to understand how an enterprise culture replaced the collectivist culture of many Western economies, we must incorporate a sense of government into our understanding of enterprise culture. Similarly, in trying to understand how private businesses moved from bureaucracies to being more market-oriented, enterprising organisations, we must also integrate a notion of government into our understanding of corporate culture. In other words, we must have an appreciation of the range of programmes, technologies, strategies and initiatives which have been drawn upon to govern the internal world of the private sector business along enterprise lines, creating an alliance between individual employees and their goals, and the goals of the organisation as a whole.

What is being suggested, therefore, is that we should understand a phenomenon such as corporate culture in aesthetically narrow terms, i.e. that ". . . the 'culture' of the business enterprise is . . . operationalized through particular practices and technologies – through 'specific measures' – which are linked together in a relatively systematic way",[33] and which aim to "govern at a distance". Such practices which are inscribed with an ethic of enterprise lead to what Salaman (1997) terms a re-engineering of the psychological relationship between employee and employer. Organisations no longer get the most out of their employees by maximising their contentment, or rationalising activity to ensure efficiency. They get the most out of employees by 'tapping into' the psychological strivings of individuals for autonomy and creativity, and harnessing them for the benefit of the organisation.[34] Work is no longer something which is imposed on individuals or undertaken for the simple fulfilment of instrumental needs. Rather it is the means of self-fulfilment, self-development and growth.[35]

The Technologies of Enterprise

Incorporating a notion of government into enterprise culture and corporate culture allows us to give 'enterprise' a technological form, i.e. understand these phenomena in terms of the range of programmes and initiatives which have sought to shape or fashion conduct in desired (enterprise) directions. Such technologies can include architechture, time-tabling, supervisory systems and payment systems.[36] One of the most common technologies used to

---

33. Du Gay, P & G Salaman, (1992) *op. cit.*, p. 626.
34. Miller, P & N Rose, (1990) *op. cit.*
35. Du Gay, P, (1991) *op. cit.*
36. Rose, N, (1992) *op. cit.*; G Salaman, (1997) *op. cit.*

institutionalise entrepreneurial behaviour in the large organisation has been the decentralisation of companies into divisions run as profit centres. In an attempt to link behaviour within a large organisation more closely with the market, large organisations have been restructured into smaller, self-contained units that function as semi-autonomous businesses.[37] It is argued that:

> ... divisionalization creates units that are simpler and less complex and thus have the potential to be more adaptable and responsive, it removes the centralized control of top corporate management over day-to-day operations, it exposes divisional senior managers directly to the requirements of the (internal) capital market regarding levels of return on investment, and it makes divisional managements more sensitive to the satisfaction of product market requirements in order to meet these performance targets...Major changes in forms of managerial remuneration, notably performance and profit-related payments, have also increased the stake of managers in entrepreneurial behaviour in recent years.
>
> (Hill, 1991:402)

Thus, such a restructuring of the large organisation suggests that, within the confines of an organisation, employees must perform their work as if they were operating within a competitive market, as if they were small-business entrepreneurs within the larger organisation who have internalised the objectives of the latter.[38] Unfortunately, as with enterprise culture in general, structural changes alone within large organisations have not been wholly successful in making them entrepreneurial, and it appears that a large organisation cannot achieve as much as a cluster of small businesses.[39] Though such structural reforms have continued, it is increasingly recognised that technologies which attempt to target the values, attitudes and self-understanding of individuals within large organisations are crucial, if such entities are to become more enterprising in their behaviour. This is a recognition that structural change by itself can not bring about the required transformation, and that some form of 'cultural engineering' which would generate an enterprising spirit should take place. This is where cultural technology as opposed to structural technology comes into play as the management of culture strives to organise the meanings individuals attribute to their employer, their work and the organisation.[40]

---

37. Hill, S, (1991) *op. cit.*
38. Salaman, G, (1997) *op. cit.*
39. Hill, S, (1991) *op. cit.*
40. Salaman, G, (1997) *op. cit.*

One particular cultural technology, which is emphasised by Peters and Waterman (1982) as a significant attribute of excellent companies with strong corporate cultures, is the notion of getting close to the customer. According to Du Gay and Salaman, (1992) the contemporary emphasis placed on the customer, as a means of assessing and defining work performance and work relations, represents an important addition to management attempts to understand and explain the essence of enterprise. This emphasis on the customer is attached to a decline in what Abercrombie (1991) calls producer culture. In producer culture, producers of a product or service will share technical knowledge of their work, have a common understanding of what counts as excellent in their field, and will be involved in an ongoing discussion about the nature and quality of the product or service. Such a culture tends to unify producers across competing companies, and moderate competition while attempting to encourage co-operation, resulting in a similarity of attitudes and values across producers *vis-à-vis* consumers. Within a producer culture, the quest to produce a 'good' product or service often outweighs commercial concerns. However, the growing importance of commercial considerations and the generation of profit, allied to an emphasis on the market, has undermined this producer culture. The latter has been replaced by a consumer culture with the enterprising consumer being actively involved in the process of consumption.[41] This consumer culture has emerged out of:

> A growing degree of sophistication and discrimination on the part of consumers . . . with a corresponding resistance to the inflated and unsubstantiated claims on the part of producers, and a more actively demanding attitude towards them. Further, the relatively anonymous and impersonal character of mass production and consumption is arguably being displaced by more differentiated and individualized goods and services, thereby providing consumers with a heightened sense of individual autonomy and choice. Flexibility and responsiveness to the consumer are nowadays genuine requirements for the producer, indicating that the preferences of consumers are to some considerable extent, generated independently and out of the producer's control: hence the increasingly 'demand' or 'market-led' character of production.
>
> (Keat, 1991:8)

In response to an increased differentiation of demand, many organisations have gone through a significant cultural change process. Research has indi-

---

41. Abercrombie, N, (1991) *op. cit.*

cated that a very common strategy adopted by organisations has been to enhance the value-added of each employee through cost reduction and dramatic quality improvements. Central to the latter is an explicit emphasis on the customer and on developing and nurturing a close and direct relationship between organisation and customer.[42] This explicit emphasis on the customer is the means by which enterprise is promoted in large organisations, with managers using representations of the customer as a way of restructuring organisations, affecting change in employees' behaviour and attitudes along enterprise lines. Compliance with customer requirements connects administrative behaviour located deep inside large organisations more directly with the market.[43]

However it must be emphasised here that a customer-oriented focus does not just apply to the external customers of a business, which is our conventional understanding of customer-supplier relations. Rather the notion of a customer-oriented focus has been implemented within the internal context of large organisations, with different departments and individuals being required to treat each other as customers. Thus:

> . . . departments now behave as if they were actors in a market, workers treat each other as if they were customers, and customers are treated as if they were managers . . . a major thrust of current programmes of organizational change is to replace management hierarchical control with simulated market control, divisions, regions, become quasi-firms, and transactions between them become those of customer or supplier or even competitor.
>
> (Du Gay & Salaman, 1992: 619-620)

Projects, which place an emphasis on getting close to the customer, such as that of corporate culture, are involved in an attempt to redefine the relationship between individuals within an organisation in terms of the customer model: employees in large organisations become each other's customers. Such an organisational device which aims ". . . to cut across internal boundaries", decentralise decision-making and promote ". . . a principled commitment to the sovereignty of the customer", acts as a force which de-bureaucratises organisational behaviour.[44] Thus the cultural technology of getting close to the customer seeks to 'enterprise up' the behaviour, values and attitudes of organisational members.

The promotion of enterprise among employees within large organisations

---

42. Du Gay, P & G Salaman, (1992) *op. cit.*

43. *Ibid.*; S Hill, (1991) *op. cit.*

44. Hill, S, (1991) *op. cit.*

requires a range of management methods which do not accentuate intrusive managerial control and give greater latitude to employees when working with customers.[45] According to Abercrombie (1991), a focus on consumption is often associated with undisciplined play and disorder. This is illustrated by the fact that the provision of a quality service or product in an enterprising manner requires that employees rely on a range of interpersonal skills and capabilities which cannot be codified, standardised, regimented or broken down into discrete elements within a company handbook.[46] If managers try to exert control in a conventional bureaucratic manner, it is likely that they may stifle those very glimmers of worker self-direction, spontaneity and impulsiveness that they are becoming increasingly dependent upon.[47]

Nevertheless, this does not mean the complete abandonment of control on the part of managers. A balance is required between the organisation's need for creativity and flexibility with regard to an uncertain external environment, and the internal need for stability, structure and certainty. The promotion of excellence, enterprise and a strong customer orientation among employees in large organisations is accomplished through the application of a careful mixture of control and worker independence, the co-existence of constant central direction and maximum individual autonomy, what Peters & Waterman (1982) have referred to as the "loose-tight" principle, what we have referred to earlier as 'governing at a distance'.[48] Governing a large organisation in an enterprising fashion means actively engaging in a "controlled de-control" where employees are rigidly controlled and allowed (even required) to display autonomous, entrepreneurial and innovative behaviour, at one and the same time.[49] Thus, the marketisation of organisations through the use of customer-focused cultural technology does not automatically imply the abdication of control or disorganisation. Markets in organisations are organised according to mechanisms of action and co-ordination, rules, assessments and sanctions,[50] with the market also defining the sort of relationship that an individual should have with him/herself, and the practices that s/he should acquire and display.[51]

45. Fuller, L & V Smith, "Consumers' Reports: Management by Customers in a Changing Economy" *Work, Employment and Society* (1991) 5: 1, pp. 1-16.
46. *Ibid.*
47. *Ibid.*
48. Thompson, G, *The Political Economy of the New Right* (London: Pinter Publishers) 1990.
49. Du Gay, P & G Salaman, (1992) *op. cit.*
50. Dubois, P, "Economic Sociology and Institutionalist Economics in France: A Trend to Convergence" *Work, Employment and Society* (1996) 10: 2, pp. 361-376.
51. Du Gay, P & G Salaman, (1992) *op. cit.*

The Links between Enterprise Culture and Corporate Culture

The concerns and values implicit in the organisational reform programme referred to above are reflective of the institutional and ethical strands of the wider construction of an enterprise culture. Starting with the institutional strand which assigns "paradigmatic status"[52] to the private sector commercial enterprise, the organisational reform programme of corporate culture embodies this dimension of enterprise culture through its restructuring of internal organisational relationships. The redefinition of the relationship between individuals within an organisation, in terms of the customer model, requires that employees behave as if they were small business entrepreneurs, with each employee becoming his/her own private sector commercial enterprise.[53] Each employee becomes a diminutive private sector firm which it is argued is the most efficient entity for the provision of goods and services. Thus the restructuring of organisations under the auspices of a corporate culture programme, means the reformulation of a large organisation into an amalgam of private sector enterprises, a form of reorganisation which contributes to the privileged position of the private sector commercial enterprise.

The second strand of enterprise culture, which focuses on behaviour that is enterprising in nature, i.e. dynamic, self-reliant, energetic, disciplined, etc., is also evident in the corporate culture reform programme. As a programme of reform, corporate culture requires that employees demonstrate a range of enterprising qualities including use of initiative, commercial sensitivity, dynamism, a customer-focus and responsibility. As with enterprise culture in general, these two strands are intricately linked in the sense that it is believed that the marketisation of organisations, such that employees behave as if they were small business owners, is more likely to promote enterprising behaviour. Nevertheless, despite this linkage, it is recognised that individuals whether (imaginary) small business owners or not must continually strive to be fully enterprising. Thus the promotion of autonomy and enterprise among large firm employees does not, as stated earlier, lead to the abandonment of control, the latter is exercised continually to ensure that individuals (as commercial entities) are fully enterprising.

The view of enterprise culture and corporate culture which is being presented here is one which focuses on the range of policies and initiatives which are used to mould and direct entrepreneurial behaviour. In Chapter 1, we suggested that attempts to create and produce an enterprise culture, through the implementation of enterprise policies and initiatives, led to the emergence of an entrepreneurial management discourse, which encourages the adoption of an enterprising management style. Likewise attempts to create

---

52. Keat, R, (1991) *op. cit.*
53. Salaman, G, (1997) *op. cit.*

and promote a strong corporate culture also contribute to the emergence of an entrepreneurial management discourse. The first dimension of this entrepreneurial management discourse emerges out of attempts to encourage employees to develop enterprising qualities as discussed above. The second dimension of this discourse centres on the acquisition and competent performance of a range of managerial skills.

Employees in large organisations who are required to act as if they are small business entrepreneurs are expected to embody the necessary management functions and activities of a successful business, as well as displaying enterprising attributes.[54] Just as businesses in general are expected to manage clients, market products and services, nurture customer relations, guarantee standards and quality, manage costs and be profitable, so must individual employees (as imaginary small business owners within the context of the large organisation) demonstrate a command of these management activities on an individual basis.[55] Employees within large organisations must, therefore, be enterprising and managerial at one and the same time.

In this chapter, we have been suggesting that there are similarities and linkages between enterprise culture and corporate culture with both concepts advocating an economic and moral renaissance through a programme of cultural change.[56] To allow us to understand how such an economic and moral renaissance comes about we have suggested that a notion of 'government' should be incorporated into both, which is 'operationalised' through a range of programmes, technologies, strategies and initiatives. The programmes and strategies of enterprise culture such as privatisation and entrepreneurial governance, and the programmes and strategies of corporate culture, such as self-managed teams, peer review, quality circles, and a focus on the customer, give life to three significant aspects of these two entities. First they both assign "paradigmatic status" to the commercial enterprise as the preferred organisational model for the provision of goods and services. Second they both revere and require enterprising attributes from individuals. Third they have both contributed to the emergence of an entrepreneurial management discourse. Both enterprise culture and corporate culture utilise a vocabulary of enterprise which acts as a decoding device between:

> . . . the most general a priori of political thought and a range of specific programmes for administering the national economy, the internal world of the firm and a whole host of other organizations from the school to the hospital. But further it enables such programmes to accord a new priority to the self-regulating capacities of individuals. . . . [The lan-

---

54. *Ibid.*
55. *Ibid.*
56. Du Gay, P, (1991) *op. cit.*

guage of enterprise] provides the relays through which the
aspirations of ministers, the ambitions of business and the
dreams of consumers achieve mutual translatability. . . .
[This vocabulary establishes] connections and symmetries
at both the conceptual and practical level, between political
concerns about the government of the productive life of the
nation, the concerns of owners of capital to maximize the
economic advantages of their companies, and techniques
for the governing of the subject . . . linking up these distinct
concerns into a functioning network.

(Miller & Rose, 1990: 24-27)

Finally it must be recognised that attempts to 'enterprise up' large private
sector organisations may be fraught with difficulties and face significant resistance. However, as stated in previous chapters, difficulties surrounding
the implementation of enterprise programmes and strategies, such as entrepreneurial governance or corporate culture, do not negate its organisational
significance. Enterprise strategies, no matter how much or how little they
have been implemented in an organisation, or no matter how much or how
little they have been successful, have gained in institutional value because
they have become the approved way of doing things. Adopting enterprise
strategies, such as developing a corporate culture or advocating a customer
focus, may contribute little material or technical benefit to an organisation,
but may confer significant legitimacy on it. Thus managers may actively use
the rhetoric of enterprise ". . . to gain legitimacy without affecting activities
at the technical core of the organization".[57]

SUMMARY OF KEY IDEAS

- The construction and formation of the enterprise culture is a task of
  cultural management, which can be understood in terms of the range of
  programmes, technologies and initiatives which are implemented to encourage an enterprising spirit.
- The link between programmes such as privatisation and attempts to create an enterprise culture are clear where such programmes are implemented directly by the state. However the link between the reform programmes of private sector organisations and the achievement of the socio-
  political objectives of enterprise culture is less clear and needs exploration.

---

57. Zbaracki, M J, "The Rhetoric and Reality of Total Quality Management" *Ad-
    ministrative Science Quarterly* (1998) 43, pp. 602-636.

- Bureaucracy has been identified as the source of the lack of enterprise in large private sector organisations. It is argued that organisations must move away from bureaucratic guarantees to entrepreneurial flexibility.

- Promoting enterprise within the large organisation requires the introduction of small business characteristics such as a flatter organisational structure and the application of market forces.

- The key to 'enterprising up' large private sector organisations lies in the cultural transformation of these entities, where individuals are required to be entrepreneurs as well as managers.

- The emphasis on culture in organisations is reflective of the increased interest in the management of meaning within organisations. Culture has been identified as the means by which the way people think, feel and act in organisations can be significantly influenced.

- The importance assigned to culture is associated with 'excellent' organisations. These companies create meaning for employees by encouraging them to believe that they have control over their future, and that their activity at whatever level of the company, has a significant impact on the success of the organisation, as well as the success of their own lives.

- The creation of a strong corporate culture (in which notions of excellence are embodied) advocates an entrepreneurial order within which dynamic enterprising individuals will flourish. This mirrors the concerns of the general enterprise culture project, i.e. an economic rebirth through cultural change.

- Corporate culture draws on a range of technologies such as a focus on the customer or self-managed teams which aim to create an alliance between individual employees and their goals, and the goals of the organisation as a whole.

- The concerns and values of organisational reform programmes, such as that of corporate culture, allied to the technologies which are implemented, are reflective of the institutional and ethical strands of the wider enterprise culture project.

The Characters of Enterprise Culture

CHAPTER 5

The Entrepreneur and Enterprise Culture

For many individuals, the path to independence and self-reliance involves asceticism and self-denial, a life of hard work and deferred gratification. Not all will succeed, and only the successful deserve moral approbation...All can learn the moral behaviour appropriate to the Great Society. But in practice the gulf remains. There is always a moral elite in capitalism, and the proof of their superior status for Hayek as well as for Mises, is economic success. Entrepreneurs deserve higher moral esteem than other individuals because, by taking risks, they are the ones who move society forward, and provide benefits and higher living standards for everyone.

(Gamble, 1996)

UNDERSTANDING THE ENTREPRENEUR

In earlier chapters we have suggested that understanding enterprise culture, the position of the entrepreneur within this, and the activity of entrepreneurship, also implies understanding a way of thinking about the practice of management. Over the past century, different conceptualisations of what a manager does, or should do, have been constructed, each attempting to develop a better form of management, which will mould and direct the conduct of managers. Contemporary treatises on management assign a privileged position to the enterprising individual, with managers increasingly being expected to behave in an entrepreneurial manner, i.e. be entrepreneurs.

Managing in an enterprising manner is profoundly different from other forms of management, particularly bureaucratic management, with the heroic role assigned to the entrepreneur being directly connected to the extreme transformation of government practices at the level of organisations and the state in recent years.[1] Within the context of this transformation, which

---

1. Du Gay, P, *Consumption and Identity at Work* (London: Sage) 1996.

we have discussed in earlier chapters, the entrepreneur is viewed as the ultimate 'enterprising' individual, with a key aim of enterprise culture being the creation of new entrepreneurs.[2]

Given the privileged role which is assigned to the figure of the entrepreneur, it is important that we understand what exactly an entrepreneur is and does. This is particularly so in the light of earlier comments that an enterprise culture will not succeed unless individuals behave in a manner conducive to the market order, i.e. act like entrepreneurs. As Weber suggests:

> . . . every type of social order, without exception, must, if one wishes to evaluate it, be examined with reference to the opportunities which it affords to certain types of persons to rise to positions of superiority through the operation of the various objective and subjective factors.

> (Weber quoted in Hennis, 1983:170)

Understanding the opportunities which are afforded to certain types of individuals, such as entrepreneurs, means developing an understanding of the various programmes, initiatives and supports which have been put in place to encourage and nurture entrepreneurs and their activities. This brings us back to the key argument of this book, that a notion of government must be incorporated into our understanding of enterprise culture, if we are to understand how such opportunities occur, and how enterprising activity and entrepreneurs are produced. Up to now, we have explored the government of enterprise and the promotion of enterprising individuals in state organisations and large organisations. In later chapters we will examine the nurturing and promotion of enterprising activity and entrepreneurs in the small business sector. In this chapter we will assess understandings of the entrepreneur and the activity of entrepreneurship, demonstrating that, despite the privileged position of the entrepreneur within enterprise culture, there is no agreed definition of what exactly an entrepreneur is or does. Recent American research which sought to explore definitions of the entrepreneur from the perspective of academics and business leaders, identified 44 different definitions and 90 different attributes of entrepreneurship.[3]

In attempting to understand what an entrepreneur and entrepreneurship is, a good starting place is to look at the etymology of the word entrepreneur which derives from two main terms: *entre* which means 'to enter' or 'to penetrate in between'; and *pren* (prendre) which means 'to take/grasp' or 'seize hold of'.[4] Thus one general understanding of the entrepreneur ". . . is one

2.   Gray, C, *Enterprise and Culture* (London: Routledge) 1998.
3.   Wickham, P, *Strategic Entrepreneurship* (London: Pitman Publishing) 1998.
4.   Chia, R, "Teaching Paradigm Shifting in Management Education: University

who *penetrates* the spaces between established boundaries and *seizes* opportunities that are otherwise overlooked by others".[5] This notion of what an entrepreneur does (i.e. identify an opportunity, exploit it, get out as quickly as possible), is clearly understandable if one takes into account descriptions of entrepreneurial activity provided by such diverse sources as Schumpeter and Marx. Schumpeter describes entrepreneurial activity as something:

> . . . that incessantly revolutionizes the economic structure from within incessantly destroying the old one, incessantly creating a new one. This process of Creative Destruction is the essential fact about capitalism. It is what capitalism consists in and what every capitalist concern has got to live in. . . . A perennial gale of creative destruction is going through capitalism.

> (Schumpeter, 1976:84)

Similarly Marx and Engels describe the nature of entrepreneurial activity as a:

> Constant revolutionizing of production, uninterrupted disturbance of all social conditions, everlasting uncertainty and agitation distinguish the (entrepreneurial) epoch from all earlier ones. All fixed, fast-frozen relations, with their train of ancient and venerable prejudices and opinions are swept away, all new-formed ones become antiquated before they can ossify. All that is solid melts into air, all that is holy is profaned, and man is at last compelled to face with sober senses, his real conditions of life, and his relations with his kind. The need of a constantly expanding market for its products chases the (entrepreneur) over the whole surface of the globe. It must nestle everywhere, settle everywhere, establish connections everywhere.

> (Marx & Engels, 1996:83)

Entrepreneurship is presented here as something very uncertain, very turbulent and the harbinger of great change. It also conveys the feeling that to survive such turbulence an entrepreneur would need to be very tough and very aggressive. This notion of the pugnacity, resilience, and strength required to be entrepreneurial is clear in a lot of the 1980s profiles of success-

---

Business Schools and the Entrepreneurial Imagination" *Journal of Management Studies* (1996) 33: 4, pp. 409-428; C Gray, (1998) *op. cit.*
5.   Chia, R, (1996) *op. cit.*, p. 413.

ful entrepreneurs. In many of these great emphasis is placed on the qualities of battle, struggle, ruthlessness, rebelliousness and rugged individualism.[6] However, despite the fact that there seems to be an understanding of the entrepreneur and what he/she does inherent to the word itself, there is, as said above, little consensus about its meaning. Within the confines of this chapter therefore we cannot do justice to the high level of diversity in this area, however the approach we will take in exploring the entity of the entrepreneur, is to examine and assess six different schools of thought on entrepreneurship drawn from Cunningham and Lischeron (1991), in terms of their relationship with the understanding of enterprise culture being presented in this book.

This approach will allow us to do three things: first to assess whether all the perspectives looked at allow for the notion of entrepreneurs being cultivated, nurtured, shaped and moulded through a series of enterprise initiatives. Second in exploring the various schools of thought, we will look at the interplay and relationship between the figures of the entrepreneur and the manager. Third we will consider the links between the various perspectives and the emergence of an entrepreneurial management discourse. Thus the perspectives on the entrepreneur outlined below will allow us to further explore the relationship between government and enterprise discussed throughout the course of this book.

ENTREPRENEURIAL SCHOOLS OF THOUGHT

Despite the lack of agreement surrounding writing on entrepreneurship, it is generally agreed that the adoption of a multi-disciplinary approach to the study of this phenomenon is beneficial. It is now accepted that a range of disciplines (including economics, sociology, psychology and management) can help shed some light on what entrepreneurship is, and what the entrepreneur does. Given the expansion of the field and the continued lack of agreement, different approaches to the entrepreneur can be presented in terms of different schools of thought. This approach to understanding entrepreneurship (i.e. using each of a range of perspectives systematically to address the same phenomenon so that different facets of it can be revealed), can be set along side wider debates on contemporary management. Of particular relevance here is the emergence of management knowledge based on radical relativism. An example of such an approach is Morgan's (1997) *Images of Organization* in which a range of perspectives are drawn upon to illuminate different facets of an organisation that one approach alone would not expose.

---

6.   Collinson, D & J Hearn, "Breaking the Silence: On Men, Masculinities and Managements" in D Collinson & J Hearn (eds), *Men as Managers, Managers as Men* (London: Sage) 1996.

Though concerns about such an approach have been expressed, research indicates that practitioners are comfortable with it.[7]

The 'Great Person' School of Entrepreneurship

Within this school the entrepreneur is conceptualised as someone who is *born* with great energy, vision, intelligence, determination, dynamism and daring. The emphasis is placed on 'born not made' characteristics and such individuals are usually presented as rich, commanding, authoritative individuals. Though many treat this school of thought with a degree of cynicism, it presents a very influential cultural image of the entrepreneur as a special type of person. Journalistic accounts in particular tend to place an emphasis on the 'master of the universe' qualities of entrepreneurs, particularly those who have achieved great commercial success from very humble beginnings.

In attempting to create an enterprise culture and entice individuals to set up in business, the 'great person' view of the entrepreneur plays an important role. The imagery of this school is extremely positive and energetic. From this perspective the entrepreneur is a hero displaying a virile, swashbuckling, flamboyant, rugged individualism. There is an extremely strong 'can do anything' aura surrounding this image of the entrepreneur. By presenting this image to potential entrepreneurs, individuals are encouraged to think of themselves as the next Richard Branson, Anita Roddick or James Dyson.

Nevertheless, the paradox of this view of the entrepreneur in relation to its contribution to the establishment of an enterprise culture, is that it suggests that enterprise culture has little real impact on these 'masters of the universe' because they will succeed no matter what. This school of thought does not allow for the notion of entrepreneurs being produced, shaped or moulded, and inherent to it is the suggestion that enterprise policies of any kind are obsolete. The achievement of social and economic objectives from the point of view of this perspective is nothing to do with the activities of government but emerges out of the activities of a finite number of 'God-like' individuals, with no guarantee that their actions will lead to outcomes beneficial to the economy as a whole. In addition, the activity of management and the figure of the manager are not even alluded to, the key figure is the superhuman entrepreneur and his/her enterprising activity.

The problems with this particular perspective are obvious. Conceptually it is simplistic and suggests that the production of enterprising activity and entrepreneurs is down to serendipity. In practical terms there are significant consequences attached to this particular understanding, in that being in awe of 'born' entrepreneurs may lead to a dangerous level of complacency among

---

7.   Palmer, I & R Dunford, "Interrogating Reframing: Evaluating Metaphor-based Analyses of Organizations" in S Clegg & G Palmer (eds), *The Politics of Management Knowledge* (London: Sage) 1996.

those interested in developing an enterprise culture. Coming back to the observation that an enterprise culture will not succeed unless individuals behave in a manner conducive to the market order, the danger of leaving the production of the 'right' type of individuals to chance is clear. In addition such a way of thinking implies that weaker entrepreneurs, i.e. those who do not live up to the great person image, may not be given the support they and their business require.

The Psychological Characteristics School of Entrepreneurship

From the perspective of this school of thought, entrepreneurs are believed to have unique values and attitudes towards work and life which differentiate them from the rest of the population. Individuals are believed to act in accordance with their values and characteristics which for entrepreneurs include honesty, responsibility, risk-taking propensity, ethical behaviour, need for achievement, locus of control, need for independence and innovative behaviour.[8] As with the 'great person' school of entrepreneurship, the focus is largely on enterprising as opposed to management characteristics and values, with the entrepreneur presented as a special type of person. The behaviour and personality derived from these enterprising values is said to develop over the early part of an individual's life largely through relationships formed in the family, school and church. Having experienced a process of cultural socialisation, the values which individuals learn and internalise stay with them and guide them throughout their life.[9]

The perspective on entrepreneurship presented by the psychological school seems to suggest that the supply of entrepreneurs is finite, i.e. limited to those who display certain characteristics. In this it shows its affinity to the 'great person' school of thought. However, the interest in culture and the process of cultural socialisation discussed within this school are significant, because it allows us to argue that the extensive development of a culture which promotes such values, and socialises individuals into them, could significantly increase the supply of entrepreneurs. Though this perspective generally assumes that entrepreneurs cannot be cultivated or trained, the process of cultural socialisation which the psychological school highlights, alludes by definition to a moulding process, where individuals acquire the 'right' values and characteristics through a range of relationships. Given this, it would seem that the psychological school, unlike the great person school, can conceptually accept the notion of enterprise policies and initiatives which aim to cultivate the 'right' type of individuals so that they hold values conducive to a market order. The question that needs to be addressed here is whether such

---

8.   Cunningham, J B & J Lischeron, "Defining Entrepreneurship" *Journal of Small Business Management* (1991) 25: 1, pp. 45-61.
9.   *Ibid.*

initiatives should be confined to the institutions which the psychological school currently acknowledges, i.e. the family, education system and church, or whether the range of institutions, and the stages at which they impact on an individual's life, should be expanded.

The Classical School of Entrepreneurship

This perspective on entrepreneurship differentiates between the figure of 'the manager' and the figure of 'the entrepreneur'. The latter is associated with innovative, creative and opportunistic behaviour, which are identified as the key elements of entrepreneurship. Emphasis is placed on 'doing' as opposed to ownership. Despite the differentiation which is made between 'the manager' and 'the entrepreneur', contemporary exponents of this perspective make strong reference to ". . . the opportunity-seeking *style of management* that sparks innovation."[10] Here we see a linkage being made between the two characters with managers being explicitly encouraged to act like entrepreneurs. The reference to management styles within this school signals a shift away from the 'born not made' trend of thinking of the 'great person' school, bringing entrepreneurship some way out of the 'magical' into the more practical realm. A key issue here is the suggestion that the population of entrepreneurs is not finite as the 'great person' school suggests. Following on from the psychological school, which suggests that entrepreneurial values can be learned, this school of thought introduces us very firmly to the notion that entrepreneurial skills can be *cultivated, nurtured* and *shaped.* The notion of a governance of enterprise begins to emerge from this particular perspective.

The Management School of Entrepreneurship

The emergence of the idea that entrepreneurial activity can (and should) be governed, shaped and moulded is clear within this school of thought, indicating a decisive shift away from the 'magical' to the 'practical'. A clear link is made between entrepreneurship and the ability of the manager to perform a number of tasks including planning, organising, budgeting, staffing, controlling and co-ordinating.[11] An emphasis is placed on the competent performance of managerial tasks, away from the mystique attached to the entrepreneur within the 'great person' school. From the perspective of this school "...entrepreneurship is a series of learned activities which focus on the central functions of managing a firm".[12] This school suggests that improving an individual's management capacity through the development of a rational cause and effect demeanour and strong analytical skills will benefit entrepreneur-

---

10. *Ibid.*, p. 51.
11. *Ibid.*
12. *Ibid.*, p. 52

ship. Within this school of thought, we are very firmly located within the notion that entrepreneurship can be shaped and moulded, and that a range of enterprise initiatives to facilitate this are crucial. We are also made aware of the very *human* nature of the entrepreneur and entrepreneurship. The possibility of failure is very real, with the management school placing an emphasis on the need to understand why businesses fail, while at the same time suggesting how entrepreneurs and their businesses can be improved.[13]

The management school of entrepreneurship clearly gives a strong impetus to the notion of enterprise education, a significant enterprise cultural technology. In many countries enterprise education has been identified as one of the most critical means by which individuals with the skills, self-understanding and psyche congenial to a market order can be nurtured. However in thinking about the impact that enterprise education has on levels and forms of enterprise and entrepreneurship, we need to also pay attention to the form that this education takes. The association between entrepreneurship and the performance of management skills made by the management school, provides us with a particular understanding of enterprise education, i.e. the inculcation of a range of technical management skills. In this it is reflective of the general vocationalist approach which is conventionally taken to enterprise education. From this perspective, education should be less academic and more oriented to the outside business world, in particular the business world of the small firm.[14] An emphasis is placed on practical experience with a resultant distinction being made between 'academic' and 'vocationally-oriented' education. However, the ability to distinguish between vocational and academic education has been queried, with commentators arguing that a clear distinction cannot be made between subjects which are practical and subjects which are deemed to be academic. According to Lynch (1992), the belief that some subjects are completely vocational and practical while other are academic and non-practical is false.

Nevertheless, even if it is possible to make such a distinction, serious reservations attach to a sole focus on vocational and technical education. The type of "new vocationalism" advocated by writers such as Gibb (1987, 1996) with its emphasis on 'hands-on' experience may have a negative effect on entrepreneurial activities. What must be recognised is that highly theoretical subjects are capable of making a crucial contribution to the innovative aptitude of an economy. A dissuasion away from academic education towards more 'hands-on' experience may mean thwarting a facet of enterprise and

---

13. *Ibid.*
14. Gibb, A, "Enterprise Culture - Its Meaning and Implications for Education and Training" *Journal of European Industrial Training* (1987) 11: 2, pp. 3-38; A Gibb, "Entrepreneurship and Small Business Management: Can We Afford to Neglect Then in the Twenty-First Century Business School?" *British Journal of Management* (1996) 7, pp. 309-321.

entrepreneurship which can make the difference between success and failure. Practical skills, management or otherwise, should not be divorced from
the conceptual framework within which they were imagined, as it is the latter
which can make such skills full of possibilities.

Thus an overemphasis on a vocational approach to enterprise education
to the exclusion of the academic may stifle rather than encourage entrepreneurship and enterprise. Too big a move away from all forms of academic
activity runs the risk of impacting negatively on creativity and innovation
within an economy. Though the business world has asserted that the values
of education and business should be more closely aligned, it may be argued
that the development of creative and innovative ideas which *serve* business,
can often best be achieved at a distance from the business world.[15] However,
this is not to suggest that we should therefore privilege an intellectual approach to enterprise education over a vocationalist approach and ignore the
practical reality of running a business. Rather, we should think about attempting to negotiate a relationship between these two conceptions of enterprise
education.

To bring creative and innovative ideas to life, one needs the technical and
practical skills which approaches like Gibb's (1987, 1996) and the management school of entrepreneurship emphasise. There is much fundamental business knowledge which can be taught to aspiring entrepreneurs, and which
can contribute immeasurably to the success of their business. Nevertheless,
to gain the most from such skills, to enable such skills to be abundant with
possibilities, to use such skills entrepreneurially, they should not be divorced
completely from a larger conceptual framework. As Chia (1996) argues, unless aspiring managers and entrepreneurs engage themselves in the subtle
play of ideas and their interaction with business situations, they will not develop a mind that is flexible and alert to business opportunities. Thus as an
effective government technology, which aims to shape and mould entrepreneurial activity, enterprise education must not only be successful in giving
individuals the skills of business, it must also stimulate ways of thinking and
the entrepreneurial imagination, which enhances our capacity to see and understand business and life situations in new ways.[16]

The Leadership School of Entrepreneurship

The notion of improving, grooming and moulding entrepreneurship is also
present in the leadership school of thought. Affinities between this school
and the 'great person' school may be identified in the emphasis that is placed
on the entrepreneur's ability to 'grab the hearts and minds' of those he/she
works with. This commitment is then used in the conversion of an enterpris-

---

15. Chia, R, (1996) *op. cit.*
16. *Ibid.*

ing idea into a material reality.[17] The 'great person' school and the leadership school present an image of the entrepreneur as a 'natural' leader who has no difficulty enticing people to subscribe to his/her vision. The emphasis here is on creativity, dynamism and daring. However, the leadership school also establishes a connection with the management school, demonstrated by the emphasis which is placed on the management of people through the acquisition of a range of skills, such as empowerment and human resource management techniques. It suggests that the clever use of such management (leadership) skills should enable the entrepreneur to obtain the commitment of employees to his/her vision. The leadership school presents an image of the entrepreneur as an individual who has no difficulty enticing people to follow his/her vision. However, the latter is achieved not through a *natural* predisposition to be a leader, as the 'great person' school suggests, rather such leadership is achieved through the acquisition of technical skills such as the ability to motivate and empower.

These two images of the entrepreneur as leader are similar but significantly different at the same time. They also represent two sides of the entrepreneurial management discourse, which we have argued emerges from the use and implementation of a range of enterprise cultural technologies. One image stresses the dynamic, daring, risk-taking, spontaneous side of this discourse, while the other stresses the rational, ordered, managed side. As argued in Chapter 1, these two sides of the entrepreneurial management discourse should not be understood as being in competition with each other. Rather they co-exist in a dialectic tension. No one side is more important than the other, yet the relationship between the two sides can be fraught.

The Intrapreneurship School of Entrepreneurship

As with other schools already discussed, the emphasis here is on the improvement and refinement of entrepreneurship, but within the confines of the large organisation, an issue we discussed in depth in Chapter 4. As a school it concerns itself with the identification and location of individuals who display entrepreneurial characteristics within the existing – and large – organisation. Its aim is to encourage these individuals to use these attributes to promote innovation within the large organisation. This school of thought advocates the adoption of a range of management techniques which can be used to isolate and develop such entrepreneurship within large organisations. One significant aspect of this school is its acceptance that entrepreneurship and enterprise can exist in many different types of organisations. However, in contrast to the other schools discussed, it presents a 'team' model of entrepreneurship whereby individuals work in semi-autonomous groups solving problems and creating opportunities.[18]

---

17. Cunningham, J B & J Lischeron, (1991) op. cit.
18. *Ibid.*

GOVERNING THE ENTREPRENEUR

The above review illustrates the lack of consensus between the various schools of thought as to the nature of the entrepreneur and entrepreneurship. The existence of different entrepreneurial schools is said to be representative of the multi-faceted nature of the entrepreneurial phenomenon, with many commentators arguing that all approaches are equally valid, each offering its own useful insights. It is suggested that to give one school of thought the 'official entrepreneurial imprimatur' over any other runs the risk of misunderstanding the essence of entrepreneurship, and mistaking or ignoring the needs of the entrepreneur.[19]

There is a positive and a negative side to this multi-perspective approach. On the positive side, we avoid defining the nature of the entrepreneur and entrepreneurship too rigidly. Neither do we privilege one way of thinking about entrepreneurship over another. An awareness of the multi-faceted nature of entrepreneurship can aid the formulation of policies which support and promote entrepreneurship. On the negative side there is the possibility that the lack of agreement surrounding entrepreneurship may hinder rather than help attempts to encourage and promote entrepreneurial activity. Nevertheless, despite the differences that exist, two significant linkages across these schools of thought can be identified, each of which contributes to the understanding of enterprise culture being developed here.

In previous chapters we have suggested that to understand enterprise culture we need to incorporate a notion of government into this phenomenon. This will allow us to understand how enterprise culture is actually produced by focusing on the range of strategies, initiatives and technologies used to create this entity. Except for the 'great person' school of thought on entrepreneurship, all other schools of thought contain within them a notion of the cultivation and grooming of entrepreneurs, which can be understood in terms of the governance of enterprise. The governance of enterprise occurs through the implementation of policies, strategies, etc. and is the means by which enterprise culture is produced. The result of such governance is the rationalisation of the subjectivity and activity of individuals, with the aim, as suggested in Chapter 1, of aligning the sense of purpose of individuals (and businesses) with the values that are designed into state and government activities.[20] This approach to understanding government activity and its relationship to individuals within enterprise culture is best appreciated, as argued in Chapter 2, in terms of Foucault's concept of *governmentality*.

---

19. *Ibid.*
20. Carr, P, "Reconceptualising Enterprise Culture" *The Conference of the British Sociological Association* (University of Reading) 1996; P Carr, "The Cultural Production of Enterprise: Understanding Selectivity as Cultural Policy" *Economic and Social Review* (1998) 29: 2, pp. 27-49.

Within the context of this concept Foucault characterises 'government' as "the conduct of conduct" which delineates an extensive ". . . domain between the minutiae of individual self-examination, self-care and self-reflection, and the techniques and rationalities concerned with the governance of the state".[21] Government from this perspective is not just about ordering and organising a range of activities and processes, it is intimately concerned with the *formation* of particular ways for people to be.[22] Contained within the schools of thought on entrepreneurship is a notion (which varies from school to school) about the way an entrepreneur should be. From this perspective, it is hoped that a combination of forces, techniques and devices, will regulate the decisions and actions of individuals, groups and organisations in relation to authoritative criteria,[23] so that individuals and organisations will behave in a manner which is conducive to the market order. Within an enterprise culture these authoritative criteria are enterprising in nature, and aim to "make up"[24] individuals along enterprise lines. "Making up"[25] individuals along enterprise lines means attempting to establish linkages and symmetries between the self-development of individuals and the increased need for a flexible and competitive economy, allowing an alignment to take place between the technologies of subjectivity and the technologies of enterprise culture.[26]

One of the consequences of the range of strategies, initiatives, and technologies implemented in an attempt to create an enterprise culture, is as said in Chapter 1, the creation of an entrepreneurial management discourse. From our examination of the six schools of thought on the entrepreneur we can see the two dimensions of this discourse emerge both within – and across – the different perspectives. The first of these dimensions places an emphasis on intuition, spontaneity, creativity, dynamism, daring and risk-taking and is clearly evident in the 'great person' school. It is also present in the psychological school, the leadership school and the intrapreneurship school. The second dimension which focuses on management and control manifests itself strongly in the classical and management schools, and is also present in the leadership and intrapreneurship schools. However, though some of the schools may emphasise one dimension over the other, the advocation of a multi-perspective approach to the understanding of the entrepreneur, sup-

21. Dean, M, *Critical and Effective Histories: Foucault's Methods and Historical Sociology* (London: Routledge) 1994.
22. Du Gay, P, (1996) *op. cit.*
23. Rose, N, "Governing 'advanced' liberal democracies" in A Barry, T Osborne & N Rose (eds), *Foucault and Political Reason: Liberalism, Neo-Liberalism and Rationalities of Government* (London: UCL Press) 1996.
24. Hacking, I, "Making Up People" in T C Heller, M Sosna & D E Wellbery (eds), *Reconstructing Individualism* (California: Stanford University Press) 1986.
25. *Ibid.*
26. Miller, P & N Rose, "Governing economic life" *Economy and Society* (1990) 19: 1, pp. 1-31; P Du Gay, (1996) *op. cit.*

ports our suggestion in previous chapters that the relationship between these two dimensions of the entrepreneurial management discourse should not be understood in terms of 'either/or', rather it should be understood as a 'both/ and' relationship. Thus the suggestion is that across the six schools of thought on the entrepreneur that we have looked at, there exists a dialectic co-existence between entrepreneurship and management.

SUMMARY OF KEY IDEAS

- In recent years an increased priority has been assigned to the entrepreneur as a particular type of person who is highly valued, and who we are all encouraged to emulate. The entrepreneur is not just a figure among other figures, he/she is a cultural hero.

- Nevertheless despite this privileged position, it is clear from any attempt to understand the entrepreneur that little or no agreement exists in the area.

- This lack of consensus has led to the emergence of a range of perspectives, each of which presents a different understanding of the entrepreneur and entrepreneurship. In exploring conceptualisations of the entrepreneur, six different schools of thought are assessed here.

- Inherent to five of the perspectives examined is a notion of the cultivation and nurturing of potential and existing entrepreneurs. One school, i.e. the 'great person' school suggests that entrepreneurs are born and cannot be cultivated. However, the image of the entrepreneur which this school presents is an image which is propagated by other schools, e.g. the leadership school, in their attempts to cultivate and nurture entrepreneurs.

- The cultivation, grooming and nurturing of entrepreneurs, which is inherent to the perspectives presented here, can be understood in terms of the governance of enterprise. This governance of enterprise occurs through the implementation of a range of policies, strategies, and techniques and is the means by which enterprise culture is produced.

- The aim of such governance is to align the sense of purpose of individuals (and businesses) with the enterprise values that are designed into state and government activities.

- One of the consequences of this process of enterprise governance is the emergence of an entrepreneurial management discourse which promotes the dialectic co-existence of entrepreneurship and management.

CHAPTER 6

The Small Business and Entreprise Culture

... the very embodiment of a free society – the mechanism by which the individual can turn his leadership and talents to the benefit of both himself and the nation. The freer the society, the more small business there will be. And the more small businesses there are, the freer and more enterprising that society is bound to be.

(Margaret Thatcher, cited in Curran, 1997:1)

THE REBIRTH OF SMALL BUSINESS

A key characteristic of the enterprise culture project is the attention that is paid to the moulding and reshaping of the identity of individuals. As argued earlier structural transformations alone, such as the privileging of the private sector commercial enterprise through programmes such as privatisation, are dependent for their success on explicit and changing conceptions of the person.[1] In other words the cultural metamorphosis which enterprise culture requires is heavily dependent on individuals' possessing a psyche which is congenial to the market order. The project of enterprise culture is 'performative', providing the means by which the nature of work can be re-imagined, means which correspond with changing notions of the disposition and orientation required of the individual who performs that work.[2]

Enterprise culture is therefore concerned with "making-up"[3] individuals in a particular way, and understanding enterprise culture means discovering how individuals are gradually and progressively constituted as enterprising persons. *Homo economicus* from this perspective is not the subject untouchable by government, rather in neo-liberal enterprise culture "*homo economicus*

---

1. Miller, P & N Rose, "Production, identity and democracy" *Theory and Society* (1995) 24 pp. 427-467.
2. *Ibid.*
3. Hacking, I, "Making Up People" in C Heller, M Sosna & D E Wellbery (eds), *Reconstructing Individualism* (California: Stanford University Press) 1996.

is *manipulable man,* man who is perpetually responsive to modifications in his environment".[4] Thus 'enterprise' is not a natural characteristic of an individual or a form of consciousness, rather it is a type of action with explicit historical and cultural conditions.[5] Nevertheless transformations in identity resulting from the project of enterprise culture, cannot be understood if studied through a broad conceptualisation of this phenomenon. Rather enterprising transformations can only be fully comprehended if addressed in terms of the practices, programmes, techniques and procedures that act upon individuals within this historical juncture, an approach, which we have argued earlier, requires a notion of government within our conceptualisation of enterprise culture. From this perspective then we can explore the way the identities and selves of individuals are configured within enterprise culture, not through "a naturalistically conceived process of socialization, but [through] the forms of interrogation, or questioning, of what we are and do within an horizon of historically specific and culturally given practices".[6]

A defining characteristic of the era of enterprise culture is the attempt that has been made to shape and reshape the identity of individuals in terms of the small business owner, an issue we have looked at previously in chapter four when discussing how employees in large organisations are encouraged to act as if they are small business owners. Small business owners are presented as cultural heroes at the heart of enterprise culture, who will not only regenerate the economy but also renew the morality and moral backbone of modern society. From this perspective the development of the small business sector will lead to the economic and moral revitalisation of society in many national contexts.[7] Attached to the reverence which is granted to the small business owner, the small business, as an organisational form, is identified as the form of private sector business which is particularly nurturing of enterprise and entrepreneurship. In fact the small business has been identified as the 'home' of enterprise and entrepreneurial activity. Throughout the 1980s, small firms in the UK (and other countries) found themselves "cast as the great hope of the twentieth century",[8] a view of small business which appears to have held through various political transitions from Margaret Thatcher to John Major to the New Labour administration which came to power in May

---

4. Gordon, C, "Governmental rationality: an introduction" in G Burchell, C Gordon & P Miller (eds), *The Foucault Effect* (Hertfordshire: Harvester Wheatsheaf) 1991.

5. Dean, M, "Governing the unemployed self in an active society' *Economy and Society* (1995) 24: 4 pp. 559-583.

6. Dean, M, *op. cit.* (1995) p. 566.

7. Lane, C, *Industry and Society in Europe: Stability and Change in Britain, Germany and France* (Aldershot: Edward Elgar) 1995.

8. Rainnie, A, "Small Firms, Big Problems: The Political Economy of Small Businesses" *Capital and Class* (1985) 25, pp. 140-168.

1997. All have been captivated by the perceived enterprise and benefits of the small firm,[9] and all have contributed to the development of a range of programmes, practices, techniques and policies, designed to encourage individuals to be enterprising by setting up a small business.

Such attention has not been confined to the UK but has also manifested itself in many European countries leading to a significant increase in levels of self-employment and start-up small businesses across Europe. Looking at levels of self-employment as a per cent of the non-agricultural workforce, it appears that between 1981 and 1991 self-employment increased from 9.6 per cent to 13 per cent in Ireland; from 17.7 per cent to 19.3 per cent in Spain; from 19.7 per cent to 22.2 per cent in Italy; from 11.6 per cent to 12.8 per cent in Belgium; with self-employment levels in France and Germany holding steady at around 10 per cent and 8 per cent respectively. Taking Ireland as an example, such percentages translate into a contemporary estimate of around 160,000 non-farm small businesses, with around 98 per cent of these having fewer than 50 employees and around 90 per cent having less than ten employees.[10] However, in assessing changes in the small business sector, the UK presents one of the most noteworthy cases, displaying significant growth in self-employment after decades of gradual decline.

There was some growth in self-employment in the UK during the 1970s but this was certainly not of the same order as the rising trend in the 1980s.[11] From 1979 to 1989 the overall number of businesses in the UK increased by two thirds, averaging at around 500 additional firms every working day.[12] By 1991, British self-employment had risen by 52 per cent, growing from 2.2 million to a total of 3.3 million, an increase of 1.1 million.[13] Research indicates that self-employment declined in the early-1990s until 1993 and since then has risen again.[14] Nevertheless, despite this dramatic change it should be noted that over 70 per cent of the growth in this sector in the UK can be attributed to one-person businesses without employees. The increase in the

---

9. Curran, J, "The Role of the Small Firm in the UK Economy" (unpublished Paper) 1997.
10. *Task Force on Small Business 1994* (Dublin: Stationery Office). Care should be taken with the cross-national comparisons here, as the figures presented are based on each country's definition of self-employment and are therefore not strictly comparable. Nevertheless they do give us some sense of self-employment trends throughout the 1980s.
11. Hakim, C, "Self-Employment in Britain: Recent Trends and Current Issues" *Work, Employment & Society* (1988) 2: 4, pp. 421-450.
12. Daly, M & A McCann, "How Many Small Firms?" *Employment Gazette* (February 1992).
13. Campbell, M & M Daly, "Self-employment: into the 1990s" *Employment Gazette* (June 1992).
14. Curran, J, *op. cit.* (1997).

self-employed *with* employees was much less.[15] By the beginning of 1996, it was estimated that there were just under 3.7 million businesses in the UK, 95 per cent of which had less than ten employees. Only 0.1 per cent (just over 3,400 businesses) employed 500 or more people, with only 6,640 of the 3.7 million employing 250 or more people.[16]

Understanding Small Business Policies in Enterprise Culture

A key component of attempts to create an enterprise culture during the 1980s was the development of a range of small business policy measures in the UK. These measures included the establishment of the Enterprise Allowance Scheme, the provision of free and subsidised advice to individuals wishing to set up in business, the provision of a range of training programmes and the supply of incubator units for start-up small businesses.[17] The conventional analysis of such policy measures has tended to centre on an evaluation of the effectiveness of these policies when judged against their own stated objectives.[18] Alternatively, the ideologies or policy framework they are held to manifest, or the role they confer on the state and the market in the allocation of resources is the focus of assessment.[19] Such an approach to the evaluation of small business policies and programmes is limited, because it cannot highlight how the cultural transformation, which enterprise culture aims to bring about, is heavily dependent on the self-actualising abilities of individuals, and their alignment with the aims and objectives of the enterprise economy within which they are located.[20] Neither can such an approach highlight how attempts are made to change attitudes, values and norms, so that individuals are able to make the right choices and respond positively to the enterprise environment which is held out to them.[21] In other words, conventional evaluations of small business policies do not illustrate how, within enterprise culture, the self-actualising individual provides the basis for the transformation of social and economic life.[22]

---

15. Hakim, C, "Workforce Restructuring in Europe in the 1980s" *The International Journal of Comparative Labour Law and Industrial Relations,* (1989-1990) 5: 4, pp. 167-203.
16. Curran, J, *op. cit.* (1997).
17. Storey, D, "Should We Abandon Support to Start-Up Businesses?" in F Chittenden, M Robertson & D Watkins (eds), *Small Firms: Recession and Recovery* (London: Paul Chapman Publishing) 1993.
18. Gray, C, *Enterprise and Culture* (London: Routledge) 1998.
19. Dean, M, *op. cit.* (1995).
20. Rose, N, "Governing the Enterprising Self" in P Heelas & P Morris (eds), *The Values of the Enterprise Culture: The Moral Debate* (London: Routledge) 1992.
21. Carr, P, "The Cultural Production of Enterprise: Understanding Selectivity as Cultural Policy" *Economic and Social Review* (1998) 29: 2, pp. 27-49.
22. Miller, P & N Rose, *op. cit.* (1995).

To allow us to do this, we must understand small business policies and programmes in terms of practices and techniques which act at a distance on the behaviour of small business owners across a range of different sites, and under the auspices of a range of different authorities.[23] Understanding the relationship between enterprise culture and small business policies, requires that the latter are conceptualised as practices and procedures that act upon individuals and their behaviour in specific domains of existence. The way in which such practices and procedures embody the dimensions of enterprise culture must also be considered. Government from this perspective:

> . . . is the historically constituted matrix within which are articulated all those dreams, schemes, strategies and manoeuvres of authorities that seek to shape the beliefs and conduct of others in desired directions by acting upon their will, their circumstances or their environment . . . [and] governmental technologies [are] the complex of mundane programmes, calculations, techniques, apparatuses, documents and procedures through which authorities seek to embody and give effect to governmental ambitions
>
> (Rose & Miller, 1992:175)

Such an approach to the analysis of small business policies and programmes highlights how practices of *governmental self-formation* are dependent upon, operate through, and create connections with practices of *ethical self-formation*.[24] Governmental self-formation here refers to the ways in which authorities and agencies endeavour to mould the conduct, ambitions, desires and abilities of designated political and social categories (here small business) with the aim of entering them into particular strategies (e.g. reducing unemployment) and encouraging them to seek particular goals (e.g. take on employees). Ethical self-formation refers to practices, routines and techniques used by individuals seeking to question, form, know, decipher and act on themselves.[25] Thus small business policies can be understood as the means by which government aims to shape small firm activity, while, at the same time, giving expression to the norms and practices required within an enterprise culture.

This approach to the assessment and analysis of small business policies brings us back again to Foucault's concept of governmentality which, according to Rose, (1993:288) "is a way of problematizing life and seeking to act upon it". Governmentality is a concept which allows us to assess how a

---

23. *Ibid.*
24. Dean, M, *op. cit.* (1995).
25. *Ibid.*

state acts on individuals, either collectively or singly, with the aim of shaping, guiding, correcting and modifying the ways in which they conduct themselves.[26] The ultimate aim of such an approach is to understand how freedom is practised. Understanding enterprise culture and the small business policies and programmes which produce it in this way, means focusing on the manner in which SME policies and techniques guide and manage the conduct of small business owners (or potential owners) in the light of the principles or goals of enterprise culture. Approaching small firm policies and programmes from this perspective means exploring:

> . . . the complexity and diversity of the relations between authorities and subjects, and the ways in which such practices have not suppressed freedom but on the contrary, sought to 'make up' subjects capable of exercising a regulated freedom and caring for themselves as free subjects.

> (Rose, 1993:288)

SHAPING ENTERPRISE ACTIVITY

In recent years the UK, like many other countries, has witnessed the proliferation of government policies and programmes designed to assist the small business sector and to encourage individuals to start up their own business.[27] According to Storey (1994), between 1979 and 1983 more than 100 measures were introduced by the Conservative government to assist small firms. The range of policies, programmes and strategies initiated during the 1980s and 1990s can be grouped under a number of headings. These include:

- **macro policies** which impact on the taxation system, the rate of inflation and interest rates;
- **deregulation** which focuses on legislative exemptions and the cutting of bureaucratic 'red tape';
- **sectoral and targeted policy initiatives**, such as policies aimed at ethnic minorities, women, community enterprise or high-tech firms;
- **financial assistance** which included programmes such as the Business Expansion Scheme/Enterprise Investment Scheme, a loan guarantee scheme, the Enterprise Allowance Scheme, Business Start-Up Scheme and grants;

---

26. Burchell, G, "Liberal Government and Techniques of the Self" in A Barry, T Osborne & N Rose (eds), *Foucault and Political Reason* (London: UCL Press) 1996.
27. Westhead, P & D Storey, "Management Training and Small Firm Performance: Why is the Link So Weak?" *International Small Business Journal* (1996) 14: 4, pp. 13-24.

• **indirect assistance** which included training initiatives, the provision of information and advice and consultancy services.[28]

Within the context of the approach being taken here to the exploration of small firm policies, it is not possible or appropriate for us to discuss each and every policy and programme initiative put in place during the 1980s and 1990s. Instead, in this chapter, we will focus on two specific policy initiatives i.e. the Enterprise Allowance/Business Start-Up Scheme and Small Business Management Development. In addition in Chapter 7 we shall explore the policy of Selectivity. Starting from the perspective that these policies are what Dean (1995) calls governmental-ethical practices, the forthcoming exploration will highlight the dual nature of these initiatives. On the one hand they try to accomplish a variety of politico-administrative goals, such as reducing unemployment levels, providing financial support for potential small businesses and attempting to ensure the efficient use of state resources. On the other "they involve practices of self-formation, practices concerned to shape the attributes, capacities, orientations and moral conduct of individuals, and to define their rights, obligations and statuses".[29] Thus understanding small business policies as one of the means by which enterprise culture is produced, we can suggest that these initiatives do more than provide financial aid for existing or potential small business. Contemporary modes of small business assistance are involved in the configuration and reconfiguration of the characteristics, abilities and competencies of small business owners as enterprising individuals.[30] They aim to fashion the aspirations, attributes, abilities and attitudes of those who come within its ambit. In addition, such small business policies also attempt to enlist individuals in their own government by requiring their collaboration in:

> . . . these practices of self-shaping, self-cultivation and self-presentation. These practices become involved not simply in governmental practices but in ethical practices, and what emerges is a kind of governmental sponsorship and resourcing of certain kinds of ethical or ascetic practice.

> (Dean, 1995:567)

In other words, small business government policies resource activities which are enterprising in nature, i.e. daring, dynamic, independent, risk-taking and demonstrating initiative, reflecting the ethical dimension of enterprise culture.

---

28. Storey, D, *Understanding the Small Business Sector* (London: Routledge) 1994.
29. Dean, M, *op. cit.* (1995) p. 567.
30. Carr, P. *op. cit.* (1998).

Enterprise Allowance Scheme and the Business Start-Up Scheme

The Enterprise Allowance Scheme (EAS) was introduced in August 1983 and was for a time the flagship operation and spearhead of the enterprise culture.[31] The objective of the EAS, and its successor the Business Start-Up Scheme (BSUS), was to give financial support to unemployed people to help them establish viable small businesses.[32] Under this particular scheme, individuals, who wanted to start-up their own business, received financial support for a period of 52 weeks. To participate in this scheme individuals had to have £1,000 to invest in a business and to be:

- aged between 16 and 64;
- unemployed or facing unemployment in the near future through redundancy;
- actually receiving benefits;
- out of work for thirteen weeks (reduced to eight weeks at a later stage).[33]

General support for the small business sector was provided as a way of dealing with unemployment, and the EAS was established to rectify an anomaly in the taxation/benefit system which discouraged unemployed people from establishing their own business. By allowing individuals to keep their benefits for a period of twelve months while they embarked on establishing a business, it was argued that the risk of setting up a small business was reduced.[34] Thus the EAS was designed to encourage unemployed individuals to give up social benefits in exchange for limited support in establishing a business.[35]

Evaluations of the EAS have for the most part centred on the material benefits gained in terms of whether the scheme has been cost-effective, whether it has increased levels of self-employment, the impact of the EAS businesses on existing businesses, and the survival rate of businesses set up under the scheme. Such evaluations demonstrate that the failure rates were higher than national self-employment rates. It was also argued that EAS businesses displaced existing small firms, and that the most successful of the EAS businesses would have started anyway. Overall, from this perspective, its record was mixed and according to Gray (1998) was unlikely to improve in its new format as the BSUS administered by local Training and Enterprise Councils. However, small firm policies, such as the EAS, should not just be

31. Storey, D, *op. cit.* (1994); Gray, C, *op. cit.* (1998).
32. Westhead, P & D Storey, D, *op. cit.* (1996).
33. Storey, D, *op. cit.* (1994); Gray, C, *op. cit.* (1998).
34. Storey, D, *op. cit.* (1994).
35. Gray, C, *op. cit.* (1998).

considered in these terms, consideration should also be given to how such policies try to mould and shape the identity of individuals who come within its ambit. In other words policies such as the EAS aimed to do a lot more than provide material support for business start-ups, it also tried to encourage individuals to take care and responsibility for their own lives by creating their own jobs. The EAS was one of a wide range of techniques and practices which tried to connect up the freedom, choices, ways of life and behaviour of individuals with a mixture of political aims, social ambitions and governmental ends.[36]

Enterprise 'Fashioning'

There are a number of questions which can be explored if we want to understand how government activities are linked to individual activities. The first question we might ask is: "What do these government practices seek to govern?".[37] Looking at the EAS it is clear that it sought to govern unemployment by removing any disincentives to paid work, such as anomalies in the tax/social benefits system, and by encouraging unemployed individuals to set up their own business as a way of finding employment.

This focus on small firms as the means by which unemployment could be 'solved' originally emerged from David Birch's work on job generation and the small business sector in America. This research suggested that the site of future job creation was more likely to be the small firm than the large firm.[38] It appeared that the former were net job generators while the latter were net losers, or at best made a modest contribution to job generation.[39] This research and its findings were replicated in countries, such as the UK, and despite qualifications made to this approach in later work,[40] its conclusions were accepted and contributed to the development of policies such as the EAS and BSUS.

According to Dean (1996:222) the materiality (here unemployment) which is governed by such policies is "drenched with thought", i.e. thought which represents an enterprise ethic. A policy such as the EAS was not just about

36. Dean, M, "Foucault, Government and the Enfolding of Authority" in A Barry, T Osborne & N Rose (eds), *Foucault and Political Reason: Liberalism, Neo-liberalism and Rationalities of Government* (London: UCL Press) 1996.
37. Questions derived from Dean, M, *op. cit.* (1995).
38. Birch, D, "Who Creates Jobs?" *The Public Interest* (1981) 65, pp. 3-14.
39. Curran, J, *op. cit.* (1997).
40. For example, C Armington & M Odel, "Small Business - How Many Jobs?" *The Brookings Review*(Winter 1982) pp. 14-17; Davis, S J, J Haltiwanger & S Schuh, "Small Business and Job Creation: Dissecting the Myth and Reassessing the Facts' Working Paper No. 4492 (Boston: National Bureau of Economic Research) 1993; Storey, D, *op. cit.* (1994).

removing disincentives to establishing a small business and providing some financial support towards this project, it also sought to manage and regulate the impact of unemployment on individuals. In particular, it sought to prevent and negate the possibility of a culture of dependency becoming ingrained which would negatively affect the disposition, attitudes and behaviour of the unemployed, in a manner which might prevent them from returning to the labour market, while at the same time contributing to an anti-enterprise culture. Policies such as the EAS promoted an ethic of enterprise among the unemployed by encouraging and supporting them to demonstrate initiative, independence and a daring risk-taking demeanour by setting up a small business. Thus the EAS (and its successor the BSUS) endeavours to govern and invalidate anti-enterprise attitudes and behaviours which could contribute to a dependent disposition.

The second question which we can ask of the EAS as a practice concerned with the guidance of conduct and the relation of "self to self",[41] focuses on the mechanics by which this scheme is implemented. Inherent to the EAS was a notion of what Dean (1995) calls *reciprocal obligation* which means that the government provided financial and advisory support on condition that the individual engaged him/herself in small business activity. Throughout the 1980s people were encouraged to move out of their unemployment status and away from the receipt of benefits into a self-employed status and the receipt of an allowance. As the EAS has evolved and developed into the BSUS, attempts on the part of government to encourage individuals to set up a small business have led to the emergence of a range of new agents called Start-Up Counsellors or Personal Business Advisors. These agents adopt a *pastoral* role (an issue which will be discussed in depth in Chapter 7) evaluating and helping to prioritise the needs of potential start-ups and existing businesses, directing them towards appropriate specialist advisers and generally helping to enhance their ability to successfully function as a small business.[42] Through such practices, the unemployed individual, who is a potential small business owner, becomes involved with and 'obeys' the directions of a range of pastoral agents, and receives an allowance on condition that s/he establishes "a particular relation to self",[43] i.e. demonstrates initiative, independence, self-reliance and a risk-taking orientation.

This leads us into the third question we can ask about the EAS: "What mode of subjectification of the individual does this policy hope to produce?" An immediate answer to this question is that it aimed to encourage and direct individuals to adopt an enterprising orientation towards themselves and their own self-governance. The EAS was concerned with moulding unemployed

41. Dean, M, *op. cit.* (1995); Dean, M, *op. cit.* (1996).
42. Dean, M, *op. cit.* (1995); Gavron, R, M Cowling, G Holtham & A Westall, *The Entrepreneurial Society* (London: Institute for Public Policy Research) 1998.
43. Dean, M, *op. cit.* (1995) p. 576.

individuals into active entrepreneurs of themselves and their lives through the establishment of a small business. To enable them to be successful at the latter, they were encouraged to avail of the range of advisory and counselling services provided by support agencies. The EAS and the BSUS place an emphasis on providing independent advice and support tailored to the peculiar needs of individual clients.[44] These policies view "each individual as a case to be managed, [supervises] the individual's relation with him or herself, neutralize[s] dependency by identifying certain risks in his or her relation to self"[45] and promotes and encourages individuals to becomes entrepreneurs of their own destiny.

Thus the EAS/BSUS is part of a wider programme of reforms which attempt to 'fashion' and mould individuals into an enterprising form, with the concerns and values implicit in such a policy being reflective of the institutional and ethical strands of the enterprise culture. This policy embodies the institutional dimension of enterprise culture through its promotion of self-employment and the establishment of a small business as the solution to unemployment. Each unemployed individual is encouraged to set up a private sector small firm which, it is argued, is the most efficient entity for the provision of goods and services. The promotion of such start-up small firms contributes to the privileged position of the private sector commercial enterprise. The second dimension of enterprise culture, which places an emphasis on behaviour that is enterprising, is also embedded in the EAS/BSUS in that the establishment of a small business requires independence, use of initiative, self-reliance and some daring.

The Enterprising Small Firm

Within enterprise culture, as discussed throughout this book, the private sector commercial enterprise has been granted a favoured status as the site where enterprising behaviour is most likely to flourish. The small business as an example of a private sector organisation has been singled out as the form of private sector business which is particularly nurturing of enterprise and entrepreneurship. However we need to be careful about making such a linkage, as it is argued that commercial enterprises, such as the small business, are not always completely enterprising. This sense of a lack of enterprise is said to be reflected in the statistical profile of the UK small business sector as discussed above. The overrepresentation of the micro-business within the UK small business sector has contributed to a distinction being made between the small business venture and the entrepreneurial (enterprising) venture.[46]

---

44. Gavron, R, M Cowling, G Holtham & A Westall, *op. cit.* (1998).
45. Dean, M, *op. cit.* (1995) p. 576.
46. Carland, J W, F Hoy, W R Boulton, & J A Carland, "Differentiating Entrepreneurs from Small Business Owners: A Conceptualization" *Academy of Man-*

The small business venture and owner is said to be characterised by a business entity which is run by an individual for the principal purpose of furthering personal goals. It is also characterised as a business entity which does not engage in new innovative practices or demonstrate an enterprising orientation, reflected in its name *trundler* or *lifestyle firm*.[47] In contrast the entrepreneurial venture and its owner (the entrepreneur) is characterised by a business entity which involves itself in enterprising activities such as growth and innovation, and is run by an individual for the principal purpose of profit and growth. The recognition that not all small businesses are completely enterprising (i.e. have an innovation and growth orientation) in their activities has contributed to a feeling that small firms should be actively encouraged to thoroughly express enterprising qualities. Thus as well as the identity of individuals being shaped and moulded in terms of the small business owner through policies such as the Enterprise Allowance Scheme/Start-Up Business Scheme, attempts are made to further shape the capacities and attributes of individuals who become small business owners, particularly in terms of their management capabilities.

According to Du Gay *et al.* (1996) the 'character' of the manager in the UK was put under the spotlight during the 1980s, with many commentators arguing that British companies were losing out to foreign competitors because of the calibre of their managers. The expression of such concern highlights how "the economic priorities of politicians and business persons have been articulated in terms of the required personal characteristics of managers".[48] Nevertheless despite the economic importance attached to the small firm during the 1980s and 1990s, it is only in recent years that the management capabilities of small business owners have come under significant scrutiny. Concerns have been expressed about the internal efficiency and business performance of small businesses and it has been suggested that high failure rates and low growth derives from poor managerial competence.[49] This has led to the introduction of a number of training initiatives in the UK based on the premise that:

> . . . training can, and should, be a powerful agent of change,

---

agement Review (1984) 9: 2, pp. 354-359; Wickham, P, *Strategic Entrepreneurship* (London: Pitman Publishing) 1998.

47. Bridge, S, K O'Neill & S Cromie, *Understanding Enterprise, Entrepreneurship and Small Business* (London: Macmillan Business) 1998.

48. Du Gay, P, G Salaman & B Rees, "The Conduct of Management and the Management of Conduct: Contemporary Managerial Discourse and the Constitution of the 'Competent' Manager" *Journal of Management Studies* (1996) 33: 3, pp. 263-282.

49. Westhead, P & D Storey, *op. cit.* (1996).

facilitating and enabling a company to grow, expand and develop its capabilities thus enhancing profitability.

(Jennings & Banfield, 1993
cited in Westhead & Storey, 1996:13)

Such training initiatives have included policies such as the Business Growth Training programme which was introduced in 1989 and consisted of a set of five types of government financial support packages for small firms. Option 3 of this programme provided financial assistance for businesses with between 25 and 500 employees, to enable them to employ consultants to help them develop their management capabilities.[50] Evaluations of such initiatives have followed the conventional route, focusing on the material benefits gained in terms of improved firm performance. However, such evaluations have found it difficult to demonstrate that the provision of management development and training in small firms clearly leads to a superior performance on the part of the recipient firm, though it has been identified that attitudes to management development vary with firm size.[51] According to Marshall *et al.* (1993:347) management development works best in larger small firms "that have the managerial capacity to make the necessary commitment and to absorb both management and business development...projects were less effective in very small firms with a small management team". Therefore from this perspective the value of such training initiatives is still open to question.[52]

However as with the EAS/BSUS, management training and development policies should not just be considered in these terms, attention should also be given to the way such policies try to shape and govern the conduct of small business managers. To explore the impact such policies have on small business behaviour we can ask the same questions[53] of them that we asked of the EAS/BSUS above. Firstly what do small business management development initiatives seek to govern? We can suggest that these policies seek to govern the business activity of small business owners in the sense of influencing the way they run and develop the business. From this perspective small business management development initiatives can be understood as an attempt to transform the way small businesses are run by encouraging small business owners to adopt certain practices (e.g. a formal management development plan, formal management practices and controls) and inclinations, which allow the

---

50. Marshall, J N, N Alerman, C Wong & A Thwaites, "The Impact of Government-Assisted Management Training and Development on Small and Medium-Sized Enterprises in Britain" *Environment and Planning C* (1993) 11, pp. 349-364.
51. Westhead, P & D Storey, *op. cit.* (1996).
52. Storey, D & P Westhead, "Management training in small firms - a case of market failure?" *Human Resource Management Journal* (1997) 7: 2, pp. 61-71.
53. Derived from Dean, M, *op. cit.* (1995).

small business and its owner to become, and to be become recognised as, an entrepreneurial venture. Management development initiatives give expression to the practices and frame of mind required of small businesses and their owners, if such businesses are to make a significant contribution to the optimal functioning of the British economy. Programmes, such as the Business Growth Training initiative, encourage small business owners to adopt an ordered and managed approach to the running of their business with the hope of ensuring the best material pay-back from their enterprise activity.

The second dimension of management development initiatives that we need to consider focuses on the mechanisms by which such programmes are implemented. Attempts by the government to encourage small business owners to adopt certain business practices has led to a huge growth in the "training industry"[54] and the number of agents who adopt a pastoral role towards small businesses involved in these training initiatives. Through the direction and guidance of these pastoral agents, small businesses and their owners are encouraged "to adopt a certain entrepreneurial form of practical relationship to themselves as a condition of their effectiveness and of the effectiveness of this form of government".[55]

This leads us into the third question which asks what mode of subjectification of the individual do management training and development initiatives hope to produce. The instant answer to this question is that it aims to inspire and guide small business owners to adopt an enterprising orientation towards themselves, their own self-governance and the running of their small firm. Enterprising here means adopting a growth and profit orientation to the business. Management development initiatives are concerned to mould small business owners into entrepreneurial business owners so as to ensure the optimal performance of the market order.

Overall, therefore, policies such as the EAS/BSUS and management development initiatives aim to change the thinking and behaviour of targeted populations. From the perspective of the EAS/BSUS the population being targeted is the unemployed with the aim of encouraging such individuals to adopt an enterprising orientation towards themselves by setting up a small business. Management training and development initiatives target established small businesses with the aim of transforming the way these businesses are run. Small business owners are encouraged to transform their businesses into entrepreneurial ventures by adopting a growth and innovation orientation towards the business and themselves. As with other enterprise policies and initiatives at which we have looked, the implementation of the EAS/BSUS and management training and development initiatives has contributed to the

---

54. Westhead, P & D Storey, *op. cit.* (1996).
55. Du Gay, P "Making Up Managers: Enterprise and the Ethos of Bureaucracy" in S Clegg & G Palmer (eds), *The Politics of Management Knowledge* (London: Sage) 1996a.

development of an entrepreneurial management discourse. Individuals are firstly encouraged to display a range of enterprising characteristics, such as daring, a risk-taking orientation, and dynamism, by setting up a small business and growing it. In addition, they are also expected to participate in this enterprising activity in an ordered manner through the competent performance of a range of management skills, demonstrating that enterprising activity embraces both entrepreneurial and managerial elements. Thus the small business policies looked at in this chapter can be understood as part of the numerous diverse techniques of government, the complex of institutions, procedures, calculations and strategies, which have sought to act upon the lives and behaviour of individuals with the aim of creating an enterprise culture, so that objectives such as economic stability and social order within a state can be achieved.[56]

SUMMARY OF KEY IDEAS

- A key characteristic of attempts to create an enterprise culture is the reshaping of the identity of individuals in terms of the small business owner.

- Such attempts have led to a significant growth in levels of self-employment and start-up small business across Europe. The UK represents one of the most noteworthy cases having experienced momentous growth in levels of self-employment.

- The UK, like many other European countries such as Ireland, has experienced a proliferation of small business programmes and policies designed to assist small business.

- Small business policies can be understood as the means by which central government tries to guide and manage the conduct of small business owners (or potential owners) according to the principles or goals of enterprise culture. Small business policies try to align the desires and ambitions of small business owners with government objectives, all within an enterprise culture.

- Small business policies can thus be understood as one significant element of a broader range of initiatives and strategies which together are the means by which enterprise culture is produced.

- Small business policies such as the Enterprise Allowance Scheme are reflective of the institutional and ethical strands of enterprise culture:

---

56. Foucault, M, "Governmentality" in G Burchell, C Gordon & P Miller (eds), *The Foucault Effect: Studies in Governmentality* (London: Harvester Wheatsheaf) 1991.

firstly through its privileging of the private sector commercial enterprise in the form of small business ownership; and secondly in its promotion of a range of enterprising attributes.

- Small business management training and development policies have contributed to the development of an entrepreneurial management discourse. Individuals are encouraged to display a range of enterprising characteristics and management skills.

CHAPTER 7

The Enterprise Adviser and Enterprise Culture

My objective for more than 25 years has been to sketch out a history of the different ways in our culture that humans develop knowledge about themselves: economics, biology, psychiatry, medicine and penology. The main point is not to accept this knowledge at face value but to analyze these so-called sciences as very specific 'truth games' related to specific techniques that human beings use to understand themselves.

(Foucault, 1988:18)

CREATING ENTERPRISE NETWORKS

A key aim of this book is to make visible the impact of enterprise culture on business activity in a range of settings, i.e. the public sector, the private sector large organisation, and the private sector small organisation. The wide-ranging nature of the conventional approach taken to enterprise culture can make this extremely difficult, and thus we have argued for an "aesthetically narrower"[1] conceptualisation of this phenomenon. Starting from the recognition that a market order will not benefit society as a whole unless it is comprised of individuals who can be *trusted* to behave in way that the market order requires, the narrower understanding of enterprise culture, which focuses on the link between it and government, allows us to explore how the self-actualising individual provides "the basis and presupposition for the formulation and evaluation of political strategies and the transformation of social and economic life".[2]

Such transformation does not come about by simply imposing a range of constraints upon individuals, rather it emerges from attempts at "making up citizens capable of bearing a kind of regulated freedom" and caring for them-

---

1.   Bennett, T, "Putting Policy into Cultural Studies" in L Crossberg, C Nelson & P Treichler (eds), *Cultural Studies* (London: Routledge) 1992.
2.   Miller, P & N Rose, "Production, identity and democracy" *Theory and Society* (1995) 24, pp. 427-467.

selves as free subjects.[3] The notion of a 'regulated' freedom requires that we move away from the range of oppositions such as state/market, public/private, domination/freedom, which have plagued the conventional understanding of enterprise culture.[4] Instead by adopting the narrow conceptualisation of enterprise culture which we are advocating, we can understand the relationship between state and individual in enterprise culture, in terms of government or action at a distance.[5] The key question for government in an enterprise culture, is how do you manage enterprise without annihilating its existence and its autonomy.[6] According to Rose and Miller (1992), one way in which you do this is through the creation and moulding of alliances and networks. Such alliances allow actors in a range of different locations to understand their position according to the same rationale and language, to interpret their aims and their destiny as in some way indissoluble. Connections are made between the problems and issues facing a range of individuals and groups in such a way that the conceptualisation and solution of one individual/group's problems is intricately linked to those of another. Therefore, from this perspective:

> Particular and local issues . . . become tied to much larger ones . . . associations are established between a variety of agents, in which each seeks to enhance their powers by 'translating' the resources provided by the association so that they may function to their own advantage. Loose and flexible linkages are made between those who are separated spatially and temporally, and between events in spheres that remain formally distinct and autonomous. When each can translate the values of others into its own terms, such that they provide norms and standards for their own ambitions, judgements and conduct, a network has been composed that enables rule 'at a distance'.

> (Rose & Miller, 1992:184)

Within the narrow conceptualisation of enterprise culture that is presented here, the relationship between state and individual or state and business should

---

3. Rose, N & P Miller, "Political Power Beyond the State: Problematics of Government" *British Journal of Sociology* (1992) 43: 2, p. 174; N Rose, "Government, Authority and Expertise in Advanced Liberalism" *Economy and Society* (1993) 22: 3 pp 283-299.
4. Carr, P, "Reconceptualising Enterprise Culture" *The Conference of the British Sociological Association* (University of Reading) 1996.
5. Thompson, G, *The Political Economy of the New Right* (London: Pinter Publishers) 1990; N Rose & P Miller, (1992) *op. cit.*
6. Rose, N. & P Miller, *ibid.*

be understood in such alliance terms. As argued in Chapter 2, the creation of an enterprise culture has not simply been about reducing government intervention, it has been about establishing a *change* in the nature of state activity which results in new ways to govern the economy and individuals/businesses within it. A key question therefore is how are such alliances created? Recourse again to Foucault's concept of governmentality which allows us to understand how a state acts at a distance on the actions of individuals/businesses with the aim of shaping and moulding their behaviour, is useful here. Foucault developed the notion of 'governmentalization' to answer questions such as: "How to govern oneself, how to be governed, how to govern others, by whom the people will accept being governed, how to become the best possible governor".[7] He argued that the modern state should not be conceptualised as an entity which has developed above individuals, ignoring their existence and what they are. Rather it should be thought of as a highly sophisticated structure "in which individuals can be integrated under one condition: that this individuality would be shaped in a new form, and submitted to a set of very specific patterns".[8]

Central to the notion of modern governmental techniques developed by Foucault is the theme of *pastorship*. It was originally a form of regulation that was peripheral to the domain of the state but has been absorbed into governmental techniques.[9] In understanding the concept of governmentality, the theme of pastorship is important as it encapsulates the idea that governmentality is a form of power which is both totalising and individualising. Totalising in the sense that pastorship can be understood as techniques which aim to rule individuals in a continuous and permanent way. Individualising in the sense that such techniques seek to enhance the conditions and qualities of life of citizens.[10] However, as well as being a material form of power in the sense of trying to order individuals in relations to things, it also works in an indirect way through the 'fashioning' of the consciousness of individuals.[11] The management of enterprise does not just focus on the technical features of this activity (e.g. financial planning or marketing in a small business), but also pays attention to the psychological features of the enterprising individual (e.g. motivation, possession of enterprising attributes). Individuals are made subject through pastorship, with the officials of pastoral

---

7. Foucault, M, "Governmentality" in G Burchell, C Gordon & P Miller (eds), *The Foucault Effect: Studies in Governmentality* (London: Harvester Wheatsheaf) 1991, p.87.

8. Foucault, M, "The Subject and Power" in H Dreyfus & P Rabinow, *Michel Foucault: Beyond Structuralism and Hermeneutics* (Chicago: The University of Chicago Press) 1982, p.214.

9. *Ibid.*; L McNay, *Foucault: A Critical Introduction* (Cambridge: Polity Press) 1994.

10. McNay, L, (1994) *ibid.*

11. *Ibid.*

power (e.g. police, hospitals, personal business advisors) creating alliances and acting as a type of interface between governmental activities and the 'self-formation' ascetic practices of individuals.

Within the context of enterprise culture, pastors play a crucial role in helping government to reconcile the need to restrict state activity while at the same time promoting and guiding private sector activities.[12] Pastors operationalise mechanisms, strategies, techniques and policies which mould the economic and social behaviour of a diverse array of institutionally distinct individuals and organisations, without destroying their formally different or autonomous temperament.[13] In acting as an interface between government and individuals/businesses, pastors have contributed to the development of self-regulation in a way that curtails the need for direct political intervention. Pastors act as 'translation devices' between the state and individuals/ businesses, shaping individual and business activity not by coercion but through a promise of improving the quality and effectiveness of their lives/businesses.[14] The operationalisation by pastors of the array of enterprise programmes and policies put in place in recent years, particularly in the small business area, is thus the means by which relations and linkages are created between the overall economic performance of the economy and the 'private' choices of individuals/businesses.[15] Thus governing from this perspective entails a reliance upon devices, e.g. small business initiatives and policies which undertake to create individuals "who do not need to be governed by others, but will govern themselves, master themselves, care for themselves".[16]

Pastors of Enterprise

A key pastoral figure within enterprise culture is the Personal Business Advisor (or enterprise advisor) who, within the UK context, is located in the national network of Business Link currently numbering over 220 outlets.[17] Since the establishment of Business Link in 1993, these outlets have become the main vehicle for delivery of support services to small business in the UK, with the Personal Business Advisor (PBA) acting as a type of interface between the

---

12. Rose, N & P Miller, (1992) *op. cit.*
13. Miller, P & N Rose, "Governing Economic Life" *Economy and Society* (1990) 19:1.
14. *Ibid.*
15. *Ibid.*
16. Rose, N, "Governing 'Advanced' Liberal Democracies" in A Barry, T Osborne & N Rose (eds.), *Foucault and Political Reason: Liberalism, Neo-liberalism and Rationalities of Government* (London: UCL Press) 1996, p. 45.
17. Lean, J, S Down & E Sadler-Smith, "An Examination of the Developing Role of PBAs Within Business Link" Paper presented as the ISBA National Small Firms Policy & Research Conference, Belfast (1997).

governmental activities of the British state, the business community locally and nationally, and the individual business owner.[18] The role of the PBA has been defined as developing and fostering long-term relationships between the PBA and the small business client to help support their development and growth. This relationship should facilitate the transfer of experience, knowledge and skills to small businesses, as well as providing them with access to first-class business support services.[19] In addition it should also be recognised that the implementation of small business policies through such relationships are the means by which expression is given to the norms and practices required within enterprise culture as we will see below. Small business policies are thus operationalised through these relationships, which provide the relays through which the objectives of ministers, the aspirations of small business and the desires of consumers achieve mutual translatability.[20]

This process of translatability and the role that enterprise advisors play in this, will be illustrated with reference to research on the small business policy of selectivity in Ireland, conducted by the author during the mid-1990s. This research centred on the operationalisation of the policy of selectivity, understood simply as the targeting of state resources at Irish small businesses most likely to grow successfully, and the economic actors who were involved in its implementation. These include state personnel working in the Irish state development agency Forbairt,[21] bank personnel working in the Irish associated banks and a group of small business owners from a variety of sectors. The research outlined here will refer exclusively to in-depth interviews with Forbairt personnel conducted during the early months of 1994. Thirteen Forbairt project executives (enterprise advisors) and managers working in the Dublin region were interviewed. Given the low numbers involved and the unrepresentative nature of the sample, the intention of this research is to illustrate the nature of the operationalisation of the policy of selectivity and its contribution to the production of enterprise culture. However, it cannot be seen as a definitive account of this process.

Within the context of the conceptualisation of enterprise culture being

---

18. Carr, P, (1996) *op. cit.*; J Binns & J Kirkham, "Do Personal Business Advisors Add Value" Paper presented at the ISBA National Small Firms Policy & Research Conference, Belfast (1997).
19. Lean, J, S Down & E Sadler-Smith, (1997) *op. cit.*
20. Miller, P & N Rose, (1990) *op. cit.*
21. Forbairt was formerly part of the Industrial Development Authority (IDA), an autonomous body with national responsibility for the implementation of Irish industrial policy. In 1993 the IDA was dissolved and reformulated as Forbairt (responsible for the promotion of Irish indigenous industry), IDA Ireland (responsible for attracting foreign investment), and Forfas (responsible for co-ordinating overall policy). Forbairt is an Irish word which has two meanings: one is growth or development, the other is wart or boil. Active consideration is currently being given to restructuring and renaming these agencies again.

developed in this book, this analysis of selectivity will show how this policy aims to do more than identify fast-growth firms or get value for state resources, it also attempts, through its advisory function, to shape and regulate the conduct of entrepreneurs. Understanding selectivity as a cultural policy in this sense we will see that it is concerned with the formation and reformation of the abilities and attributes of small business entrepreneurs. Conceiving of selectivity and other small business policies in cultural terms allows us to comprehend how enterprise culture is produced, so that the self-actualising abilities of individuals are aligned with the aims and objectives of the enterprise economy within which they are located. Within this context, the Forbairt personnel who operationalise the policy of selectivity can be understood as adopting the pastoral role of enterprise advisor, assessing the needs of individuals and their businesses who approach them for aid, through the application of selectivity criteria to business proposals.

Selectivity

Within the UK context selectivity measures have been in existence since the 1972 Industry Act. The trend towards selectivity was further emphasised during Margaret Thatcher's reign in government. During the 1980s, efforts were made to move state support for business away from automatic non-discriminatory grants to a system of discriminatory and non-automatic support.[22] Prior to 1984/1985 applicants for state support received grants more or less automatically as long as they filled in the correct forms and met a range of minimal requirements, and applications for grant support were not scrutinised in any significant way. However, with the introduction of selectivity, this approach to industrial support changed significantly.[23] The move away from automatic non-discriminatory grants to a non-automatic selective discriminatory system also implied more *scrutiny* of businesses applying for grant aid. This involved assessing the viability of projects, determining whether the projects met government technological and employment objectives, and follow-up studies of businesses which received support. In addition state support agencies and the personnel within them adopted the role of enterprise advisor (akin to a business consultant) through the provision of a range of business advice.[24]

The emergence of selectivity as a significant policy within the Irish industrial policy arena can be traced to the Telesis Report (1982), the White Paper on Industrial Policy (1984), Review of Industrial Performance (1990), the Culliton Report (1992), the Moriarty Task Force Report (1992), and the subsequent response by the Department of Employment and Enterprise (1993)

---

22. Thompson, G, (1990) *op. cit.*
23. *Ibid.*
24. *Ibid.*

to the latter two reports. The general argument of all of these policy documents is that blanket support for new firms and business in general is inefficient, and that a policy of selectivity is more appropriate, giving the best value for money in terms of state resources. In this only a few chosen firms are eligible for state support but this support is said to make a significant contribution to the growth and development of the business,[25] as well as making a meaningful contribution to the national economy.

According to the 1990 Review of Industrial Performance, there was little economic justification for the state supporting large numbers of start-up companies, or expanded small industries, if they make no significant contribution to the national economy. The general view was that state resources should be targeted where they can generate the highest return, rather than be squandered (through blanket support) where the return is at most marginal, and at worst detrimental to the long-term interest of the economy.[26] Such a view was supported by commentators such as Storey (1994) and Storey and Johnson (1987, 1987a) who conducted research on small business within the UK context (and which will be discussed in Chapter 8). It was also borne out in the interviews for the selectivity research of this author, with respondents stating that "it was much worse in the past", when the emphasis was on "volume" and they were "inundated with . . . projects". This created a situation where enterprise advisors within Forbairt were in favour of "discrimination" as the following quotations illustrate:

> There was a time when we got a lot of applications. I mean you'd have sectors or projects that might be in vogue, for example bottled water. As soon as Ballygowan started becoming well known everybody and anybody that had a swampy patch in their backgarden wanted to do bottled water and that's a fact and that went on for years. Now there isn't that much...chips sorry potato chips was another one. Every now and then you get these little waves of projects, I suspect that maybe in the next year or two you'll have recycling, I reckon we'll be inundated with recycling projects . . . all the problems with rubbish disposal and all that, we're going to get them coming out of the woods.

> . . . it was much worse in the past when the IDA was hell bent, and particularly in the small business area, on volume, put through proposals. There was a famous saying: "if it moves grant aid it and if it doesn't move give it a kick in

25. MacDonald, R & F Coffield, *Risky Business? Youth and the Enterprise Culture* (London: The Falmer Press) 1991.
26. Kinsella, R, W Clarke, D J Storey, D Mulvenna & D Coyne, *Fast-Growth Small Firms: An Irish Perspective* (Dublin: Irish Management Institute) 1994.

the arse and grant aid it". There was . . . there's always
more enthusiasm at grassroots level and Project Officer level
for discrimination and for the ability if you like to refuse,
than it was higher up where it was seen as a political imperative to be active.

It might be suggested that reflected in these arguments in favour of selectivity are Foucaultian sentiments, that such a policy should aim to develop aspects of individual entrepreneurs and their companies, which not only
strengthen their business, but also strengthen the wider economy and state.
In this context Forbairt personnel adopt the pastoral role of enterprise advisor acting as a type of interface between governmental endeavours and the
self-formation disciplinary practices of individuals. Within the interviews here
respondents presented themselves as the "interface" between the individual
firm and a "formal sanctioning . . . decision making board"[27] as follows:

The individual project officer is very much the interface with
the individual company through all the contacts and chan-
nels, and who is ultimately responsible for presenting . . .
writing and presenting a case which gets the formal sanctioning from a decision making board.

This advisory and 'shepherding' role was emphasised throughout the interviews with all respondents presenting themselves as small business advocates, whose role was not only to guide applicants through the selectivity
process by "encouraging them to get information", but to "fight the case" to
a higher board as follows:

I have taken proposals to board and I haven't gotten through
the . . . maybe there was x, y and z and they weren't quite

---

27. The power of the Irish government here is refracted through the Industrial Development Act 1986, and it is from this legislation that the power of the IDA as
an instrument of government derives. It is also from this legislation that the
restructured development agencies, i.e. Forbairt, IDA Ireland and Forfas derive
their power. According to the Act the IDA is an autonomous body which has
national responsibility for the implementation of industrial development policies. This responsibility includes the provision and administration of grants and
financial facilities for industry; to advise the relevant Minister on the future
development potential of Ireland; and to give advice and guidance to those who
are contemplating establishing a new business or expanding an existing one.
Further the Act states that the IDA may perform any of its functions through
members of staff authorised to do so. This includes the delegation of its grant
making powers to a *board or committee* constituted by the IDA or any of the
Authority's staff members. These powers are now bestowed on Forbairt, IDA
Ireland and Forfas.

> happy, and I would . . . its probably deferred which has hap-
> pened to me and if I felt really, really strongly about it, and I
> felt that maybe it wasn't coming across the way it should
> have, I would go back and do more research with the com-
> pany, and go back and fight the case because of what I felt
> were the strengths and weaknesses of the company, and I
> have done it and it has worked.

Nevertheless it must be recognised that these agents are not only 'caring' for the welfare of the companies and entrepreneurs they are working with, they are also 'governing' and 'exploiting' them in the sense of 'encouraging' firms to behave and present themselves in a particular way. This recognition captures the essence of governmentality as being a form of individualisation and a form of totalisation "in which human beings are regarded as both self-governing citizens *and* members of the flock who are governed, members of a self-governing political community *and* members of the governed population".[28] Thus the argument we are making here is that our understanding of enterprise culture should focus on how attempts are made to align the sense of purpose of small business entrepreneurs, with the values that are designed into state activities, and the role policies, such as selectivity, play in this. Within enterprise culture these values can be understood as the priority given to the economy in terms of the progressive enlargement of the market, and the requirement that individual and commercial entities display enterprising qualities.[29]

The process of alignment is facilitated through the relationship between state enterprise advisors (pastors) and individual entrepreneurs. Such 'pastors' can be conceptualised as 'cultural specialists' who within the context of enterprise culture implement its 'cultural techniques', i.e. those agents who are actively involved in enterprise culture creation through the implementation of policies such as selectivity. The next section explores how further data drawn from interviews with Forbairt personnel supports the narrower understanding of enterprise culture proposed in this book, and the role policies, such as selectivity, play in its creation. This will be done by focusing on the way in which selectivity attempts to shape and mould the entrepreneurial activity of Irish small business in enterprise culture terms.

---

28. Dean, M, *Critical and Effective Histories: Foucault's Methods and Historical Sociology* (London: Routledge) 1994, p.185.
29. Du Gay, P, *Consumption and Identity at Work* (London: Sage) 1996; P Du Gay, (1996a) "Making Up Managers: Enterprise and the Ethos of Bureaucracy" in S Clegg & G Palmer (eds), *The Politics of Management Knowledge* (London: Routledge) 1996.

Selectivity and the 'Cultural Production' of Enterprise

Attempts to construct an enterprise culture in countries such as Britain and Ireland have centred on the privileging of 'the market'. As discussed in Chapter 1, the creation of such a culture for enterprise comprises of two interwoven strands: an institutional strand and an ethical strand. The former privileges the private sector commercial enterprise, while the latter places an emphasis on 'enterprising' qualities such as risk-taking, self-reliance and a daring spirit. Entrepreneurs are also expected to perform competently a range of managerial skills including planning, organising, budgeting, staffing, controlling, co-ordinating, to enhance the strength of the business and allow it to negotiate the growth process successfully.

Within the discourse of economy and enterprise, these strands are intricately entwined. This is demonstrated by the strong belief that it is within the institutional context of the commercial enterprise (as a business entity), that individuals are likely to demonstrate the ethic of enterprise (as an activity). However, as suggested in earlier chapters, despite the linkage that exists between the institutional and ethical strands of enterprise, there would seem to be a suggestion that commercial enterprises are not always completely enterprising, and therefore must be encouraged to express enterprising qualities thoroughly. It is here that the unrecognised cultural dimension of policies, such as selectivity, comes into play, in that entrepreneurs are required to exhibit such characteristics when attempting to access state resources. If they do not exhibit 'enterprising' characteristics they are actively encouraged to acquire them, particularly 'enterprising managerial' characteristics, which can include "a lot of gathering information from outside sources and seeking a lot of expert advice" as the following illustrates:

> . . . often you can get a person coming in at a fairly early stage . . . what you're probably doing is encouraging them to get information. It is something that becomes essential as you go along but not . . . you don't throw somebody out the door just because they haven't quite got the right answers. . . . In other words you're saying 'look there's information needed here, we need to work together to get that'.
> . . . So there [can be] a lot of gathering information from outside sources and seeking a lot of expert advice on it where we feel that you [entrepreneur] don't know it yourself.

Such 'encouraging' is what Du Gay (1996b: 19) refers to as "a material-cultural process of formation or transformation whereby ('encouraging') the adoption of certain habits and dispositions allows an individual to become – and to become recognised as – a particular sort of person". Thus a policy such as selectivity gives expression to the practices and habits required of

Irish organisations and individuals for the optimal functioning of the Irish market economy, and is one of the means by which the conduct of Irish small business entrepreneurs is shaped, moulded and regulated.

The commitment to attempts to influence, shape and regulate entrepreneurial conduct emerged in all the interviews with respondents stating that selectivity is "not just about giving money"; it is about giving "proper advice on how to structure the company"; "bringing a lot of expertise and help"; making "sure that all the bases have been covered"; giving "whatever non-monetary assistance we can, directed towards building up the company", as the following illustrates:

> I think we have a lot of expertise in start-up situations and how you structure them, what's important, what might make them work and I think our ability to appraise, and also to help individuals. One of the things you often find with people in a start-up situation, often they don't have a network of people who can advise them very well and we can give them that network as well. I mean we know a lot of very good accountants who have been very helpful, given proper advice on how to structure the company. We know the banks that are friendly to deal with, we know where the experts are in various industries that people should talk to. So we're often expanding their network and their knowledge which is very important, because people can work in isolation . . . it can be very difficult, and they may be operating from a basis of knowledge that is slightly flawed, in that case they need experts and quality.

Another respondent stated:

> I think what we often bring to the product, I think, is you know very good experience and judgement of parallel situations . . . it's not just about giving money. It's about bringing a lot of expertise and help, and where people often need access to extra expertise and part of what we do is maybe introduce them to the right people who maybe have that expertise.

Such views were unanimously supported as follows:

> Generally they will have gaps in their information, so before they actually start-up and spend the kind of money that they're going to spend on start-up, we encourage them to fill in the gaps in their information...We have control not so much over whether they're viable or not, but we're putting

> money in, we want to make sure that all the bases have been covered and that's part of our role.
>
> We like to feel we offer a range of services, advice, and brokering contacts and generally trying to give whatever non-monetary assistance we can, directed towards building up the company.

In implementing the policy of selectivity, small business entrepreneurs are 'encouraged' to acquire and apply a range of managerial skills which are said to be crucial for successful entrepreneurship. From the above quotations, we can see the strong emphasis that is placed on the strengthening of managerial skills in the belief that this will enhance the commercial viability of businesses which request state support. This is seen as beneficial for the entrepreneurs involved and the Irish economy in general. In requiring "that all the bases have been covered", Forbairt personnel are actively involved in moulding and shaping the way in which Irish small business entrepreneurs 'do business', i.e. they are 'businessing' businesses,[30] and ensuring that Irish small business is as 'enterprising' as possible. Through a variety of interlinked practices and routines (e.g. requiring entrepreneurs to provide a range of information on the proposal or expecting entrepreneurs to adhere to a set range of criteria), selectivity as a form of government encourages entrepreneurs:

> . . . to adopt a certain entrepreneurial form of practical relationship to themselves as a condition of their effectiveness and of the effectiveness of this form of government. In other words, this form of government 'makes up' the governed as entrepreneurs of themselves, as enterprising sorts of persons'
>
> (Du Gay, 1996a:22)

Therefore within the context of an "aesthetically narrower" definition of enterprise culture which conceives of this phenomenon in terms of practices and techniques of conduct, the policy of selectivity can be understood as one of the means by which Irish entrepreneurs are 'fashioned', so as to ensure the optimal performance of the market order. Thus we can understand policies such as selectivity as the site of enterprise cultural production.

This shaping and moulding of Irish small business entrepreneurs becomes clearer if we examine the criteria around which the policy of selectivity is operationalised, as inherent to these criteria are the institutional and ethical strands of enterprise culture. The official criteria benchmark for the Irish

---

30. Peters, T, *Liberation Management* (Basingstoke: Macmillan) 1992.

policy of selectivity is the Industrial Development Act 1986. This sets out strict rules for grants, setting limits for grant assistance; focusing assistance on internationally trading companies and the development of export markets; and requesting firms to provide new employment, increase local value added and improve research and development.[31] The list of criteria provided by this legislation, around which entrepreneurs, who approach state agencies, such as Forbairt, must 'fashion' themselves, contains a mixture of what can be called 'development' (potential employment, growth orientation, trade on international markets, import substitution), and 'enterprising' (business plan, equity, commercial viability) criteria.[32] It should be noted that two types of 'enterprising' criteria are used in the selectivity process. The first type here refers to private sector management skills. It can be suggested that this emphasis on commercial management skills is connected to the institutional dimension of enterprise culture which privileges the private sector commercial enterprise and private sector commercial practices. The second type of 'enterprising' criteria used in the selectivity process (discussed in detail below) places an emphasis on enterprising attributes and is reflective of the ethical dimension of enterprise culture.

Looking at Table 1[33] below we can see that, though there is some variability in selection procedures across the Forbairt 'pastors', a fairly clear pattern emerges. For the most part the majority tend to place more emphasis on the 'enterprising' aspects of business ventures as opposed to their 'development' aspects. A majority of respondents cited 'enterprising' criteria such as 'business plan' (92 per cent), 'cash flow projections' (85 per cent), 'market research' (78 per cent), 'management team' (78 per cent), 'individual appli-

---

31. Drudy, P J, "From Protectionism to Enterprise: A Review of Irish Industrial Policy" in A Burke (ed.), *Enterprise and the Irish Economy* (Dublin: Oaktree Press) 1995.

32. Labelling the various criteria as either 'development' or 'enterprising' was in the main unproblematic, i.e. the orientation of each criterion was clear. However some of the criteria namely 'growth orientation' and 'trade internationally' could have been assigned to either category. For the purposes of this research they were placed in the 'development' grouping, largely because encouraging indigenous business to grow through international trade is a key aim of industrial policy, as it is believed that this will contribute to the overall development of the Irish economy.

33. A listing of the criteria (derived from the 1986 legislation and pilot interviews) drawn upon by Forbairt personnel when assessing business proposals was constructed. Respondents were asked to indicate the importance they attach to each of the criteria when judging business proposals as follows: 'very important', 'important', 'worth considering', 'of limited importance' and 'not at all important'. The respondents were also asked to rank the criteria. The results of this exercise are presented in Tables 1 and 2. The figures in brackets refer to the number of respondents.

cant' (62 per cent), 'entrepreneur's equity' (62 per cent) 'over capacity in sector' (92 per cent), as important or very important. In contrast, less emphasis was placed on the 'development' criteria. Of particular significance here is the lack of importance attached to 'potential employment' as a criterion, rated by only 16 per cent as important or very important. This *should* be surprising as one of the strongest justifications presented for implementing a selectivity policy, is the need to identify those firms with the greatest employment potential, so that state resources can be targeted at them.[34]

However, in my view, the lack of attention paid to 'potential employment' as a criterion is indicative of the strong 'enterprise' ethos surrounding a policy such as selectivity. It would appear that the original ethos of industrial policies in Ireland was a 'development' one, illustrated by an article published in a Irish journal called *Administration* in 1972 which announced that "the IDA's job is to create jobs".[35] However by the 1990s, the move to an 'enterprise' ethos was clear exemplified in policy documents such as the Culliton Report (1992), the data contained in this paper, and comments such as one made by a former chairman of the IDA, a Mr Martin Rafferty in 1993. He stated: "We do not create jobs, we provide the incentive. Our project analysis has become more professional and rigorous."[36]

Table 1: Forbairt Rating of Selection Criteria

Selection Criteria	Very Important %	Important %	Worth considering %	Of limited importance %	Not important %
Business Plan	77(10)	15(2)	8(1)	—	—
Cash Flow Projections	54(7)	31(4)	15(2)	—	—
Market Research	39(5)	39(5)	15(2)	8(1)	—
Management Team	39(5)	39(5)	23(3)	—	—
Individual Applicant	39(5)	23(3)	39(5)	—	—
Entrepreneur's Equity	8(1)	54(7)	8(1)	31(4)	—
Overcapacity in Sector	69(9)	23(3)	—	—	8(1)
Sector Per Se	23(3)	39(5)	15(2)	15(2)	—
Potential Employment	8(1)	8(1)	54(7)	23(3)	8(1)
Growth Orientation	15(2)	46(6)	15(2)	15(2)	8(1)
Trade Internationally	23(3)	31(4)	31(4)	8(1)	8(1)
Import Substitution	8(1)	31(4)	38(5)	8(1)	15(2)
Economic Climate	—	23(3)	31(4)	23(3)	23(3)
Political Considerations	—	—	—	31(4)	69(9)

34. Storey, D J & S Johnson, *Job Generation and Labour Market Change* (London: Macmillan Press) 1987; D J Storey & S Johnson, (1987a) *Are Small Firms the Answer to Unemployment?* (London: Employment Institute) 1987.
35. McLoughlin, R J, "The Industrial Development Process: An Overall View" *Administration* (1972) 20: 1, pp. 27-38.
36. Murphy, C, "IDA is Dead, Long Live IDA" *The Sunday Tribune* 18 July 1993.

Therefore. in implementing a policy such as selectivity, the emphasis has shifted towards developing a system of selection rules that will identify viable businesses, largely by encouraging commercial enterprises to thoroughly express 'enterprising' qualities. Other 'development' criteria such as 'growth' and 'trade internationally', which were given a strong *rating* by 61 per cent and 54 per cent respectively, could as said earlier be categorised as 'enterprise' criteria.

In Table 2, the pattern of placing overall emphasis on the 'enterprising' profile of a business venture as opposed to its 'development' profile (e.g. amount of employment it provides) is further illustrated. The Forbairt respondents were asked to rank the criteria listed in order of importance when assessing a business proposal where 14 = most important and 1 = least important. Ranking here means ordering the criteria in terms of which criterion each project executive looks at first, second, third, etc., when assessing individual business proposals. This ranking was collapsed into three categories as follows:

- 1 to 5 = low ranking;
- 6 to 10 = middle ranking;
- 11 to 14 = high ranking.

As with Table 1, a clear trend emerges. The majority of Forbairt respondents are more likely to give 'enterprising' as opposed to 'development' criteria a high ranking as follows: 'business plan' (92 per cent), 'cash flow projections' (61 per cent), 'market research' (46 per cent), 'management team' (69 per cent), 'individual applicant' (85 per cent), 'entrepreneur's equity' (39 per cent), and 'over capacity in sector' (38 per cent). In contrast the 'development' criteria are only highly ranked by a minority as follows: 'potential employment' (15 per cent), 'growth orientation' (15 per cent), 'trade internationally' (15 per cent) and 'import substitution' (0 per cent).

In requiring that entrepreneurs adhere to 'enterprising' criteria the Forbairt 'pastors' are attempting to influence and direct how entrepreneurs run their businesses by encouraging them to fully express 'enterprising' qualities.

The 'enterprising' qualities discussed here largely refer to the performance of a range of managerial skills. However as part of the process of selectivity, Forbairt personnel also actively assess the 'enterprising' character of the individual applicant. The importance of the individual was signalled in Tables 1 and 2 where the criterion 'individual applicant' was rated and ranked highly. This assessment of the individual is mainly based on whether the entrepreneurs they are dealing with are 'enterprising' in the sense of demonstrating initiative, a daring spirit, self-reliance and "dynamism". Their perception of this will influence "how much faith" they can have in the management skills and management documentation which the entrepreneur submits as the following illustrates:

Table 2: Forbairt Ranking of Selection Criteria

Selection Criteria	High Ranking %	Middle Ranking %	Low Ranking %
Business Plan	92(12)	8(1)	—
Cash Flow Projections	61(8)	31(4)	8(1)
Market Research	46(6)	46(6)	8(1)
Management Team	69(9)	31(4)	—
Individual Applicant	85(11)	15(2)	—
Entrepreneur's Equity	39(5)	39(5)	23(3)
Overcapacity in Sector	38(5)	54(7)	8(1)
Sector Per Se	23(3)	31(4)	46(6)
Potential Employment	15(2)	46(6)	39(5)
Growth Orientation	15(2)	70(9)	15(2)
Trade Internationally	15(2)	62(8)	15(2)
Import Substitution	—	31(4)	69(9)
Economic Climate	—	23(3)	77(10)
Political Considerations	—	—	100(13)

. . . you never capture it on paper. The guy never does himself justice on . . . in his document and its only till you meet them, meet the person, get a feel for their personality, their dynamism etc. to make an informed view on how credible they are . . . how much faith you can have in the numbers that are down there in the business plan . . . if the project officer forms a view that the entrepreneur isn't credible he will be forever finding . . . finding you know ways to turn him down and then it can be a messy scenario.

Two other respondents supported these sentiments as follows:

I would say that if someone comes to me with a good idea and their plans are fine but if I don't think that they have the experience for it that's one thing and if I don't think they have the capability of doing it either . . . it's very difficult for me to say I think your project is great but I don't think you'll be able to do it . . . that can be difficult because you're telling somebody they've a great idea but you're really saying it would be better without you almost.

. . . you look at the plan and the figures and you do the assessment on that, you get a fairly good idea of how commercially viable the project is going to be, but the missing bit is how good the promoter is. You know it's judgement too and you have to kind of live with people a bit to find out whether they're really capable . . . a good promoter that's a

> key one because a good promoter can survive a bad project
> but seldom will a good project survive a bad promoter.

A question may be raised here as to the exact nature of these criteria. For example it might be argued that the criteria around which selectivity is operationalised is *bureaucratic* in nature as opposed to *enterprising*. However, in my view, the nature of the criteria can be understood as both bureaucratic *and* enterprising at one and the same time, i.e. bureaucracy in the form of Forbairt is using 'enterprise' as the means to perform its task which is to identify businesses which can be allocated state funds. This can be connected to the 'governmentality' shift of selectivity from a 'development' orientation to an 'enterprise' orientation mentioned above. It can be suggested that such a shift materialised in response to the criticism of Forbairt (formerly the IDA) which commenced in 1982 as a result of the Telesis Report. This 'critical evaluation' of the performance of the state development agency continued into the 1990s and may be one of the reasons why the increased emphasis on 'enterprise' emerged. Within the context of this criticism the benefits of this approach for the Forbairt bureaucracy are threefold:

- Forbairt gains legitimacy through its enterprising orientation.

- Forbairt's promotion of an enterprise culture and attempts to actively make individuals behave in an 'enterprising' manner contributes to its own survival. This is largely because it can present itself as a crucial component of attempts to create an enterprise culture in Ireland.

- The emphasis placed on 'enterprise' can be used by Forbairt as a means to secure resources. The number of support agencies has rapidly increased in Ireland in recent years. Within this context attempts by Forbairt to develop its business relevance through the promotion of 'enterprise' can help it maximise its funding.

The adoption of 'enterprise' by the Forbairt bureaucracy in the performance of its tasks should not necessarily surprise us given the recent insertion of market reasoning and entrepreneurial governance into the state and state-related agencies. As argued in Chapter 3 this requires that organisations that are not themselves private businesses, think and function as if they were, i.e. state organisations and individuals within them are criticised for not being enterprising. The twist here is that these self-same organisations and individuals are firstly suggesting the same thing about private sector commercial businesses, and secondly requiring that private sector businesses demonstrate their 'enterprise' credentials if they want to access state resources.

From this analysis we can see the clear 'enterprise' ethos which surrounds the operationalisation of the policy of selectivity. This is clear firstly in the emphasis that is placed on enhancing the commercial viability of business proposals and secondly in the attention that is paid to the daring, dynamic qualities of entrepreneurs that come within its ambit. The production of enterprise culture through the implementation of policies such as selectivity which embody the dimensions of this phenomenon contributes to the development of an entrepreneurial management discourse which promotes the dialectic co-existence of entrepreneurship and management. Entrepreneurs must be willing to subject themselves to such enterprise 'fashioning' if they want to access state resources. Thus, in Foucaultian terms, selectivity is one of the means by which the subjectivity and activity of entrepreneurs is rationalised in the sense of making entrepreneurs and their enterprise "fully enterprising".

Producing Enterprise Culture

To understand 'enterprise culture' it is important that we have an appreciation of the centrality of 'enterprising' individuals for the possibility of this form of social order. Allied to this we must understand how such 'enterprising' individuals are cultivated to ensure the optimal performance of the market economy. It is here that a narrow conceptualisation of 'enterprise culture', which focuses on the link between culture and government, can prove useful. Understanding this phenomenon as the ensemble of norms and techniques of conduct, that enable the self-actualising capacities of entrepreneurs to become aligned with, and provide the basis for, the optimal performance of the market economy, allows us to assess the actual practices of the cultural production of enterprise. Within this context the operationalisation of the policy of selectivity and other small business policies can be understood as a series of enterprise cultural techniques which attempt to shape and regulate the personal capacities of Irish entrepreneurs. The aim of such cultural technology is to "translate the goals of political, social and economic authorities into the choices and commitments of individuals".[37]

However, even a suspicion that applicants may be 'deceitful' in the sense of fraudulently presenting themselves as 'enterprising', does not negate the argument that Forbairt tries to mould the behaviour of Irish entrepreneurs. Whether an enterprise culture is *truly* created or business people are *truthfully* enterprising is not the issue. Rather it is that Forbairt through its deeds actively sets out to imbue entrepreneurs with an ethic of enterprise, and is using 'enterprise' as the means to perform its tasks. Nevertheless, what does need to be taken into account is the possibility of resistance on the part of those subject to a policy such as selectivity, and recognition that the pastoral process outlined above does not go unchallenged. The reflexive character of modern life in general and modern business life in particular, implies a continuous examination and reformation of practices of government and

---

37. Rose, N, "Governing the Enterprising Self" in P Heelas & P Morris (eds), *The Values of the Enterprise Culture: The Moral Debate* (place: publisher) 1992, p.159.

self in the light of new information, which constitutively alters their character. In addition it must be understood that the enterprise order which such practices can produce is a selection, and each selection by its very nature will arouse anger and prompt rebellion.[38]

What needs to be constantly remembered, and has been emphasised in earlier chapters, is that government is inherently problematic and that the desire to govern has to be understood less in terms of its success and more in terms of the difficulties surrounding its operationalisation.[39] Reality is too unruly to be apprehended by any perfect knowledge. Technologies, programmes, systems produce unintended consequences, are often put to uses for which they were not intended, or are unable to produce the technical conditions necessary to make them a success.[40] The enterprise 'order' created through the implementation of a range of enterprise policies is bound to experience problems in its operationalisation. Any alternative 'order' to enterprise would also experience similar problems. New 'orders' create new problems even if they remove the old ones.

Selectivity as a policy can, therefore, be understood as a government rationality which attempts to imbue entrepreneurs with an ethic of enterprise, and as such is a site of enterprise cultural production. Forbairt personnel who operationalise this policy can be understood as adopting a pastoral role of enterprise advisor, assessing the enterprising qualities of entrepreneurs who approach them for state aid, through the application of selective criteria to business proposals. The aim of this process is to cultivate and promote enterprise within individuals' lives in such a way that the market economy performs optimally, thus strengthening the Irish State.

SUMMARY OF KEY IDEAS

- A key concern for government in enterprise culture is how do you create and manage enterprise without destroying its existence and autonomy.

- The creation of an enterprise 'order' does not come about through the imposition of a range of restrictions and constraints on individuals and businesses. Rather it emerges through the 'fashioning' and moulding of people and firms capable of carrying a 'regulated' freedom. Such 'fashioning' occurs through the operationalisation of enterprise policies and strategies.

- Foucault's concept of 'governmentality' is useful here as it allows us to understand how the state, through the implementation of enterprise poli-

---

38. Bauman, Z, *Life in Fragments* (Oxford: Blackwell Publishers) 1995.
39. Miller, P & N Rose, (1990) *op. cit.*
40. *Ibid.*

cies and programmes, acts at a distance on the conduct of individuals/ businesses, with the aim of 'fashioning' their enterprise behaviour, without excessively controlling it or eradicating it.

- Central to the concept of 'governmentality' is the theme of pastorship. Pastors, through the creation of alliances, implement a range of enterprise strategies, techniques and policies which aim to shape the social and economic behaviour of a diverse variety of institutionally distinct individuals and organisations, without destroying their autonomy.

- A key pastoral figure within enterprise culture is the Personal Business Advisor (PBAs) whose role has been defined as developing and fostering long-term relationships between PBAs and small business clients.

- The implementation of small business policies through PBA-small business alliances is the means by which expression is given to the norms and practices required within enterprise culture.

- Selectivity is one such policy which gives expression to the norms, rules and customs of an enterprise culture. The policy of selectivity does not just attempt to identify entrepreneurial small firms or get value for state resources as conventional accounts of this policy suggest. It also attempts through its advisory function to shape and direct the conduct of entrepreneurs.

CHAPTER 8

Growth and Entrepreneurship in Enterprise Culture

In recent times there has been a substantial shift in interest and emphasis in the field of small business towards a focus on the growing business in particular. This shift has been evident in policy-making, in the application of small business support, and in related research and commentaries. Fast-growing small firms have been described as 'gazelles', 'fliers', 'growers' and 'winners', and the targeting of effort towards them has been described as 'picking', 'stimulating' or 'backing' winners'.

(Bridge *et al.*, 1998:162)

GOING FOR GROWTH

Many conventional discussions of the emergence, promotion and value of enterprise within contemporary social and economic life, are suffused with representations of the post-war 'welfare state' as a malevolent and loathsome force. The call for an enterprise order is set within the context of a discussion which emphasises the inefficiencies, incompetence and injustices of an enlarged State.[1] However, as argued earlier, such an approach to understanding the relationship between the state and individuals/businesses in enterprise culture, does not adequately characterise the diverse ways in which state power is exercised in present-day life. Neither does it acknowledge or highlight the increasing governmentalisation of the contemporary business world.[2] Thus to move away from oppositions, such as state versus individual, which characterise conventional accounts of enterprise culture we have suggested, taking a lead from Bennett (1992, 1998), that enterprise culture should be conceptualised in terms of:

---

1. Rose, N & P Miller, "Political Power Beyond the State: Problematics of Government" *British Journal of Sociology* (1992) 43: 2, pp. 173-205.
2. *Ibid.*; T Bennett, "Putting Policy into Cultural Studies" in L Crossberg, C Nelson & P Treichler (eds), *Cultural Studies* (London: Routledge) 1992.

. . . a historically produced surface of social regulation whose distinctiveness is to be identified and accounted for in terms of :

(i)   the specific types of attributes and forms of conduct that are established as its targets;
(ii) the techniques that are proposed for the maintenance or transformation of such attributes or forms of conduct;
(iii) the assembly of such techniques into particular programs of government;
(iv) the inscription of such programs into the operative procedures of specific cultural technologies.

(Bennett, 1992:27)

Bending this perspective to our own purposes, we can suggest that the vast array of small business policies and support put in place over the past twenty years, operate as enterprise culture technologies which are involved in influencing and 'fashioning' the formation of the entrepreneur and his/her business. The suggestion is that the emergence and development of small business policies, programmes, etc. have been a key factor in the shaping of contemporary enterprise and entrepreneurship. In Chapter 6 and 7 we have explored the shaping and moulding activities of small business policies, such as the Enterprise Allowance Scheme/Business Start-Up Scheme and Selectivity, demonstrating how these policies embody and produce the institutional and ethical dimensions of enterprise culture. However in considering the way that small business policies act as enterprise culture technologies, producing and creating the phenomenon of enterprise culture, it is crucial that we explore another dimension of these programmes, i.e. the emphasis placed on *growth* as an emblem of enterprise activity.

Exploring the embedding of a growth ethic within small business policies as a means of encouraging small businesses to be 'fully enterprising', illustrates an interesting paradox. In earlier chapters we have argued that the restructuring of large organisations along enterprise lines requires that employees behave as if they were small business owners, which can be understood as an attempt to introduce small firm flexibility into the large organisation. Similarly, the changes introduced into the public sector, for example the introduction of fund holding among general practitioners, requires that family doctors behave like owners of small businesses which they have to develop.[3] However, the preference for the fast-growth small firm which grows into a large business, over the small firm which stays small, illustrates the para-

---

3.   Bosanquet, N & C Salisbury, "The Practice" in I Loudon, J Horder & C Webster (eds), *General Practice Under the National Health Service 1948-1997* (London: Clarendon Press) 1998.

doxical relationship between small and large within the UK enterprise culture. Firstly, large firms are criticised for being large and encouraged to be enterprising in their management orientation, understood as the introduction of small business management within their boundaries. At the same time, small businesses are given substantial support only when they undergo the growth process and become large.

The Promotion of the 'Growing' Small Business

According to Storey (1994), the failure of UK small businesses to grow into large businesses may be the basis for the country's long-term poor economic performance. Despite the fact that it is argued that the UK economy would benefit substantially from a population of efficient and resilient small and medium-sized businesses which resemble the German Mittelstand, comments such as Storey's illustrate that within countries, such as the UK, small businesses are only valued if they demonstrate a propensity to grow large. Though research has emphasised that the small business sector can make significant contributions to levels of competitiveness, dynamism, innovation and employment, it is also emphasised that such benefits are only likely to occur in the *growing* small business as opposed to the *non-growth* small business. Small businesses which choose to stay small tend to be a denigrated entity, in countries such as the UK and Ireland, reflected in the name ascribed to them, i.e. 'trundlers'.[4] The emphasis that is placed on growth within these countries can be attributed to two things: firstly to the historical value placed on the large business unit allied to a denigration of the small business sector; and secondly to contemporary small business research, much of which has argued that resources used to support and develop the small business sector, should be focused on those with optimal potential understood as growth firms.

'Giantism'

To understand fully the emphasis that is placed on *growing* small businesses within the UK economy, we must take account of the dominant trend of 20th century capitalism, i.e. the ascendance of big business and the promotion of an ethos of 'giantism'. Large firms able to exploit economies of scale and scope were viewed as superior to small firms in practically every aspect of economic performance, i.e. productivity, job security, compensation and technological progress. 'Giantism' can generally be understood as the championing of large business, through processes such as the promotion of concentration in business ownership. It is important largely because it contributed to

---

4. Storey, D J, "Should We Abandon Support to Start-Up Businesses?" in F Chittenden, M Robertson & D Watkins (eds), *Small Firms: Recession and Recovery* (London: Paul Chapman Publishing) 1993.

the hegemony of the large firm as a business entity, and has influenced the policy orientation taken to the small business.[5]

After the Second World War, governments actively encouraged the rationalisation of their industrial structures. Fearful of competitive disadvantage with trading rivals, governments such as the French and British, promoted mergers and takeovers.[6] It was argued that, for industry to remain competitive, it must develop managerial enterprises, i.e. large industrial concerns where decisions on operations and investment are taken by a hierarchy of salaried managers, governed by a board of directors.[7] Within the British context, small firms were conceptualised as characteristic of the early phases of industrialisation and unlikely to play a significant role in the economic future of the country. Although the creation of a significant sector of large, publicly-quoted companies can be dated from the end of the 1920s, Britain experienced significant concentrations of large, managerial enterprises in a number of industries in the post-war period.[8] Thus as competition between countries moved out of the military sphere into the economic arena, large firms were viewed as essential for competitiveness because of cost advantages of scale and scope.

The result of such championing led to an increase in the number of large-sized firms. From the 1960s onwards, Britain's industrial structure underwent massive change, with large companies accounting for an increasing proportion of industrial output. Experiencing several waves of mergers during the 1960s and 1970s, Britain attained the highest degree of capital concentration of any advanced society, bypassing even the USA.[9] The rapid expansion of the corporate sector coincided with the contraction of the small business sector, resulting in a somewhat unbalanced industrial structure in Britain.[10] By the late-1960s 75 per cent of net assets held by publicly quoted companies in Britain were owned by the 100 largest firms. Between 1911 and 1971 the domination of large-scale bureaucratic enterprises resulted in a 50 per cent decline in the number of business proprietors in the UK. The growth of the corporate economy led to the almost complete demise of the entrepreneurial middle class within Britain. By 1976 the 100 largest firms in Britain accounted for 42 per cent of the output of manufacturing industry,

5. Weiss, L *"Creating Capitalism: The State and Small Business Since 1945* (Oxford: Basil Blackwell) 1988.
6. Samuels, J M & P A Morrish, "An Analysis of Concentration" in C Levicki (ed.), *Small Business: Theory and Policy* (Beckenham: Croom Helm) 1984.
7. Chandler, A, "The Enduring Logic of Industrial Success" *Harvard Business Review* (March-April 1990).
8. Samuels, J M & P A Morrish, (1984) *op. cit.*
9. *Ibid.*
10. Lane, C, "Industrial structure and performance: common challenges – diverse experiences" in J Bailey (ed.), *Social Europe* (Essex: Longman Group UK Ltd) 1992.

while also accounting for nearly 50 per cent of UK employment.[11] Thus
'giantism' contains two assumptions with regard to small business: firstly
that a preponderance of big business is important for capitalism and secondly
that small business is inferior.

Despite the championing of the small business from 1979 onwards in the
UK context, the experience of 'giantism' and the ethos it propagated has had
a lasting impact on how we view and understand the small business sector.[12]
Although it is recognised that small businesses are not big businesses writ
small, and that every small business is not necessarily an embryonic big business,[13] resources and support for the small business sector are embedded in
the notion of 'small businesses to grow large'. Within the context of an
economy such as that of the UK, small businesses although increasingly appreciated, are not valued because they are small, despite the ascription of
advantages such as flexibility to them. Rather they are valued for their potential to grow into large businesses which it is argued will make a significant
economic contribution to the UK economy in the form of increased employment, exports, innovation, etc. This is not to say that small businesses which
stay small are totally 'written off', but it suggests that the small firm as a
business entity is valued for its growth potential rather than its small size –
small is beautiful but big is better.

As suggested earlier, we therefore see a paradox inherent in the thinking
surrounding the promotion of small business in general, the position of the
large business in the contemporary British economy, and the relationship
between the small and large firm. The 1980s and 1990s have been characterised by calls for the decentralisation of decision-making and a flattening of
managerial hierarchies because of the perceived need for quicker and more
flexible reactions to constantly changing market demands.[14] However, despite this fact, to be 'fully enterprising' a small business is encouraged to
grow into a large (bureaucratic?) organisation. The history of 'giantism' and
the paradoxical legacy of this philosophy has had a lasting impact on the
British small business sector. Despite the rehabilitation and the subsequent
reversal in fortune of the British small business sector in the 1980s, the 'large'
bias has not been eradicated, indeed it is at the centre of any evaluation which
is undertaken of British small business performance. Notwithstanding, the
fact that over 95 per cent of businesses within the UK context fall within the
small firm category, the UK cannot be called a small firm economy, largely
because small businesses are only really valued if they can grow into large

11. Samuels, J M & P A Morrish, (1984) *op. cit.*
12. Weiss, L, (1988) *op. cit.*
13. Bridge, S, K O'Neill & S Cromie, *Understanding Enterprise, Entrepreneurship and Small Business* (London: Macmillan Business) 1998.
14. Lane, C, *Industry and Society in Europe* (Aldershot: Edward Elgar) 1995.

organisations. Thus as Weiss (1988) argues small business is admired and applauded not for what it *is* but rather for what it will *become.*

Research into the 'Growth' Activities of the Small Firm

According to Johnson (1990) regardless of the proliferation of small business policies and initiatives since 1979, the volume of small business research and publication of such research in serious academic journals, only began to significantly advance in the late-1980s. A key theme of much of this research is the growth of small businesses. It is thus important that we are clear about what we mean by 'growth' when looking at this process in small firms. One of the most conventional measures of growth is an increase in employment. Growth has also been interpreted as the introduction of a broader product range by a company, or an increased number of patents or of customers, none of which automatically imply greater turnover, profitability or employment.[15] An increase in the value of investments made in a business can also be interpreted as a measure of growth. It must be appreciated that 'growth' can be understood in a number of ways.[16]

Different stakeholders have different growth priorities. For government, growth in employment is usually a primary goal. Allied to this, growth in export turnover or in import substitution is also important. For shareholders, growth is interpreted in terms of enhanced dividends and an increase in share value. For owner-managers, growth in the range of products, market share, or the income generated by the business can be more important than increasing employment.[17] For researchers, the growth of businesses for the most part centres on changes in employment levels, though this should not be automatically assumed. Within the context of enterprise culture, small business policies which promote growth aim to ensure that the growth goals of government (e.g. job creation, export growth, technological advancement and regional balance) are pursued and achieved alongside the growth goals of other actors (e.g. owner-managers whose goals include profits, customer numbers, asset growth and security).[18] Understanding small business policies (and other enterprise policies) as an attempt to ensure the simultaneous achievement of different sets of goals, lies at the heart of the conceptualisation of enterprise culture which this book is advocating. Neo-liberalism and the creation of an enterprise culture are not simply about the promotion of a non-

---

15. Daly, M, "The 1980s - A Decade of Growth in Enterprise" *Employment Gazette* (March 1991) pp. 109-34; S Bridge, K O'Neill & S Cromie, (1998) *op. cit.*
16. *Ibid.*
17. *Ibid.*; R Kinsella, W Clarke, D J Storey, D Mulvenna & D Coyne, *Fast- Growth Small Firms: An Irish Perspective* (Dublin: Irish Management Institute) 1994.
18. Johnson, S, "Small Firms Policy: An Agenda for the 1990s" paper presented to the 13th National Small Firms Policy and Research Conference, Harrogate (1990).

interventionist state. Rather they are about creating a distance between state institutions and other social actors, while at the same time 'acting upon' and influencing the activities of individuals/businesses, with the aim of aligning the goals of different sectors of the economy.[19]

Despite the policy emphasis placed on growth, the amount of research on the growth activities of small businesses is not as extensive as the research on new firm formation. Nevertheless, three categories of growth research can be identified. Firstly research which develops stage models of small firm growth, identifying various stages of small firm development, e.g. start-up, survival, growth, expansion and maturity. Secondly research which focuses on the barriers to growth and considers how best these can be removed. Such barriers can be internal (e.g. lack of motivation and management skills) or external (e.g. lack of finance, competition levels) to the small business. Finally research which concentrates on the characteristics – and predictive modelling – of growth companies, an approach to the issue of small firm growth which is the most persistent, and which from a research point of view understands growth in terms of increases in employment.[20] The characteristics/predictive modelling research on growth is facilitated by a policy environment which places an emphasis on increasing employment levels, while at the same time getting 'value for money', and has given rise to the policy of selectivity discussed in Chapter 7.

Based on extensive analysis and evaluation of the performance of the UK small business sector, commentators such as Storey (1993) argue that policies which aim to multiply the formation rate of new small firms, are unlikely to be designated as good use of public money, in contrast to policies which aim to help growing businesses to grow faster. Much research has demonstrated that small firms have a very high failure rate, with a very high percentage closing within the first four years of business. Allied to this, research has emerged from a number of sources to indicate that only a low percentage of small firms, produce a large percentage of the jobs created in this sector.[21] A study of firms in the south east of England which were established between 1980 and 1982, indicated that 18 per cent of all firms accounted for 92 percent of total jobs created.[22] Similarly, research on firms in other parts of the UK concludes that job generation in small firms is heavily concentrated among a few, with 50 per cent of jobs being created by 4 per cent of new businesses over a decade.[23]

---

19. Rose, N & P Miller, (1992) *op. cit.*
20. Freel M S, "Towards an Evolutionary Theory of Small Firm Growth" paper presented at the ISBA National Small Firms Policy & Research Conference, Belfast (1997); S Bridge, K O'Neill & S Cromie, (1998) *op. cit.*
21. Storey, D J, (1993) *op. cit.*
22. *Ibid.*
23. Storey, D J, *The Entrepreneurial Firm* (London: Routledge) 1985; D J Storey,

These findings have led to a differentiation being made between the small 'lifestyle' or 'trundler' firm, and the small 'gazelle' or 'flyer' firm. The former is viewed as a non-entrepreneurial firm, and the latter as an entrepreneurial firm, discussed in Chapter 6. From the perspective of this dichotomy it is argued that 'gazelles' contribute to the fulfilment of *industrial policy* objectives in the sense of demonstrating a willingness and an ability to grow; showing a potential to generate additional economic endeavours through activities such as exporting; and possessing a propensity to add to the country's stock of human and physical capital through training and the development of new technology.[24] By contrast, it is suggested that 'trundlers' do not contribute to the achievement of economic objectives, but rather it is asserted that they contribute to the achievement of *social* objectives, such as the provision of aid to unemployed people, with the aim of helping them to create their own jobs by setting up a small business.[25] A key consequence of this research has been a shift in government attention away from start-up firms per se, to start-up firms and established firms with growth potential. Though the Business Link network seeks to counteract the disadvantages which all small businesses face, to aid all firms that want to enhance their performance, and to encourage those who wish to establish a small business; it specifically seeks to target companies that demonstrate a potential to grow and employ between 10 and 200 employees.[26] Despite calls for a re-balancing of government support towards the start-up firm,[27] the current approach which privileges those small businesses with the potential and management desire to grow still dominates.

GROWTH AND ENTERPRISE CULTURE

To understand the place of *'growth'* within enterprise culture, it is important to comprehend that it is not a policy per se in the same sense as for example the Enterprise Allowance Scheme/Business Start-Up Scheme. Rather it is a dimension of the enterprise culture phenomenon, *embodied* in enterprise culture policies and initiatives, a dimension which has gained in prominence during the 1990s. Adopting the perspective of Keat (1991), we have argued

(1993) *op. cit.*; D J Storey, *Understanding the Small Business Sector* (London: Routledge) 1994; D J Storey & S Johnson, *Job Generation and Labour Market Change* (London: Macmillan Press) 1987; S Johnson, (1990) *op. cit.*

24. Johnson, S, (1990) *op. cit.*
25. *Ibid.*
26. Priest, S J, "A Survey of Business Link Services'. Paper presented at the ISBA National Small Firms Policy & Research Conference, Belfast (1997).
27. Gavron, R, M Cowling, G Holtham & A Westall, *The Entrepreneurial Society* (London: Institute for Public Policy Research) 1998.

throughout the course of this book, that enterprise culture is composed of two interwoven strands. A first strand which privileges the private sector commercial enterprise, and a second strand which privileges enterprising qualities. However, despite the suggestion that it is within the private sector enterprise that individuals are more likely to demonstrate enterprising qualities, it is recognised that commercial enterprises do not always express enterprising qualities thoroughly. Within the context of the UK enterprise culture, a thorough expression of enterprising qualities means going for growth historically and contemporaneously.

Growth as an expression of enterprise emerges strongly from an extensive "labour of inscription" which has rendered the reality of small business into a calculable form.[28] Research into, and analysis of, the small business sector has transformed small firm activity into information about the birth rate of small business, the death rate of small business, small business turnover rates, levels and types of small business employment, etc. By means of small business research, the reality of the small business world has been made "stable, mobile, comparable, combinable".[29] Such business research is not a neutral recording activity. Rather it is an activity which has allowed the world and perceived reality of the small business to be debated and scrutinised in a particular way, with decisions being made about what is and is not enterprising activity. It is from such inscription activity that growth has been identified as a badge of enterprise. Thus we can suggest that enterprise culture is composed of three interwoven strands, an institutional strand, an ethical strand and a growth ('fully enterprising') strand, which manifests itself largely in the small business sphere. Small business policies, therefore, not only embody and produce the institutional and ethical strands of enterprise culture, they also embody and produce the growth strand, with a view to shaping and moulding the entrepreneurial activity of small business owners. For example the promotion of selectivity discussed in Chapter 7, is a specific policy approach which embodies the growth dimension of enterprise culture, in that its key aim is to target state resources at small businesses which are most likely to grow successfully. Nevertheless despite the emphasis that is placed on growth, it is long recognised that though 'governing' for growth makes perfect sense in theory, there are great practical complications involved in implementing such a policy.[30]

---

28. Rose, N & P Miller, (1992) *op. cit.*, pp. 185.
29. *Ibid.*
30. Burton, J, *Picking Losers...?* (London: Institute of Economic Affairs) 1983; C Hakim, "Identifying Fast-Growth Small Firms" *Employment Gazette* (1989) 9:1, pp. 29-41.

Problems Involved in Operationalising the Growth Dimension

In an analysis of work conducted by commentators such as Storey, Hakim (1989) argues that, even though it may appear that the growth firm is discernibly different to other firms in terms of larger workforces, assets and funds, measured in absolute terms, there is no real difference between growth and non-growth firms in terms of relative profitability. In fact it appears at times that the non-growth firms have a higher rate of return on assets and investment. This then makes it extremely difficult to identify which small firms resources should be targeted at. In addition, given the fact that markets and economic conditions are likely to become increasingly unpredictable and experience enormous change over shorter time-spans, the task of implementing policies such as selectivity which embody the growth dimension of enterprise culture, is likely to become more and more difficult. Thus it has been argued that:

> The selection of new businesses or new technologies to back with taxpayer's money is essentially a matter of judgement, hunch and gambling. Government cannot draw up 'scientific' advice for the simple reasons that no such 'scientific' expertise exists.

> (Burton, 1983:33)

Thus despite the time, energy and effort which is devoted to such initiatives, it is important that we remember that government is likely to be an innately failing operation.[31] The notion that something like enterprise can be managed unproblematically and regulated is a mirage. Reality, according to Miller & Rose (1990), is too unruly to be apprehended by any perfect knowledge. Unintended consequences, or the inability of technologies and programmes to produce what is intended, means that attempts to manage and govern enterprise, need to be understood less in terms of success, and more in terms of the difficulties surrounding their operationalisation.[32] The universe of small business programmes and initiatives is heterogeneous, antagonistic and competitive. In successfully managing one aspect of enterprise, small business programmes and policies can create problems for other aspects. Though the many technologies of enterprise culture aim to shape and mould the enterprising activities of the individuals that come within their ambit, "persons or events always appear to escape those bodies of knowledge that inform governmental programmes, refusing to respond according to the programmatic logic that seeks to govern them".[33]

---

31. Rose, N & P Miller, (1992) *op. cit.*
32. *Ibid.*
33. *Ibid.*, pp. 190.

Nevertheless, notwithstanding the difficulties involved in the operationalisation of small business programmes, as with other enterprise strategies discussed earlier, we should not underestimate their significance, or the contribution they make to the formation of an enterprise culture. 'Written into' the vast array of small business initiatives in the UK are the dimensions of enterprise culture, i.e. the institutional strand, the ethical strand and the growth strand. With regard to the growth strand, though significant concern has been expressed about the possibility of identifying firms which have the potential to grow, this concern has largely centred on whether it is right and proper for state agencies to discriminate between small businesses. Very little questioning of the growth orientation per se has occurred. As with the other dimensions of enterprise culture, i.e. the privileging of the private sector and the promotion of enterprising qualities, growth is accepted as axiomatic. The only questioning that occurs is the means by which growth can be generated.

Exploring the Equation of Growth with Enterprise

The argument we are creating suggests that enterprise culture is a highly significant government device, which aims to influence, mould and shape the activities of individuals/businesses in a range of settings, through action at a distance. A programme of government, such as that of enterprise culture, involves itself in shaping individuals and businesses along enterprise lines, holding out specific notions of how they should behave and think of themselves, notions which are embedded in the vast array of small business policies and initiatives. As suggested earlier, one notion of enterprise which small business policies embody is that of growth. Within the UK context, to demonstrate that they are behaving in an enterprising manner, small businesses are actively encouraged to grow, those small businesses which resist growth are defined as being 'non-enterprising'. This emphasis on growth is also present in other European countries, for example Germany and Ireland.

Germany, particularly western Germany is populated by small and medium-sized enterprises referred to as *Mittelstand* companies, which have played a significant part in the development and progression of the German economy. As a sector they are heavily involved in exporting activity making a significant contribution to Germany's overall export income. Like the UK, Germany has been very concerned to develop and promote a dynamic small businesses sector, aiming support at businesses with a growth orientation.[34] However, unlike the UK where extensive support for small business has only developed since the 1970s, resources and policies directed at *Mittelstand* companies have been a central part of economic and social policy in Ger-

---

34. Bannock, G & H Albach, *Small Business Policy in Europe* report for the Anglo-German Foundation (London: AGF) 1991.

many since the Second World War. In addition the ethos – 'help for self-help' – which underlines German small business support, is one which seeks to compensate small firms for the drawback of small size as long as these firms are willing to upgrade continuously and achieve the highest standards of competition. In contrast, British small business policy is largely concerned with removing or compensating for market imperfections.[35] One clear result of such differences in policy approach is that Germany tends to have 'macro', i.e. larger sized, small businesses compared to the micro size of British small business. Germany has fewer self-employed individuals without employees, and a higher number of small businesses with between 5 and 99 employees.[36] Thus though the UK and Germany both place an emphasis on growing small businesses, this emphasis manifests itself in different ways, leading to variations in the moulding and shaping of small business in the British and German context.

The Republic of Ireland is also characterised by a growth orientation, with the Irish enterprise culture programme of government placing an emphasis on small business growth as a means of demonstrating an enterprising orientation. As with the UK, the stress placed on growth as an enterprising activity is associated with an analysis of the small business sector which highlights its perceived weaknesses. It is suggested that, by 1984, there were 5,245 Irish owned manufacturing companies employing 147,000 people, compared to 806 foreign owned companies employing 92,000 people. At this time only 282 Irish owned firms employed over 100 people, with only 105 of these companies employing more than 200 people. Thus 95 per cent of companies had less than 100 employees.[37] Other studies which emphasise the critical importance of a tiny number of small firms for job creation mirror studies conducted in the UK and USA contexts. For example research conducted by O'Farrell (cited in Task Force on Small Business, 1994) found that the vast majority of 2,000 manufacturing plants opened up between 1973 and 1981 were still small by 1981, with 53 per cent employing fewer than 11 people in 1981, and only a little over 5 per cent employing more than 100. A later study of small businesses in Ireland, both north and south, stated that of every 100 small business start-ups, only 30 survive for more than ten years, and further that the vast bulk of jobs are created by only three or four firms out of this 30.[38]

It would seem that analyses of small business sectors in countries like Britain and Ireland, centre on the effect firm size has on a firm's ability to not only survive, but also engage in 'enterprising' activities. According to Storey

35. *Ibid.*; C Lane, (1995) *op. cit.*
36. Bannock, G & H Albach, (1991) *op. cit.*
37. NESC, *The Role of the Financial System in Financing the Traded Sectors* (Dublin: NESC Report No. 76) 1984.
38. Kinsella, R, W Clarke, D J Storey, D Mulvenna & D Coyne, (1994) *op. cit.*

(1994), if a small business wants to survive and embark on enterprising activities it should grow. However, research is emerging which suggests that we should be careful about associating survival and enterprise solely with growth. Looking at the issue of small business survival first, contemporary research suggests that it is not unequivocally small size per se which affects perceptions of the failure rates of the small business sector. Rather different definitions of failure impact on reported failure rates across various industry sectors, indicating that definition is a crucial factor in measuring and reporting small business failure rates.[39] A reliance on definitions which emphasise extreme notions of failure, such as bankruptcy and discontinuance of ownership (which includes every change in ownership or closure), are biased against certain industry sectors, and can inflate failure rates. In contrast definitions of failure which are more 'middle of the road', such as 'failed to make a go of it', are less likely to result in outcomes that are biased.[40]

Turning to the issue of 'enterprising' activity, if a firm does survive, analyses carried out on the small business sectors in the UK and Ireland suggest that the smaller the business the less likely it is to engage in enterprising activity, such as exporting. The assumptions underlying this reasoning are that large firms are more likely to have idle resources which can be directed towards exporting; that large firms will have achieved economies of scale which strengthen their international price competitiveness; and that large firms have a greater ability to judge, manage and carry the risk associated with exporting.[41] However, despite the fact that much research suggests that exporting as an enterprising activity is positively related to firm size, there is also much ambiguity in this area. According to Philp (1998), if a broader range of factors, such as the commitment, attitudes and attributes of a firm's management, and the firm's perceived competitiveness in the marketplace are considered, then firm size as a highly indicative discriminator of export propensity *decreases* in importance, and does not appear to contribute significantly to signalling the likelihood that a firm is an exporter. Such research signals that perhaps we should be careful about automatically making the assumption that to be 'enterprising' (for example engaging in international trade or innovation) a small firm must grow. This suggestion is reinforced if we explore the position of the small firm within other European countries, for example Italy.

39. Watson, J & J Everett, "Small Business Failure Rates: Choice of Definition and Industry Effects" *International Small Business Journal,* 17: 2, pp. 31-45.
40. *Ibid.*
41. Philp, N E, "The Export Propensity of the Very Small Enterprise (VSE) *International Small Business Journal* (1998) 16: 4, pp. 79-93.

Enterprise and the Small Firm in Italy

Unlike Britain and Ireland, Italy has a vast and vigorous small firm economy where small capital is not just 'surviving' or considered to be only functional for large firms, it contributes massively to the economic development of the country and to employment. This applies particularly to the central and north eastern regions of Italy, referred to as the Third Italy or NEC (North-East-Centre) model of Italian development.[42] Brusco (1986) identifies three different models of small firms within Italy. Firstly, the traditional artisan which focuses on the local market usually of non-standardised goods, and can rely for its competitive advantage on low labour costs. Secondly, the dependent subcontractor associated with the decentralisation of large and medium-sized firms and relies on cheap labour for competitive advantage. Finally, small firms located predominately around Emilia, Veneto, Tuscany and the Marche (i.e. the Third Italy or NEC). In considering this third type of small firm, what is important is not the characteristics of one single small company, but "the characteristics of the industrial structure of which the small firm is a part".[43] Storey & Johnson (1987) refer to this as the Bologna model, an area in Italy which stretches from the Venetian provinces in the north through Bologna and Florence, to Ancona in the centre-east. Dotted across the Third Italy are centres of sophisticated manufacturing industry, based on complex systems of small firms producing everything from knitted goods (Carpi), to textiles (Prato), special machines (Parma, Bologna), agricultural equipment (Reggio Emilia), hydraulic devices (Modena), shoes and electronic musical instruments (Ancona). As this description suggests, the Bologna model of small firm activity usually occurs in a small town where a single industry sector dominates the economy.[44]

This area is characterised by specialist workshops and small factories, where industrial exports, job and wealth creation have increased at a rate well above the national average. Within this context small firm formation is not related to the decentralisation of production by large firms, rather it represents a pattern of intensive networking among small businesses usually in traditional consumer goods. The area in which the small business develops is referred to as an industrial district which is characterised by horizontal linkages between firms. Throughout the 1970s and 1980s there was a marked

---

42. Weiss, L, (1988) *op. cit.*; B Invernizzi & R Revelli, "Small Firms and the Italian Economy: Structural Changes and Evidence of Turbulence" in Z J Acs & D B Audretsch (eds), *Small Firms and Entrepreneurship* (Cambridge MA: Cambridge University Press) 1993.
43. Brusco, S, "Small firms and industrial districts: The experience of Italy" in D Keeble & E Wever (eds), *New firms and regional development in Europe* (London: Croom Helm) 1986.
44. Storey, D J & S Johnson, (1987) *op. cit.*; L Weiss, (1988) *op. cit.*; B Invernizzi, & R Revelli, (1993) *op. cit.*

growth in industrial districts in Italy, particularly in the central and northern regions.[45] A key feature of this model is co-operative competition. In looking at the Bologna model we are not considering independent small firms in the traditional artisan sense, nor may they be seen as subcontractors of large firms, rather we are focusing on the development of an industrial system composed of inter-linked but independently owned production units.[46]

Characteristics of an Industrial District

Industrial districts are not just a concentration of firms operating within the same sector or out of the same geographical region. Rather an industrial district is part of a network of firms which through a process of specialisation and subcontracting divide among themselves the various parts of the production process. It is usually organised according to the following principles:

- *Flexibility:* As flexible entities, small firms in the Third Italy actively exploit market niches and maintain a responsive and skilled labour force.

- *Specialisation and co-ordination:* The efficiency of small firms within an industrial district is collective in nature, with no one individual firm bearing the costs and risks involved in research and development, design, training, production, marketing, etc. All of the various activities which contribute to the production of a product or service are located in one area, with individual firms maintaining their independence, while at the same time co-ordinating their activities to achieve maximum efficiency.

- *Competition and co-operation:* Industrial districts are characterised by consensual co-operation. Firms producing similar goods do compete with each other but there is a high level of co-operation, with co-operative activities helping to improve the competitive capacities of small firms within the network. Such co-operation can take a number of forms such as subcontracting, dividing up orders, working together to produce designs and the joint procurement of resources.

- *Endogenous regional development:* Development of a region is an internal process rather than being externally sought. It centres on the creation of a regional identity which could be cultural, economic and political.

- *Business is based on the notion of community:* Trust and co-operation between firms is supported and reinforced by the social community.

---

45. Trigilia, C, "Italian industrial districts: Neither myth nor interlude" in F Pyke & W Sengenberger (eds), *Industrial Districts and Local Economic Regeneration* (Geneva: International Labour Studies) 1992.

46. Storey, D J & S Johnson, (1987) *op. cit.*; L Weiss, (1988) *op. cit.*

- *Competent entrepreneurship:* It is frequently the case that individuals setting up a new business come from the ranks of experienced, senior employees in existing businesses. Firms within an industrial district can act as a very important support to potential entrepreneurs.
- *Labour:* Labour is conceptualised as a resource not a cost, a dynamic factor of production within industrial districts. The skill levels of the labour force are high, supported by widespread expertise within the community and the education system.
- *Local government and state:* Local authorities promote the development of networks, adopting the role of social co-ordinator, bringing together different groups to develop commonly agreed programmes of action for a region.

(Weiss, 1988; Sengenberger & Pyke, 1992)

Industrial districts have a good record on job creation with firms tending to be competitive on the world market, making use of advanced technology, having an innovative capacity and paying high wages. Many explanations for the emergence of this model of small business formation and activity tend to centre on the peculiar nature and characteristics of the Third Italy region.[47] These characteristics include firstly a tradition of share-cropping which it is argued contributes to the transmission of technical skills, the ability to exploit pooled resources, and the development of a range of business skills and managerial capacities. These include investment abilities, bookkeeping, wages and co-operation skills, all of which are useful in the management of a small business. Secondly, towns are said to play a role in the development of industrial districts, acting as places of commerce, trade and financial organisation. Thirdly, the previous existence of a large firm or branch of a large firm in an area introduced the technical and professional competence needed to run a business. When a branch of a large company closed down in an area, it has been replaced by a local firm set up and run by former workers. Thus from this first company, other companies develop in the district. Finally, the school system which exists in the industrial district areas, provides workers with the necessary skills. The combination of these four elements, spread among the populations of the industrial districts, is deeply embedded within the social texture of the region.[48]

According to Brusco (1982, 1986) the nature of this region as outlined here is the primary reason for the development of the phenomena of industrial districts, with local government at most accelerating an already existing process. Thus this perspective suggests that industrial policy incentives will

---

47. Brusco, S, (1986) *op. cit.*; B Invernizzi & R Revelli, (1993) *op. cit.*
48. *Ibid.*

find it extremely difficult to reproduce the industrial district experience in other areas or countries. However Weiss (1988) argues against this viewpoint, suggesting that the significance of nationally specific resources is often exaggerated, with the role of the state and its policy initiatives being downplayed. In particular what is downplayed or ignored, is that a state can adopt an approach to small business which places an emphasis on *small to stay small*, i.e. firms are born small and ordained to remain small. From Weiss's perspective what is particularly important about Italian industrial districts is that their development and success is due to a very different ethos, and that the Italian state had a big role to play in developing this ethos.

In stark contrast to the British situation, small business policy in the Bologna model is not imbued with a *small to grow large* ethos, rather Italian small business policy places an emphasis on supporting *small business to stay small*. As a special category in Italian law, the small manufacturing business has been the target of numerous benefits. The qualification for benefits crucially centres on firm size, where size is defined in terms of number of workers employed. By remaining small, companies retained benefits they would lose by expanding, a situation which is the exact opposite to the UK where firms secure benefits through growth. As well as promoting an ethos of *small to stay small*, Italian small business support also promotes co-operation, in that collaboration and joint ventures are privileged in virtually all activities. This has allowed small firms to achieve economies of scale in a range of areas such as administration, purchasing and marketing.[49] The success and proliferation of industrial districts is likely to have occurred through a mixture of social/cultural characteristics and state initiatives, with this mixture being in especially good supply in the Third Italy. Though industrial districts have developed in the north west and south of Italy also, they are more prevalent in the central and north eastern regions.[50] However, in considering the reasons for the development of industrial districts, the recognition of a policy approach which values small businesses for being small, and backs this up with a precise targeting of benefits, is what is significant for us.

Contrasting the Italian small business sector to that of the UK, Weiss (1988) suggests that the UK would have significant problems in implementing the Italian approach to small business because it entails a radical departure from market principles and deregulation. She argues that the promotion of small business in the UK is associated with the privileging of market discipline and minimum state regulation. However Weiss's conceptualisation of the contemporary relationship between small business and the state, emerges out of the conventional understanding of enterprise culture in which state and individual/business are pitted against one another. In contrast adopting an understanding of enterprise culture which incorporates a notion of gov-

49. Weiss, L, (1988) *op. cit.*
50. Trigilia, C, (1992) *op. cit.*

ernment into it, and gives full recognition to the increased governmentalisation of contemporary British business life,[51] suggests that the feasibility of the UK government shaping, moulding and 'fashioning' British small business along Italian lines is not completely impossible. In fact networks, alliances and partnerships are being increasingly promoted and developed, as we will explore fully in a later chapter.

As we have seen within contemporary enterprise culture, organisations located in a range of sectors have been problematised largely in terms of their lack of enterprise, a shortcoming which it is argued embodies their weaknesses and their failings.[52] For public sector organisations to become 'fully enterprising', they have been privatised; for large private sector organisations to become 'fully enterprising', they are encouraged to promote enterprising qualities with each employee becoming a diminutive private sector firm; for small firms to become 'fully enterprising', they are encouraged to pursue growth. All of these 'models of action' are based on a notion of enterprise which is embedded in a range of policies and initiatives, and which is "a consciously contrived style of conduct".[53] What this means is that individuals in a range of settings are encouraged to adopt, and are involved in adopting, certain practical relations to themselves so that they can make appropriate use of their freedom.[54] For small firms, making appropriate use of their freedom means *growing* the business. However, in looking at the Italian case, we can observe that making appropriate use of freedom for small business, does not automatically mean growth. In Italy the proper use of liberty for the small firm means remaining small and being involved in collaborative relationships with other businesses.

By exploring a contrasting national context which adopts a very different approach to the small business sector to that of the UK, we can further highlight the importance of incorporating a notion of government into our understanding of enterprise culture. The strategies and policies drawn upon in the Italian context, for the direction of the conduct of small business, are cultural techniques which have sought to rationalise and act upon the behaviour of small business, with the aim of aligning state and business goals. However in looking at the Italian situation, we can see that a very different institutional context, and distinct cultural technologies (i.e. different small business policies) produce a unique cultural configuration of enterprise, which is quite a contrast to that of the UK. Though the Bologna model is facing a series of

51. Rose, N & P Miller, (1992) *op. cit.*
52. Rose, N, "Governing the Enterprising Self" in P Heelas & P Morris (eds), *The Values of the Enterprise Culture.* (London: Routledge) 1992.
53. Burchell, G, "Liberal Government and Techniques of the Self" in A Barry, T Osborne & N Rose (eds), *Foucault and Political Reason: Liberalism, Neo-liberalism and Rationalities of Government* (1996) pp. 24.
54. *Ibid.*

new challenges such as international competition, escalating uncertainty and instability and increased competitiveness from large firms due to new technology which tends to reduce the costs of flexibility,[55] a consideration of the form of enterprise it creates is worthwhile. The purpose of presenting it is not to set Italian microcapitalism in opposition to giantism, or to suggest that it is inherently better (or worse). Rather, firstly, it reinforces the importance of incorporating a notion of government into our understanding of enterprise culture, as we have seen that different governmental technologies, leads to a different enterprise cultural configuration. Secondly, it acts as a starting point from which the often unquestioned adherence to a giantism philosophy can be evaluated and reflected on. Our exploration of the Italian context brings home to us the fact that although attempts to create an enterprise culture are strongly related to the historical and social context of a country, they are also based on "artificially arranged or contrived forms of the free, *entrepreneurial* and *competitive* conduct of economic-rational individuals".[56] As argued on previous occasions, enterprise culture will not succeed in the sense of producing the best results for society unless individuals behave in a manner conducive to the market order. However, the form of individual behaviour which is beneficial to this order is not a 'given' of human nature, rather the conduct of free individuals/businesses is moulded and shaped according to a set of very definite patterns, which vary from one social context to the next and which gives rise to different cultural permutations.

SUMMARY OF KEY IDEAS

- Enterprise culture in countries such as the UK is characterised by an emphasis on growth as an emblem of enterprise activity.

- The emphasis on growth emerges out of an ethos of 'giantism' which can simply be understood as the championing of large business and the assumption that small business is inferior.

- The ethos of 'giantism' has had a lasting impact on how we view and understand the small business sector, in that resources and support for small business are embedded in a notion of 'small to grow large'. Small businesses are not valued for their small size, rather they are valued for their potential to grow into large businesses.

- The emphasis on growth is further reinforced by contemporary research into the small business sector. A key characteristic of this research is that it has suggested that only a small proportion of small firms make

---

55. Trigilia, C, (1992) *op. cit.*
56. Burchell, G, (1996) *op. cit.*, pp. 23-24.

any significant contribution to the national economy, and these firms are growth oriented.

- Growth forms a third strand of the enterprise culture phenomenon, along with the institutional and ethical strands, and is embodied in enterprise culture policies.

- This emphasis on growth lies at the centre of any evaluation which is undertaken of small business performance in terms of its ability to survive and engage in 'enterprising' activities. However research, particularly research on the small business sector within other countries, suggests that we should be careful about assuming that to be 'enterprising' a small business must grow.

- Italian small business has contributed substantially to the economic development of Italy. This has occurred within the context of a state approach which places an emphasis on 'small to stay small', i.e. small businesses start small and *remain* small. Thus for a business to be 'fully enterprising', it does not automatically have to grow.

- Contrasting the Italian situation to that of the UK highlights the importance of incorporating a notion of government into our understanding of enterprise culture, as it highlights how different governmental technologies lead to different enterprise cultural configurations.

Contemporary Issues and Enterprise Culture

CHAPTER 9

The Female Entrepreneur and the Gender of Enterprise and Entrepreneurship

All that anybody knew for sure on 4 May 1979 was that a new person now lived at 10 Downing Street, that she was a woman, and that her name was Margaret Thatcher.

(*The Observer*, 25 April 1999)

MEN, WOMEN AND ENTERPRISE

The ethical strand of enterprise culture requires that individuals procure and display a range of characteristics, such as having a daring spirit, taking risks, being self-reliant and dynamic, so that they can demonstrate that they are enterprising. The ultimate enterprising individual is the entrepreneur, a category of person who has been given a privileged position within enterprise culture. Individuals in general are encouraged to be entrepreneurial in all areas of their lives, with managers in particular being required to manage in an entrepreneurial manner, i.e. be entrepreneurs. As suggested in Chapter 5, a key aim of enterprise culture is the creation of new entrepreneurs, with a range of programmes, initiatives and supports put in place to promote, cultivate and mould entrepreneurs and their activities. The proliferation of such programmes signal that a significant concern of the state in enterprise culture is the problematising of individual existence, in recognition of the fact that a market order will not succeed unless individuals can be trusted to behave in a way that the market order requires.[1] Nevertheless a central concern for the architects of enterprise culture:

---

1. Gordon, C, "The Soul of the Citizen: Max Weber and Michel Foucault on Rationality and Government" in S Lash & S Whimster (eds), *Max Weber, Rationality and Modernity* (London: Allen & Unwin) 1987; D Marquand, "The Paradoxes of Thatcherism" in R Skidelsky (ed.), *Thatcherism* (Oxford: Basil Blackwell) 1988.

> .....is the maintenance of collective conditions that nurture an active individual *Lebensfuhrung* (understood as the conduct of life), while resisting the latter's subsumption into a rigid, pervasive, collective-pastoral supervision and *reglementation* of life.

(Gordon, 1987:307)

If enterprise culture is all about the steady and progressive constitution of individuals as 'enterprising' persons, i.e. entrepreneurs, a key question is how do we understand the character of the entrepreneur. In Chapter 5 we looked at six different schools of thought on the entrepreneur, assessing their similarities and differences around the dialectic co-existence of entrepreneurship and management. However, as with other analyses, this consideration of the entrepreneur and entrepreneurship was presented in *agendered* terms, and could be accused of what Mulholland (1996) refers to as parodying a notion of neutrality. The facade of neutrality manifests itself in the emphasis that is placed on assumed entrepreneurial qualities, such as total commitment, leadership, management capabilities, a long-term strategic orientation, ruthlessness, financial acumen and risk taking; a range of characteristics which are more likely to be attributed to men rather than women without acknowledging this. The result of such an approach, manifest in most considerations of the entrepreneur and entrepreneurship, is a taken-for-granted representation of such enterprise activity as an essentially masculine exercise, monopolised by men and excluding women.[2]

Understanding Female Entrepreneurship

Given this background, a key question we may ask is, how do we understand the activity of female entrepreneurs and their position within enterprise culture, remembering that a major consequence of the promotion of entrepreneurship and small business in recent years is the significant increase in the numbers of women in business. Though data on the exact level of female entrepreneurship is difficult to find as much of the information on self-employment is not broken down by gender, those that do exist indicate that, from a low starting point in 1980, increasing numbers of women are starting up their own business. The result of this trend is that the rate of increase in

---

2.   Mulholland, K, "Entrepreneurialism, Masculinities and the Self-Made Man" in D Collinson & J Hearn (eds), *Men as Managers, Managers as Men* (London: Sage) 1996; R Reed, "Entrepreneurialism and Paternalism in Australian Management: A Gender Critique of the 'Self-Made' Man" in D Collinson & J Hearn (eds), *Men as Managers, Managers as Men* (London: Sage) 1996.

female-owned businesses in the 1980s was substantially higher than that of men.[3]

In the UK in 1980, women in self-employment on their own account comprised only 4 per cent of the total female paid labour force, making up 20 per cent of the self-employed and employer sector.[4] Between 1981 and 1987, a 70 per cent increase in the number of self-employed women was recorded, compared to a 30 per cent increase in the number of self-employed men.[5] By the end of the 1980s the rate of increase in female owned businesses in percentage terms was 81 per cent compared to 51 per cent for men.[6] Thus by 1991 the number of women in self-employment had increased by 140 per cent since 1979, a trend which was projected to continue throughout the 1990s.[7] Similar trends were evident within the USA. During the 1980s the number of self-employed women increased five times faster than the numbers of self-employed men, and three times faster than the number of female employees.[8] Research undertaken in the 1990s indicates that almost half of all new businesses in the USA are started by women. In 1990, more than 3.5 million women in the USA owned their own business, generating over US$40 billion a year.[9] It has also been estimated that within the next decade, 40 per cent of all businesses in the US will be owned by women.[10]

As suggested earlier, entrepreneurship tends to be presented as a gender neutral activity with much of the literature in this area being routinely addressed at men, working under the assumption that entrepreneurialism is solely a male endeavour.[11] However though some commentators suggest that research into female entrepreneurship is still limited, it is true to say that the literature on female enterprise has expanded in line with the increased number of women opting for self-employment during the 1980s and 1990s.[12] For the

---

3. Rosa, P, D Hamilton, S Carter & H Burns, "The Impact of Gender on Small Business Management: Preliminary Findings of a British Study" *International Small Business Journal* (1994) 12: 3, pp. 25-32.
4. Goffee, R. & Scase, R. 1985: *Women in Charge* (London: Allen & Unwin).
5. Stephens, M, "She's the Boss" *Employment Gazette* (October 1989) pp. 529-533.
6. Daly, M, "The 1980s – A Decade of Growth in Enterprise" *Employment Gazette* (March 1991) pp. 109-134.
7. Gray, C, *Enterprise and Culture* (London: Routledge) 1998.
8. Loscocco, K A, J Robinson, R H Hall & J K Allen, "Gender and Small Business Success; An Inquiry into Women's Relative Disadvantage" *Social Forces* (1991) 70: 1, pp. 65-85.
9. Rossman, M L, *The International Businesswoman of the 1990s: A Guide to Success in the Global Marketplace* (New York: Basic Books) 1990.
10. *The Sunday Business Post* (February 1997).
11. Mulholland, K, (1996) *op. cit.*
12. Cromie, S & J Hayes, "Towards a Typology of Female Entrepreneurs" *The Sociological Review* (1988) 36: 1, pp. 87-109; S Johnson & D J Storey, 93: 'Male

most part, this literature has tended to focus on the problems and challenges facing the female entrepreneur.[13] Within this context, considerations of gender tend to just be 'added on' to the apparently gender neutral account of entrepreneurship. This is done by expanding our consideration of this area to examine the possibility that traditional cultural norms about male and female roles in society (particularly in the realm of the family), may create a situation where it is harder for women than men to participate in enterprising activities such as setting up a small business. The general suggestion is that though all entrepreneurs face a range of hurdles when entering into the world of business, female entrepreneurs can face additional gender-related problems which can have a profound impact on the success and viability of their business.

However, there are problems with this approach to understanding the relationship between gender and enterprise, particularly within the context of an understanding of enterprise culture which explores the steady and progressive constitution of individuals as 'enterprising' persons. If, as said earlier, a key aim of enterprise culture is the nurturing of the entrepreneur as the ultimate 'enterprising' person, it is important to recognise that the contemporary promotion of the entrepreneur has led to a reincarnation of the 19th century entrepreneurial ideal,[14] which is irredeemably male, and which:

> . . . portrays the entrepreneur as a self-made man, a paternalist employer working initially beside **his** employees and becoming a captain of industry, through **his** own enterprise and hard work [my emphasis].
>
> (Allen & Truman, 1993:5)

In other words, entrepreneurship has historically been connected to certain physical and other personal attributes, and these are male. Thus given that an enterprise mode of being is presented as the model "not only for the conduct of economic activity, but for the totality of human action [with] [i]ndividual citizens [being] entrepreneurs of themselves and their lives, [with the] indi-

---

and Female Entrepreneurs and their Businesses: A comparative study" in S Allen & C Truman (eds), *Women in Business: Perspectives on Women Entrepreneurs* (London: Routledge) 1993; D Deakins, *Entrepreneurship and Small Firms* (Berkshire: McGraw-Hill) 1996; P Rosa, D Hamilton, S Carter, & H Burns, (1994) *op. cit.*; S A McKechnie, C T Ennew & L T Read, "The Nature of the Banking Relationship: A Comparison of the Experiences of Male and Female Small Business Owners" *International Small Business Journal* (1998) 16: 3, pp. 39-55.

13. McKechnie, S A, C T Ennew & L T Read, (1998) *op. cit.*
14. Marquand, D, "The enterprise culture: old wine in new bottles?" in P Heelas & P Morris (eds), *The Values of the Enterprise Culture: The Moral Debate* (London: Routledge) 1992.

vidual life . . . structured as a cluster of enterprises, both economic and non-economic",[15] and embedded in this model is a taken-for-granted maleness, it is imperative that we explore this dimension of enterprise cultural technologies. Thus, rather than treating enterprise and entrepreneurship in a bizzarely neutered, asexual fashion, we will expose the gendered nature of enterprise. In particular, we will highlight the 'fashioned' masculinity of the entrepreneurial management discourse produced by enterprise culture, and how the masculine values of individualism, competitiveness and aggression are seen to be emblems of enterprise activity. From this perspective we can question the naturalisation of entrepreneurialism as male,[16] demonstrating how masculine values and assumptions are embedded in enterprise culture policies and initiatives.

MASCULINITY AND ENTREPRENEURIALISM

A number of the schools of thought on entrepreneurship, such as the 'management' school and the 'leadership' school, are suffused with masculine values in a taken-for-granted way, with management and leadership being conventionally associated with men as opposed to women. However, in exploring the issue of masculinity and entrepreneurialism, a good starting point is the 'great person' school of entrepreneurship which presents the entrepreneur as a dynamic 'master of the universe'. Emphasis is placed on the highly masculine values of individualism, aggression, competition, drive, perseverance, vision, single-mindedness and decisiveness.[17] Though (as outlined in Chapter 5) there are problems with this school of thought, it presents a very powerful cultural image of the entrepreneur, one which is saturated with masculine values and which holds an important position within enterprise culture. If the ultimate success of enterprise culture is bound up with – and dependent on – redefining the types of personal identities and qualities individuals are expected to possess, the 'great person' school represents the cultural image of the entrepreneur to which individuals are encouraged to aspire.

Throughout the 1980s, this was reflected in numerous journalistic profiles of 'captains of industry' who were regularly portrayed as 'heroic', with an emphasis being placed on the qualities of 'battle', 'struggle' and 'conquest'. The masculine, abrasive, autocratic styles of entrepreneurs, such as

---

15. Gordon, C, (1987) *op. cit.*, pp. 314.
16. Mulholland, K, (1996) *op. cit.*
17. Cunningham, J B & J Lischeron, "Defining Entrepreneurship" *Journal of Small Business Management* (1991) 25: 1, pp. 45-61; D Collinson & J Hearn, "Naming Men as Men: Implications for Work, Organization and Management" *Gender, Work and Organization* (1994) 1: 1, pp. 2-22.

Iacocca and Maxwell, were highly valued and acclaimed as the best means of securing business success.[18] Such a view of entrepreneurship can be associated with what Kerfoot and Knights (1993) refer to as "competitive masculinity" which is characterised by:

> . . . a way of relating to the world wherein everything becomes an object of and for control . . . [a] form of control . . . [which] equates with reason, logic and rational process; generates and sustains a hierarchy imbued with instrumentalism, careerism and the language of 'success'; stimulates competition linked to decisive action, 'productivism' and risk-taking.

> (Kerfoot & Knights, 1993:671)

A key component of this masculine approach to entrepreneurship is the separation of the public and the private spheres, freedom from the obligations and responsibilities of the latter and the adoption of a 'breadwinning' role. Entrepreneurs (usually male) from this perspective should be protected from all but the most cursory domestic work, leaving them free to build up and develop their businesses.[19] However, the ability of female entrepreneurs to avail of such a separation and to privilege work responsibilities over home responsibilities is highly restricted. For women in business, managing the balance between the demands of a family and a company can be extremely difficult. In fact the demographic characteristic with the largest variance between male and female entrepreneurs is marital status. Research indicates that the vast majority of male entrepreneurs tend to be married with a stay-at-home spouse who makes an important or large contribution to the management of their husband's business.[20] However whether married or not, female entrepreneurs face a cultural disadvantage in that they often do not receive the support and labour provided by a spouse (though Rosa *et al.*, (1994) in their study suggest this is changing), something which a majority of male entrepreneurs do, and which is often crucial for a business, particularly at the start-up stage.

Many male-owned firms could not survive without the unpaid contribution of a spouse, both at home and in the business, a contribution which male entrepreneurs appear to rely on heavily, and which has a significant positive impact on the viability of businesses run by men. Thus women suffer the 'double whammy' of being less likely than men to have help from a spouse

---

18. Collinson, D & J Hearn, "Breaking the Silence: On Men, Masculinities and Managements" in D Collinson & J Hearn (eds), *Men as Managers, Managers as Men: Critical Perspectives on Men, Masculinities and Managements* (London: Sage) 1996.

19. Reed, R, (1996) *op. cit.*; K Mulholland, (1996) *op. cit.*

20. Rosa, P, D Hamilton, S Carter & H Burns, (1994) *op. cit.*

with their businesses, and more likely to have home responsibilities which require time away from the firm.[21] It could be suggested, therefore, that a key difference between male and female entrepreneurs is that the realm of the private colonises the public sphere of business for women, often having a negative impact. In contrast for men, the paradox of being able to separate the public and private realms, is that the public world of their firm colonises the private sphere to the benefit of their business.

Research into Female Entrepreneurship

Commentators such as Goffee and Scase (1985) and Cromie and Hayes (1988) have argued that one main motivation for a large number of women setting up in business is the ability to construct working hours around domestic and childcare responsibilities. Such a motivation for the establishment of a business is reflected in the typologies of female entrepreneurs developed by these commentators. Looking at the intersection between two sets of factors, i.e. commitment to entrepreneurial ideals and acceptance of traditional gender roles, Goffee and Scase (1985) develop a four-fold typology of female entrepreneurs as follows.

Typology One of Female Entrepreneurs	
Conventionals	High commitment to entrepreneurial ideals. High attachment to traditional gender roles.
Domestics	Low/moderate commitment to entrepreneurial ideals. High attachment to traditional gender roles.
Innovators	High commitment to entrepreneurial ideals. Low attachment to traditional gender roles.
Radicals	Low commitment to entrepreneurial ideals. Low attachment to traditional gender roles.
	(Goffee & Scase, 1985)

Likewise Cromie and Hayes (1988) develop a three-fold typology based around the possession of childcare responsibilities as follows.

---

21. Goffee, R, & R Scase, *Women in Charge* (London: Allen & Unwin) 1985; K A Loscocco, J Robinson, R H Hall & J K Allen (1991) *op. cit.*; S Johnson & D J Storey, (1993) *op. cit.*

Typology Two of Female Entrepreneurs

Innovators   These highly educated entrepreneurs have a strong commit-
              ment to their business, significant management experience
              and no childcare responsibilities.

Dualists   For these entrepreneurs, a key motivation for setting up a busi-
              ness is the management of child care responsibilities. Though
              these entrepreneurs have good educational credentials, some
              managerial skills and wish to remain in paid employment,
              priority is given to their children.

Returners   Setting up a small business is seen as a means by which these
              entrepreneurs can return to paid work after raising their chil-
              dren. These entrepreneurs tend to lack employment experi-
              ence, have few managerial and technical skills and a low level
              of educational attainment

                                              (Cromie & Hayes, 1988)

However, one problem with the approach taken to female entrepreneurs by
these two sets of commentators, is that the issue of business ownership for
women is set within the context of general labour market difficulties that
women experience, and presented as a possible solution to these difficulties.
Though there is an acknowledgement of the range of problems and difficulties that women in business face as women, these are understood as being
'outside of' entrepreneurship per se, being located in wider social processes.
Little consideration is given to the nature or gender of entrepreneurial activity itself. In fact Goffee and Scase (1983:635) suggest that women enter into
business ownership "to reject male-imposed identities", without considering
the [male] identity of entrepreneurship and the implications of this for female (and male) entrepreneurs. Thus, despite the construction of these
typologies around the issue of domestic responsibilities, there is little consideration given to the difficulties female entrepreneurs experience in establishing a strict separation of home and work, so as to embody this masculine
dimension of enterprise.

The only female entrepreneurial 'type' who can make this separation in
both typologies is the 'innovator', who does not carry traditional domestic
and childcare responsibilities. This type of entrepreneur is most similar to
her male counterparts but does not receive spousal support for the business
which as said above is often crucial to its success particularly at the start-up
stage. In fact the representation of female entrepreneurs in terms of a range
of 'domestic' types by Goffee and Scase (1985) and Cromie and Hayes (1988)
is itself masculine in two ways. Firstly, in that the typologies themselves "constitute a masculine and/or managerial preoccupation with the control of the

world and the meanings in it; a totalizing exercise intended to achieve a kind of closure".[22] Secondly, by evaluating female entrepreneurs experience of business ownership in terms of the reconciliation of home and work responsibilities, it reinforces the difficulties female entrepreneurs have in not being able to make the strict separation between the public and the private spheres as their male counterparts can, in not being able to adopt this 'masculine' enterprising mode of behaviour.

A focus on the issue of domestic responsibilities is reflective of the prominence of gender-stereotypical explanations in understanding the female experience of entrepreneurship, and how it differs from that of the male. From the point of view of this perspective, differences between male and female in terms of socialisation, training, the burden of domestic responsibilities and other experiences, ultimately shape their involvement with activities such as entrepreneurship. A key aim of such an approach is to question the apparent neutrality of a range of criteria which the successful entrepreneur is supposed to possess. Studies of growth (defined as entrepreneurial) companies have suggested that the founders of such firms tend to be male; aged between 35 and 44; have relatively more formal qualifications than non-growth firms; have managerial experience in the private sector in both small and large companies; and are less likely to be unemployed at start-up.[23] Starting with the right gender, male entrepreneurs are more likely to 'measure up' to this profile than female entrepreneurs. Research in the 1980s and early-1990s indicates that women are less likely than men to have had relevant training or experience prior to setting up a business and are more likely to be unemployed. Men are more likely to have operated their business on a part-time basis before setting up full-time. This can mean that women set up businesses in activities and at times which appear to be not entirely 'logical' or 'rational', when compared with the start-up process undergone by male entrepreneurs.[24]

Another significant area of contrast between male and female entrepreneurs is the sector in which they locate their businesses. Women's businesses, which tend to be both smaller and newer than men's, are predominantly located in the services sector, particularly in retail, catering and other services. In contrast men are more likely to be located in manufacturing, construction, transport and high technology sectors.[25] The sectoral profile of female entrepreneurs can impact on women's experience of running a business. For example it may have a negative impact on their ability to obtain finance for the firm. Research indicates that access to finance is a problem for entrepre-

---

22. Collinson, D & J Hearn, (1994) *op. cit.*, p. 9.
23. Kinsella, R, W Clarke, D J Storey, D Mulvenna & D Coyne, *Fast-Growth Small Firms: An Irish Perspective* (Dublin: Irish Management Institute) 1994.
24. Johnson, S. & Storey, D.J. 1993: *op cit.*
25. *Ibid.*; K A Loscocco, J Robinson, R H Hall & J K Allen, (1991) *op. cit.*

neurs, however it appears to be a bigger problem for women than for men. The profile which female entrepreneurs present and the sector in which they are most likely to be located are often considered to be high risk for banks.[26] From a bank's point of view, the potential market profitability of a business is very important in terms of return. Given the sectors women locate in, market profitability is likely to be lower than for men. Retail, catering and certain other service sectors are perceived by banks to be high risk (usually sectors which reflect the traditional, caring role of women) largely because they have low entry barriers, and low turnover and profits.[27]

There is a perception that, despite the high start-up rate among women, they are likely to set up businesses which are non-profitable, marginal and targeted at the domestic market, a perception heavily influenced by the sector in which the majority of female businesses are located. Such businesses are not always commercially attractive.

Exposure and familiarity with a chosen market, previous managerial experience, significant levels of family support, all within a (somewhat) dynamic sector, have been demonstrated as key factors in determining the success of a business. However, these attributes are more likely to figure in the cultural capital of men than women. The, often lower, educational qualifications of women and the fact that they tend to be older and have less work experience than men, creates a situation where they are viewed as a high risk and are less likely to get bank finance than men.[28]

However as with the division between home and work life, such factors cannot be seen as purely neutral or objective as they are strongly associated, as suggested above, with the construction of gender roles within society, and the cultural expectations which society in general has of women (and men). The apparent 'objective' profile which a female entrepreneur presents is linked to socialisation and cultural experiences, such as family responsibilities, education and gender segregation in the labour force. In addition, the popular association made between men and entrepreneurship means that female entrepreneurs are often perceived as not possessing the characteristics needed for success in business. Such a perception can have serious practical consequences, presenting another difficulty for women when trying to acquire financial support. A bank, when giving financial support to a business, considers both business factors and the personal qualities of the entrepreneur, and the perceptions which bank managers have of entrepreneurs should not be

26. Koper, G, "Women entrepreneurs and the granting of business credit" in S Allen & C Truman (eds), *Women in Business: Perspectives on women Entrepreneurs* (London: Routledge) 1993; S A McKechnie, C T Ennew & L T Read, (1998) *op. cit.*
27. *Ibid.*.
28. Rees, T, *Women and the Labour Market* (London: Routledge) 1992; G Koper, (1993) *op. cit.*

underestimated. As suggested above, entrepreneurial characteristics, such as ambition, perseverance and resolution, are not usually attributed to women, with the result that women are not perceived as 'having what it takes' to be a successful entrepreneur. It is clear from research[29] that often what will cause a bank manager to support a business person is determined more by feelings about the entrepreneur than the so-called neutral business plans and cash flow projections. What this suggests is that differences between male and female entrepreneurs cannot be taken solely at face value.

Various warnings have been attached to these type of gender-stereotypical explanations with some commentators arguing that there is "a tendency to assign primary causal status to gender in discussions of women and work outcomes but to the work situation in similar studies of their male counterparts".[30] The suggestion is that within the context of entrepreneurship and small business, care should be taken with interpretations which place an emphasis on gender-based contrasts between male and female. It is argued that situations can arise where observed differences which appear to be gender-based are actually due to sectoral or other structural characteristics,[31] leading commentators such as McKechnie *et al.* (1998) to suggest that the key challenge facing researchers in this area is the disentangling of the effects of gender from other structural differences.

Such a call is linked to the tradition in this area of seeing gender as something which, as said earlier, is 'added on' to a gender neutral account of entrepreneurship. Structural characteristics, such as sector, business size and financial characteristics, are seen as neutral, while the issue of the public-private divide is seen to be gendered. As Rosa *et al.* (1994:27) suggest "the further decisions are removed from the domestic and social domains, the less likely that direct gender effects are detectable, and the more likely that sectoral competitive forces are shaping the management process". The suggestion here is that though it is still acknowledged that gender can have a significant impact on the experience of owning and managing a business, it only manifests itself in certain areas. From this point of view, the gendered nature of domesticity and the fact that male and female experience this differently is acknowledged, while structural characteristics are believed to be experienced in the same way by both male and female because these are not thought to be gendered. The overall suggestion is that women's experience of small business and their level of success will be commensurate with that of their male counterparts if they hold the same structural position. Thus "gender differences should be interpreted as occurring within a framework of underlying

---

29. Carr, P, "Reconceptualising Enterprise Culture" Unpublished PhD thesis, Trinity College, Dublin (1996); K A Loscocco, J Robinson, R H Hall & J K Allen, (1991) *op. cit.*

30. Loscocco, K A, J Robinson, R H Hall & J K Allen, (1991) *op. cit.*, pp 69-70.

31. Rosa, P, D Hamilton, S Cartern& H Burns, (1994) *op. cit.*, p. 26.

commonality",[31] and that commonality from this perspective is the world of small business and enterprise. A call for such 'disentangling' appears to be supported by research which either suggests that the level of difference between male and female entrepreneurs is declining, or sometimes where differences do exist, female entrepreneurs seem to get a better deal than their male counterparts.[32] However, the danger with this move towards disentanglement is that there is a strong likelihood that gender will again be lost in this process, and that we will be brought back to an agendered world of enterprise and entrepreneurship. To avoid this it is important that we recognise that embodied in the enterprise culture policies which create the contemporary small business world is an enterprise ethic which can be characterised as masculine.

GENDER AND ENTERPRISE CULTURE

In Chapter 8 we argued that growth is a dimension of enterprise culture which is embodied in enterprise culture policies and initiatives. Within countries like the UK, organisations, such as small firms, are encouraged to demonstrate that they are 'fully enterprising' through the growth of the business. A key aim of that chapter was to highlight the pursuit of growth as an emblem of enterprise. In looking at the relationship between gender and enterprise culture, we can similarly explore the maleness of this phenomenon. Our suggestion is that, embodied in the modes of training, classification systems, administrative practices, forms of expertise, initiatives and strategies which make up the enterprise culture programme of governance, is a form of masculinity which Kerfoot and Knight (1993) call "competitive masculinity", and Collinson and Hearn (1994) refer to as entrepreneurialism. This form of masculinity is characterised by a 'hard-nosed' and highly competitive approach to business. However, in contrast to the growth dimension of enterprise culture, entrepreneurialism masculinity is not pursued as an explicit objective, rather it is a taken-for-granted, often unacknowledged element of enterprise. The exploration of the relationship between gender and enterprise in this chapter aims to contribute to "the disruption of the taken-for-granted"[33] maleness of enterprise and entrepreneurship. Thus what we are suggesting is that embedded in the legal, administrative and institutional practices of enterprise culture which aim to promote an enterprising form of life is an often unrecognised form of masculinity.

---

32. McKechnie, S A, C T Ennew & L T Read, (1998) *op. cit.*; P Rosa, D Hamilton, S Carter & H Burns, (1994) *op. cit.*
33. Dean, M, "A Genealogy of the Government of Poverty" *Economy and Society* (1992) 21: 3, pp. 215-247.

The overall suggestion is that when looking at enterprising activity, such as entrepreneurship, it is important to remember that the labour embedded in the setting up and running of a business, is often decisively linked to the (male) gender of the entrepreneur. Therefore, taking up the argument developed throughout the course of this book, we are suggesting that enterprise culture is a historically specific government device, which through an extensive set of practices seeks to synchronise dimensions of the state, the business world and individual lives. The aim of such synchronisation is the promotion of enterprising forms of the conduct of life, and embedded in the notions of how this mode of government encourages individuals/businesses to 'fashion' themselves along enterprise lines, is a gendered image of entrepreneurship.

In looking at the phenomenon of enterprise culture, we have suggested that it is comprised of a number of dimensions which are operationalised by a range of technologies, initiatives and strategies. One key structural dimension is the privileging of the private sector commercial enterprise, with the organisational form of the small business being identified as the mode of private sector business which is highly supportive of enterprise and entrepreneurship. As argued above, most discussions of the experience of running a small business, and the structural issues which attach to this, such as the organisational form of the small business, sectoral location, business age, size and growth rate tend to be presented in agendered terms in most "malestream"[34] small business writing. However we need to be careful of accepting the idea that such structural factors are neutral as conventional writing does unquestioningly, or as those in favour of 'disentangling' structure and gender currently argue.

Where the gender of such structural factors has been explored, it has been argued that structural contrasts between the businesses of male and female owners are due to gendered socialisation and cultural experiences. However, as discussed earlier, though this argument can have some explanatory merit, one problem with it is that as an explanation of the link between entrepreneurialism and gender, it lies outside of enterprise itself. In contrast what we would like to suggest is that, if we understand enterprise culture as a task of cultural management which tries to ensure that individuals relate to and become subjects of the enterprise project,[35] becoming a subject of enterprise means involving oneself in activities (such as setting up a small business and adopting enterprising characteristics) and traits (such as risk-taking, leadership, a daring spirit, etc.) which are conventionally associated with maleness. This association is demonstrated in the work of McKechnie *et al.* (1998) who suggest that the level of similarity that they observed between

---

34. Mulholland, K, (1996) *op. cit.*
35. Du Gay, P, "Enterprise Culture and the Ideology of Excellence" *New Formations* (1991) 13, pp. 45-61.

male and female entrepreneurs may be due to an increasing number of female entrepreneurs possessing a predominance of male traits.

However, if we are clear about the link between masculinity and enterprising traits, how does masculinity link to the structure of business entities such as small firms? We can propose that the link is made through the encouragement of small businesses to express enterprising qualities thoroughly, and to demonstrate this expression through the growth of the business and the striving for profit. The suggestion is that a thorough expression of these masculine enterprising traits in order to be 'fully enterprising', is connected to a preference for the fast-growth small firm over the small firm which stays small. If we accept that enterprising qualities are gendered and male, then we can also suggest that the 'product' of such traits, i.e. a growth firm is also gendered and male. Thus growth (which links to other structural variables, such as size of business, age of business, sector, etc.) as a structural variable is associated with the enterprising male traits of ambition, daring, leadership, competitive spirit, etc. and can itself be understood as being male. Approaching the issue of gender and its relation to enterprise in this way, allows us to explore how the maleness of entrepreneurship not only impacts on women but also excludes some men, privileging male entrepreneurs with fast-growth firms over male entrepreneurs with 'trundler' firms, ranking the former as 'fully enterprising' and the latter as non-enterprising. Thus we might suggest that two models of small business enterprise development can be identified. Firstly, a 'male' model which places an emphasis on growth and profit and, secondly, a 'female' model which centres on a notion of a small firm staying small established for reasons other than profit. Male entrepreneurs who develop fast-growth firms and 'innovator' female entrepreneurs exemplify the former, while male entrepreneurs with small, small businesses and other categories of female entrepreneurs such as 'domestics', 'returners', 'conventionals', who also run small, small businesses, embody the latter.

The Impact of the Female on Enterprise

Up to now we have explored the impact of the masculinity embedded in enterprise and entrepreneurship on female and male experiences of business ownership. However, it might also be useful to consider whether the increased number of female entrepreneurs has contributed to a feminisation of enterprise as a counterbalance to its traditional masculinisation. Has the increasing numbers of female entrepreneurs contributed to a redefinition of entrepreneurial ideals in a more pro-female direction? We can explore this issue with particular reference to the entrepreneurial management discourse, which has emerged out of the creation of an enterprise culture through the implementation of enterprise policies, strategies and initiatives. The maleness of this discourse clearly emerges if we look at the two dimensions it is comprised of. The first dimension places an emphasis on the possession of enterprising qualities and is more likely to be perceived as masculine for the reasons outlined above. The second dimension focuses on management activities and also has a strong masculine perspective attached to it. As well as promoting and valuing enterprising attributes, such as leadership, dynamism, daring, etc., this discourse promotes and values economic efficiency and managerial control, which we have seen when looking at enterprising initiatives such as entrepreneurial governance in the public sector. Within the context of this entrepreneurial management discourse:

> . . . ..men as managers identify with other men who are as competitive as themselves, willing to work at a similar pace, endure long hours, be geographically mobile and meet tight production deadlines. These requirements tend to exclude some men who are not considered 'man enough' or predatory enough to satisfy them and most women, whose employment . . . is often seen as incompatible with entrepreneurial concerns.

> (Collinson & Hearn, 1994:14)

Entrepreneurial management has led to a redefining of managerial qualities, with individuals now expected to perform their job in an entrepreneurial manner, to be proactive, forward-looking change masters. In large organisations, individuals are expected to work to annual targets, to receive performance pay, to apply for jobs rather than expect to be promoted unasked, to become miniaturised enterprises.[36] In small organisations, business owners are expected to develop an entrepreneurial business through the active, unceasing pursuit of opportunities and growth of the business. Women are not excluded as women from this entrepreneurial management discourse as long as they can adopt the required competitive and individualistic traits.[37] However, with women's entrance into management and business ownership in significant numbers, is there a possibility that a demasculinisation of enterprise and the entrepreneurial management discourse will occur?

Optimistic visions of a redefinition of entrepreneurial management in a more 'pro-female' direction because of increased numbers of female entrepreneurs and managers, and an increased emphasis on the non-hierarchical firm, are probably contradicted by other features of the enterprise era, such as the emphasis on competition, downsizing and business process re-engi-

---

36. Halford, S & M Savage, "Restructuring Organisations, Changing People: Gender and Restructuring in Banking and Local Government" *Work, Employment and Society* (1995) 9: 1, pp. 97-122; G Salaman, 1997: 'Culturing Production" in P Du Gay (ed.) *Production of Culture/Cultures of Production.*
37. Halford, S & M Savage (1995) *op. cit.*

neering. According to Grint (1998:559), the latter is a violent and destructive form of organisational restructuring, characterised by aggressive and confrontational language, contributing to "the resurgence of explicit masculine aggression in managerial discourse". The violence of management emerges in language such as "brutal competition", "aggressive expansion" and "lean and mean".[38] The emergence of entrepreneurial management is linked to a new form of organisational masculinity which is characterised by a "workaholic 'macho' ethos".[39]

The masculinist imagery, which has always attached to management as an occupation, has not declined with the emergence of new management forms, such as entrepreneurial management. Rather the latter has been created around a new form of organisational masculinity.[40] Management, and the masculinity attached to it, is not a fixed and unitary category, instead it is an invented category which is a product of the cultural meanings which attach to certain attributes, abilities, dispositions and forms of conduct, which managers are supposed to hold, at certain historical moments.[41] In the 'historical moment' of enterprise culture, the apparatus[42] of enterprise, which includes regulations, administrative measures, architectural arrangements, policies, etc., shapes and moulds the conduct of individuals/businesses, along enterprise lines, and embedded in this is an entrepreneurial masculinity described above. As mentioned above, women are not excluded as women from the world of enterprise and the entrepreneurial management that it produces. However, the robust demarcation of the public and private spheres which is embedded in entrepreneurship, and which women cannot always easily avail of, may make it difficult to participate on these masculine terms. Only those women (and men) who can comply with a masculine entrepreneurialism are likely to be recognised as entrepreneurs and to be called 'fully enterprising'.

38. Caulkin, S, "Work: A Glass Ceiling made of Lead" *The Observer* (3 January 1999).
39. Halford, S & M Savage, (1995) *op. cit.*
40. Collinson, D & J Hearn, "Breaking the Silence: On Men, Masculinities and Managements" in D Collinson & J Hearn (eds), *Men as Managers, Managers as Men* (London: Sage) 1996.
41. Nixon, S, "Exhibiting Masculinity" in S Hall (ed.), *Representation: Cultural Representations and Signifying Practices* (London: Sage) 1997.
42. Hall, S, "The Work of Representation" in S Hall (ed.), *Representation: Cultural Representations and Signifying Practices* (London: Sage) 1997.

SUMMARY OF KEY IDEAS

- Enterprise culture can be understood as the consistent and continuous constitution of individuals as entrepreneurs. However most analyses of the entrepreneur tend to be presented in unacknowledged male terms, which can present some difficulty when trying to understand the position of the female entrepreneur in enterprise culture.

- A notable consequence of the creation of an enterprise culture is a significant increase in the numbers of female entrepreneurs.

- Though the literature on female entrepreneurship has risen in line with the increased numbers of women in business, gender is presented as something which is 'added on' to considerations of entrepreneurship and not integral to it.

- The figure of the entrepreneur is saturated with male values. If a key aim of enterprise culture is to re-define the types of identities and qualities individuals are expected to possess and these are male, the latter should be highlighted and explored.

- A key component of entrepreneurial masculinity is the robust separation of the public and private sphere, something which many female entrepreneurs find difficult to do.

- Research into female entrepreneurship often places an emphasis on the reconciliation of home and work duties, categorising business women in terms of how they negotiate the public/private divide, an approach which is itself masculine.

- Recent research has argued that gender issues such as domestic responsibilities and their impact on a business, should be disentangled from 'neutral' structural factors such as size of firm, age. etc. However we need to be careful of this move towards disentangling, as gender may be lost in the process.

- Understanding enterprise culture as a task of cultural management, we should recognise that individuals/businesses are encouraged to adopt a range of traits and qualities such as risk-taking, daring-spirit, leadership, which are conventionally associated with maleness.

CHAPTER 10

Co-operation and Enterprise Culture

Trust . . . should be understood specifically in relation to risk. . . . Trust is related to absence in time and in space. There would be no need to trust anyone whose activities were continually visible and whose thought processes were transparent, or to trust any system whose workings were wholly known and understood. It has been said that trust is "a device for coping with the freedom of others". . . . Risk and trust intertwine, trust normally serving to reduce or minimise the dangers to which particular types of activity are subject.

(Giddens, 1991:30-35)

CO-OPERATION, NETWORKS AND ENTERPRISE

We have argued throughout the course of this book that a notion of government must be incorporated into our conceptualisation of enterprise culture. The purpose of such incorporation is to allow us to highlight the pivotal position that the governance of subjectivity occupies within enterprise culture. Such 'enterprise' governance has not occurred through the development of an all-powerful, all-seeing central state whose agents attempt deliberately to survey and control all subjects. Rather the enterprise government of subjectivity has occurred through the development and expansion of a complex array of enterprise technologies, some of which we have discussed in earlier chapters.

In exploring the development of enterprise culture, we have suggested that the moulding, shaping, integrating and enhancing of the subjectivity of individuals in an enterprising manner has been central to the creation of the enterprise culture phenomenon. The success of enterprise culture is heavily dependent upon the existence of particular types of individuals who do not require continual external supervision. 'Rolling back the state' in enterprise culture, therefore, means the translation of external constraint into an 'enterprising' internal constraint upon the behaviour of the individual. It means the development of individuals who are prepared to demonstrate initiative, take responsibility for their actions, and for whom the ethic of enterprise is part of their mental fabric.[1]

The economic vision which the architects of enterprise culture created is one which places particular stress on the individual: on individual responsibility, on individual initiative, on individual freedom, on individual enterprise in a market context.[2] Within this economic vision the market is a spontaneous co-ordination device where individuals enter and leave the exchange like strangers, involving themselves in relationships that entail limited personal involvement.[3] A market is open to all individuals:

> . . . but while it brings people together, it does not establish strong bonds of altruistic attachments. The participants in a market transaction are free of any future commitments. The stereotypical competitive market is the paradigm of individually self-interested, noncooperative, unconstrained social interaction'.
>
> (Powell, 1990:302)

From this perspective, economic transactions are not characterised by the social or family obligations of the individuals involved. Rather of more importance is the rational calculations of individual gain, an outlook that has today denied the very existence of 'society' in favour of its individual elements.[4] Thus implied in the notion of the market as a method of co-ordination is the existence of individuals capable of calculation and in possession of information "on all the possible states of the world, on the nature of the actions which can be undertaken and on the consequences of these different actions, once they have been undertaken".[5] However, according to Callon (1999), such market co-ordination experiences problems when ambiguities about the states of the world, the action that can be taken and the expected consequences of these actions, multiply. Given that the existence of such uncertainties is the rule and not the exception in the contemporary business world, an important question to explore is how are individuals within a mar-

---

1. Rose, N, *Governing the Soul: The Shaping of the Private Self* (London: Routledge) 1989.
2. Cohen, A P, "The Personal Right to Identity: A Polemic on the Self in the Enterprise Culture" in P Heelas & P Morris (eds), *The Values of the Enterprise Culture* (London: Routledge) 1992.
3. Callon, M, "Actor-Network Theory – The Market Test" in J Law & J Hassard (eds), *Actor Network Theory and After* (Oxford: Blackwell Publishers) 1999.
4. Granovetter, M, "Economic Action and Social Structure: The Problem of Embeddedness" *American Journal of Sociology,* (1985) 91: 3, pp. 181-510; A P Cohen, (1992) *op. cit.*
5. Callon, M, (1999) *op. cit.*, p. 184.

ket setting able to calculate and 'do business' with one another if no permanent or lasting information on the future exists?[6]

Within a context of massive uncertainty, lack of information, rapid changes
in technology and an increasingly competitive environment, co-operation in
the form of *inter-firm networking* is often presented as the means by which
intricate transactional and co-operative inter-dependence among companies
is regulated and co-ordinated.[7]

Nohria (1992) identifies three main reasons for the increased attention
that is being paid to the issue of networking. Firstly the emergence of the
'new competition' which includes the rebirth of small business, the increased
presence of Asian economies such as Japan or Korea in the world economy,
and the emergence of new industries such as computers and biotechnology.
Secondly, internal restructuring of large organisations which increasingly it
is argued adopt a network mode, and thirdly recent technological development.

Increasingly the term *'network'* is used to describe an assortment of contemporary organisational entities involved in co-operative relationships. These
range from large, multinational companies to small, entrepreneurial firms,
manufacturing to service companies, and regional economies such as the Third
Italy to national economies such as those of Japan. Not only is the term *'network'* employed to describe the make-up of some existing organisations, it is
also used normatively.[8] Though co-operative relationships of one sort or another are not a recent phenomenon, it would appear that, in the contemporary
business world, such relationships are viewed as a strategic necessity and not
just as a strategic option.[9] The network organisation is presented as the organisational form firms *must* adopt if they wish to compete and survive in
today's business world, with commentators, such as Castells (1996), arguing
that networks constitute the new social morphology of our time. A recent
newspaper article adopted a similar logic and suggested that the European
Union should develop a network form (Network Europe) which would promote co-operation and competition between European states at one and the
same time.[10] Given the increased attention that is being paid to networks as a

6.   *Ibid.*
7.   Grandori, A & G Soda, "Inter-Firm Networks: Antecedents, Mechanisms and
     Forms" *Organization Studies* (1995) 16: 2, pp. 183-214; P Smith Ring & A H
     Van de Ven, "Structuring Co-operative Relationships Between Organizations"
     Strategic Management Journal (1992) 13, pp. 483-498.
8.   Nohria, N, "Is a Network Perspective a Useful Way of Studying Organizations?"
     in N Nohria & R G Eccles (eds), *Networks and Organizations: Structure, Form
     and Action* (Boston: Harvard Business School Press) 1992.
9.   Mulcahy, A, "Irish Indigenous SMEs Co-operating to Compete: A Short Run or
     Long Run Phenomenon" (Unpublished dissertation, Department of Management
     and Marketing, University College Cork) 1997.
10. Leonard, M, "New Europeans" (*The Guardian*, 4 September 1999).

form of co-operation both in journalistic and research terms, allied to the association that is made between networks and small firms, the aim of this chapter will be to explore the concept of 'network' and its association with enterprise culture and the entrepreneurial management discourse.

THE EMERGENCE OF THE NETWORK ORGANISATION

The concept of 'network' is in the anomalous position of being old and new at one and the same time. Old in the sense that interest in notions and forms of co-operation can be dated since the 1950s, with much been written on the issue of strategic alliances, joint ventures and partnerships. New in the sense that notions of co-operation and networks have been rejuvenated with the aim of strengthening the small business sectors of various countries and regions, while at the same time providing a means by which large firms can prosper in an increasingly competitive business world.[11] As mentioned above, networks can be found in a wide diversity of industries and organisational forms and despite differences between them, they are all characterised by complex, multidimensional durable relationships where horizontal forms of exchange are of the utmost importance.[12] In general, a network has been defined as a relationship where partners are:

> . . . engaged in reciprocal, preferential, mutually supportive actions. A basic assumption of network relationships is that one party is dependent on the resources controlled by another, and that there are gains to be had by the pooling of resources. In essence, the parties to a network agree to forego the right to pursue their own interests at the expense of others.

> (Powell, 1990:303)

Though a variety of network forms which can be described in these terms can be identified in and between large firms (some of which we will make brief reference to), we will for the most part focus on co-operative relationships among small firms, and the strong interest which is currently expressed in this, particularly by state bodies such as development agencies.

Contemporary discussions of networks where firms are viewed as differentiated units which need to be co-ordinated, and networks themselves are understood as integration mechanisms which connect separate units to each

---

11. Nohria, N, (1992) *op. cit.*; A Mulcahy, (1997) *op. cit.*
12. Powell, W W, "Neither Market nor Hierarchy: Network Forms of Organization" *Research in Organizational Behavior,* (1990) 12, pp. 295-336.

other, can be connected to two adversarial characterisations of networks.[13] The first is one which places inter-firm networks on a market-hierarchy continuum, suggesting that it is a hybrid form of organisational structure which lies between market transactions at one end and highly centralised, hierarchical organisational forms at the other. The placing of networks on this continuum arises out of a general question which asks in what circumstances are economic activities likely to be performed within the boundaries of a hierarchical organisation instead of by market processes.[14] The response is that, where economic transactions occur regularly and are costly in terms of time, energy or money and involve a high degree of uncertainly, they are more likely to be performed efficiently within hierarchically organised companies. In contrast where economic transactions can be characterised by discrete contracts, are unlikely to recur, and are relatively inexpensive and straightforward, they will occur within a market context.[15]

However, such a dichotomous view which places markets at one end of a continuum and hierarchies at the other, with networks lying somewhere in between has been questioned. According to Powell (1990), understanding the relationship between markets, networks and hierarchies in terms of a continuum, suggests that markets are the starting point out of which all other forms of exchange and co-ordination evolve, and such an understanding of markets in economic exchange is a distortion of historical and anthropological evidence. Similarly, the suggestion that hierarchies are an evolutionary end-point of economic exchange and co-ordination is also a historical inaccuracy. A review of the history of economic exchange demonstrates that it "is a story of family businesses, guilds, cartels, and extended trading companies – all enterprises with loose and highly permeable boundaries".[16] This leads us to the second characterisation of a network which suggests that it is a third type of organisational form identifiable by its own attributes and properties which are qualitatively different from markets and hierarchies.[17] In response to this approach, Nohria (1992) suggests that to state that an organisation has a network form is a tautology because from a network perspective all organisations can be characterised as networks anyway. However, Nohria (1992) further argues that the benefit of adopting a network-as-form perspective is that it encourages us to analyse networks on their own terms instead of viewing them as a simple hybrid variant of markets and hierarchies.

Thus starting from a position which accepts the network-as-form approach and subsuming a range of contemporary co-operative forms under the general heading of 'inter-firm networking', much research attention has been

13. Grandori, A & G Soda, (1995) *op. cit.*
14. Granovetter, M, (1985) *op. cit.*
15. Powell, W W, (1990) *op. cit.*; P Smith Ring & A H Van de Ven, (1992) *op. cit.*
16. Powell, W W, (1990) *op. cit.*, p. 298.
17. Grandori, A & G Soda, (1995) *op. cit.*; W W Powell, (1990) *op. cit.*

spent on identifying different types of networks and the factors which influence their development. The result has been a proliferation of typologies of co-operative relationships and network forms among large firms, between large and small firms and among small firms, which would be too numerous to outline here. However, we can focus on the constitution of networks, allowing us to explore the type of networks that can exist among organisations, particularly small firms. For the latter, networks are viewed as being particularly useful and valuable as the weakness, which often accompanies small size, can be offset by the support provided by a strong, flexible network. Three main types of constitution can be distinguished in exchange networks, i.e. control, co-ordination and co-operation.[18]

Exploring Network Organisations: Control

It would be naive to assume that all network relationships are harmonious in nature. According to Powell (1990), each point of contact in a network can be a point of discord and conflict as well as agreement and rapport. Given this, it is important to remember that networks are not only characterised by co-operation, give-and-take and exchange, they also involve relationships distinguished by power and dependency.

The existence of the latter means that many companies experience a certain amount of trepidation when entering into co-operative relationships with other organisations, particularly given research estimates which suggest that up to 60 per cent of all strategic alliances fail.[19]

Co-operation, which is characterised by constraint and coercion, is more likely to be found among some small-firm/large-firm networking relationships. The constitution of many networking relationships between large and small firms is one of control. Here, by 'control' we mean quasi-hierarchical relationships where one company (usually the large one) dominates the other(s).[20] In such a situation the relationship between a large and small firm can often be one of forced co-operation where an asymmetrical dependency exists between the large and small firm.[21] Within such relationships, small firms tend to complement and serve the interests of the large firm, the latter attempting to 'pass on' costs and/or risks to the small firm, which often acts as a type of shock absorber within the network. Such a network can be char-

---

18. Szarka, J, "Networking and Small Firms" *International Small Business Journal* (1989) 8: 2, pp. 10-22.
19. Powell, W W, (1990) *op. cit.*; R E Spekman, T M Forbes, L A Isabella & T C MacAvoy, "Alliance Management: A View From the Past and a Look to the Future" *Journal of Management Studies* (1998) 35: 6, pp. 747-772.
20. Szarka, J, (1989) *op. cit.*
21. Pyke, F, "Co-operative Practices Among Small and Medium-Sized Establishments" *Work, Employment & Society* (1988) 2: 3, pp. 352-365.

acterised by a mutual lack of trust with power largely residing in the hands of the large organisation.[22]

Exploring Network Organisations: Co-ordination

The constitution of a network characterised by co-ordination is one where a 'leading' or 'hub' company arranges and integrates the value-added chain of the network. The superiority of the 'hub' firm in areas such as marketing, technology or size is what places it in the lead position. However, it should not be assumed that the firms which are being 'co-ordinated' are in a totally dependent position, as the lead firm cannot easily replace the expertise of the other companies if it is lost. In fact involvement in such a network on the part of a 'hub' company is often motivated by managers' desire to access specialised resources such as tooling and skilled labour, which are only available outside their own organisation.[23] Because of this, 'co-ordinated' firms (which are often small) have a greater capacity to exercise choice over design, price and delivery issues, than is possible in a network characterised by control.[24] The supplier group system characteristic of the car and electronics industries in Japan can be understood as a type of co-ordinated network. A supplier group system is a network of large and small companies arranged in a pyramid, where the large company at the top is responsible for final assembly of the product and co-ordinates with a first tier of smaller companies which produce major components and sub-assemblies. This first tier in turn co-ordinates work with a third and sometimes fourth tier of smaller companies which specialise in increasingly narrow tasks, and so on.[25]

Though the connections between firms involved in this type of network are vertical, they should not be viewed as dependent. 'Hub' companies within these supplier group networks often supply co-ordinated firms with financial and technical support which enables the small firms to upgrade their operation on a regular basis.[26] The network relationships which small firms in Japan have been involved in with large firms over the past three or four decades have allowed them to move away from a position of asymmetrical dependency. By the 1980s up to 80 per cent of subcontractor firms were in-

22. Rainnie, A, "Small firms: between the enterprise culture and 'New Times'" in R Burrows (ed.), *Deciphering the Enterprise Culture* (London: Routledge) 1991; A Rainnie, "Just-In-Time, Sub-Contracting and the Small Firm" *Work, Employment and Society* (1991) 5: 3, pp. 353-375.

23. Harrison, B & M R Kelley, "Outsourcing and the Search for Flexibility" *Work, Employment and Society* (1993) 7: 2, pp. 213-235

24. Szarka, J, (1989) op. cit.

25. Howard, R, (1990) "Can Small Business Help Countries Compete?" *Harvard Business Review* (November-December 1990) pp. 88-103.

26. *Ibid.*

volved in the design of products, deciding on product price, exchanging production information with their network partners, and receiving payment within two months as opposed to nine or twelve months.[27] According to Szarka (1989), the existence of a constantly changing marketplace which requires firms to be continually flexible, innovative and creative, has led to a situation where the small subcontractor has to be a more equal partner in the design and production process, to ensure competitive advantage for all partners involved.

Exploring Network Organisations: Co-operation

A co-operative network is one where the partners are equal and involved in a symmetrical relationship which is characterised by trust and mutual dependence. Howard (1990) refers to these type of networks as 'republics' with the classic example being the industrial districts of the Third Italy which we discussed in Chapter 8. Horizontal connections exist between the members of such a network which are usually regionally concentrated and sectorally related. Networks within the Third Italy, allow small businesses to compete globally, some in state-of-the-art technological niches. Howard (1990) gives the example of a robotics manufacturer with sixteen employees which is involved in a network with five other small companies (none of which has more than twenty employees) and one large company – Siemens, which produces world class robotics for the diesel engine industry.

In such networks, strategic direction and co-ordination is often provided by a 'broker' which is either a public body or a private membership organisation.[28] Balancing co-operation and competition is a key concern of this type of network (it is also an issue for the co-ordinated network but not the controlled network) and means ensuring that members of the network can achieve their shared objectives while at the same time maintaining some control over their own futures.[29] It is often the case that a company belongs to more than one network at the same time, for example being a supplier in one network while pursuing a joint research and development agenda in another. The 'social and institutional embeddedness' of these networks can have a significant impact on their viability. Webs of pre-existing relationships and connections, shared cultural values and a supportive institutional framework, impact strongly on the capacity and willingness of firms to involve themselves in networks where the constitution is one of co-operation.[30] Such co-operative networks are not just occurring between large and small firms or among small

---

27. Perrow, C, "Small-Firm Networks'. In N. Nohria & R.G. Eccles (eds), (1992) *op. cit.*

28. Howard, R, (1990) *op. cit.*; J Szarka, (1989) *op. cit.*

29. Leonard, M, (1999) *op. cit.*; J Szarka, (1989) *op. cit.*

30. Granovetter, M, (1985) *op. cit.*; J Szarka, (1989) *op. cit.*

firms, they are also becoming more common among large organisations. Large companies are collaborating not just on a once-off basis, but involving themselves in multidimensional long-term linkages where all partners contribute capital, technology and managerial expertise.[31]

'FASHIONING' THE ENTERPRISING NETWORK

Earlier we outlined a number of reasons for the contemporary interest in co-operation and networking. We suggested, following Mulcahy (1997), that one reason for this interest is that many development agencies at both the European and national level advocate the establishment of network relationships between small firms, as a means of building up and enhancing their competitive position within a globalised business world. Given this, it is important that we continue what we have done in earlier chapters with other enterprise phenomena, such as entrepreneurial governance, privatisation, small business enterprise technologies, and locate our consideration of network initiatives within the wider ideological and political context of attempts to create an enterprise culture.

From this perspective, policies and practices which encourage networking can be understood as part of the wider range of enterprise governmental techniques which produce enterprise culture. However, whereas other enterprise governmental techniques adhere to a competitive logic, networking techniques subscribe to a logic which aims to maintain a creative tension between co-operation and competition. Within the Irish context, such network techniques include programmes such as *Technology Transfer and Business Partnerships*, an initiative which specialises in promoting strategic alliances between firms both within Ireland and abroad. The aim of the programme is to develop and strengthen the technical innovative capacity of companies involved in advancing new or improved products, through the establishment of partnerships or acquiring new technology through joint ventures or licensing.[32] A second network initiative is the *National Linkages Programme*, the key aim of which is to establish linkages between indigenous small firms and multinational companies setting up in Ireland. A third initiative is the *Inter Firm Co-operation Networks Pilot Programme*, the aim of which is to encourage Irish small firms to co-operate in strategic activities such as marketing or product/process development.[33]

How should we understand the emergence of enterprise technologies which concentrate on the promotion of networks between small firms? Following on from Miller (1998) and his discussion of accounting and the emergence of

---

31. Howard, R, (1990) *op. cit.*; W W Powell, (1990) *op. cit.*
32. Mulcahy, A, (1997) *op. cit.*
33. *Ibid.*

new practices within this profession, we can suggest that new enterprise technologies such as networking initiatives arise out of a process of *problematising* existing practices. According to Miller (1998):

> 'Problems' have to be made recognizable, a particular perception has to form . . . a measure of agreement has to be reached as to the nature of the problems identified, a consensus has to form that something needs to be done, and another way of calculating that fits the problem identified has be to made available.

(Miller, 1998: 175)

Existing enterprise technologies, such as the Enterprise Allowance Scheme or the Business Expansion Scheme in the UK, have been criticised for not giving rise to a small business sector in which the majority of firms are growth orientated. In response to this the suggestion is emerging that initiatives that promote enterprising networks between small firms (as discussed in chapter eight) will allow businesses to trade as if they were a growth company. In addition participation in a network may alert a small business to new opportunities and through identification of these opportunities small businesses involved in the network may grow. Thus participation in a network may lead to the growth of individual small businesses.

The problematising of existing practices may emerge from within business itself. For example, firms may recognise that competing successfully within the contemporary global economy may be more easily achieved through networking as opposed to growth, merger or acquisition. Alternatively, the problematising of existing practices may emerge from institutionalised actors, such as regulatory bodies or government agencies who suggest that a problem exists which needs to be dealt with.[34] Within the enterprise context in countries such as the UK or Ireland, the problem as mentioned previously is the micro nature of small businesses and the lack of growth orientated businesses. The solution being offered is the establishment of networks among small firms, a solution which is being applied to government agencies themselves in the UK as a means of delivering support to small businesses in a more efficient manner. According to Deakins (1999), the more formal the network among government agencies, the more likely it is that these agencies will be able to break away from generalist start-up advice for small firms, a type of advice which has characterised small business support in the past. Research in the Ireland highlights the fact that the impetus for the development of network initiatives has not come from Irish government agencies,

---

34. Miller, P, "The Margins of Accounting" in M Callon (ed.), *The Laws of the Markets* (Oxford: Blackwell Publishers) 1998.

rather it has originated in the European Union which provides funding for a range of network initiatives.[35]

As with other enterprise culture technologies, networking initiatives can be understood as one of the means by which the dimensions and values of enterprise culture are operationalised. In addition, such networking initiatives contribute to the production and evolution of the entrepreneurial management discourse. The first dimension of this discourse, which places an emphasis on the procurement and enactment of enterprising attributes such as risk-taking, flexibility, daring and creativity, is enhanced through involvement in networks. The second dimension, which focuses on management activities, encourages the development of an 'alliance mindset',[36] which requires the development of additional management skills. Individuals and businesses are not only expected to perform a range of management tasks, such as organising, co-ordinating, planning, controlling etc., competently, they must also possess skills which will allow them to network socially within and between companies to secure commitment to an organisational network. An adeptness to relate to others, leadership skills and the ability to work outside of prescribed guidelines and routines are also required.[37] The establishment of networks requires that management skills extend beyond what is normally required. Network initiatives encourage individuals and businesses to recognise that:

> . . . command and control and/or management by fiat will not work. Alliance management spans the boundaries of independent firms which agree to work together, to collaborate. Compromise, influence, and trust emerge as key operative terms – one cannot dictate. One must gain the partners' agreement on mutually achievable goals and must enact processes to achieve these goals.
>
> (Spekman *et al.*, 1998: 765)

The Problem of Enterprise Government

As with other enterprise technologies, networking initiatives have the dimensions of enterprise culture 'written into' them which contributes to the emergence and production of enterprise culture and the entrepreneurial management discourse associated with this. Nevertheless, as suggested in earlier chapters, it is important to remember that 'government' as an activity is a

---

35. Mulcahy, A, (1997) *op. cit.*
36. Spekman, R E , T M Forbes, L A Isabella & T C MacAvoy, (1998) *op. cit.*
37. *Ibid.*

"congenitally failing operation".[38] Difficulties attached to the various enterprise technologies which make up the government of enterprise, often mean that the production of enterprise culture is often something which occurs in an imperfect and contentious manner. Particular problems can attach to the enterprise technology of networking as the tension between co-operation and competition is not always easily resolved. Enterprise culture is competitive and individualistic and the implementation of co-operative initiatives within such a context can lead to strong contradictory pressures. Managing the tension between competition and co-operation can be extremely difficult particularly in a context which is competitive and individualistic.

Nevertheless, despite the difficulties attached to the enterprise technology of networking, the emergence of such strategies and policies, and the importance attached to them by state development agencies at European and national level, signals the fluidity and mobility of the practices which contribute to the production of enterprise culture. Enterprise initiatives, strategies and practices are criticised on an ongoing basis for not achieving what they originally set out to do. For example as stated earlier a key criticism which is often made of current enterprise technologies targeted at small firms is their apparent inability to nurture a significant number of growth orientated small businesses. Inherent to the emergence of networking strategies is the suggestion that such an enterprise technology would remedy the defects of a small firm sector largely comprised of micro businesses offering '. . . something more, something different, something better'.[39]

The development of a range of networking enterprise initiatives, particularly in the UK and Irish context, can be understood as something which happens at what Miller (1998) refers to as the 'margins' of an area of expertise. The identification of a problem, such as the lack of growth-orientated small businesses, and the development of 'solutions' to these problems is the means by which a body of practices (in this case enterprise practices and technologies) is formed and re-formed. As seen in earlier chapters, one solution, which has been developed and implemented to deal with this problem of a low number of growth small businesses, is selectivity. Networking initiatives such as the *Inter Firm Co-operation Networks Pilot Programme* in Ireland can be understood as the advent of another solution, and one which might appear to more easily marry the aspirations of individual small business owners and state development agencies.

For our purposes, the importance of the emergence of initiatives such as networking is that it highlights the way in which different calculative enterprise practices have been developed within a certain historical context. Enterprise technologies, such as the Enterprise Allowance Scheme, embodied

---

38. Miller, P & N Rose, "Governing Economic Life" *Economy and Society* (1990) 19: 1, pp. 10-11.
39. Miller, P, (1998) *op. cit.*, p. 175.

the ideal of widespread small business ownership, with individuals creating and providing jobs for themselves and others. However, the problem of a high failure rate and lack of small business growth led to the emergence of other enterprise technologies such as selectivity and networking. The development and evolution of the calculative practices of enterprise, demonstrates how the creation of an enterprise culture "is itself an ensemble of devices and ideas formed at particular times and in particular locales, rather than an immutable and universal"[40] phenomenon. Thus what is highlighted is that the calculative practices and rationales of enterprise "have been assembled in an ad hoc fashion in relation to historically and geographically localized concerns and issues".[41]

SUMMARY OF KEY IDEAS

- Within enterprise culture significant stress is placed on individual responsibility, initiative and freedom in a market context. The market is a spontaneous co-ordination device where individuals interact with limited personal involvement.

- For such a market to work successfully, individuals must be capable of rational calculation and be in possession of extensive information. However where ambiguities about the world exist, difficulties with market co-ordination emerge.

- Within a context of massive uncertainty and limited information, inter-firm networking is presented as the means by which interaction among companies is regulated and co-ordinated.

- In recent times networking has been presented as the only means by which firms can survive and thrive in the contemporary business world.

- Networks can be found in a wide variety of industries and organisational forms and are characterised by complex, multidimensional, durable relationships where horizontal forms of exchange are key.

- A key reason for the current interest in networking is that many development agencies at both a European and national level advocate the establishment of network relations among small firms as a means of enhancing their competitive position within a globalised economy.

- Policies and practices which encourage networking can be understood as part of a wider range of enterprise governmental techniques.

- New enterprise practices such as the networking initiatives arise out of a process of problematising existing practices.

---

40. *Ibid.*, p. 177.
41. *Ibid.*, p. 190.

- A key concern of many state agencies involved in supporting and promoting small firms is the lack of growth businesses. The solution being offered is networking.
- Networking initiatives contribute to the production and evolution of the entrepreneurial management discourse particularly through the development of an "alliance mindset".

CHAPTER 11

Internationalisation or Globalisation of Enterprise Culture

> The world economy is changing in fundamental ways. The changes add up to a basic transition, a structural shift in international markets and in the production base of advanced countries. It will change how production is organized, where it occurs, and who plays what role in the process.
>
> (Cohen & Zysman, 1987:79)

A GLOBAL WORLD?

In recent years, much has been written about the emergence of a 'borderless' world. In such a context it is argued that activities and occurrences throughout the world are merging and combining in an extremely precipitous manner. This continuous, rapid, often volatile convergence of events is said to lead to the development of a single, integrated sphere, where a range of influences including economic, social, cultural, technological and business activities, traverse the traditional boundaries of regions, nations, national cultures, time, space and sectors, with enhanced ease.[1] It is suggested that the globalisation of the world economy has led to "an intensification of patterns of global inter-connectedness" and contributed to the creation of an environment characterised by colossal turbulence, volatility and uncertainty. In such a milieu it is argued that the only organisations and individuals that will survive, thrive and prosper are those that are increasingly enterprising and creative, relying less and less on bureaucratic structures and practices, and more and more upon entrepreneurial forms and behaviour.[2] In addition, globalisation

---

1. Parker, B, "Evolution and Revolution: from International Business to Globalization" in S R Clegg, C Hardy & W R Nord (eds), *Handbook of Organization Studies.* (London: Sage) 1996.
2. Du Gay, P, G Salaman & B Rees, "The Conduct of Management and the Management of Conduct: Contemporary Managerial Discourse and the Constitution

theorists suggest that the increased level of interdependence and interconnectedness within the world economy, has created a situation where nation states and national governments are subsumed and dominated by a global economy propelled by ungovernable world market forces.[3]

However, from the perspective of this book, which argues for the incorporation of a notion of government within our conceptualisation of enterprise culture, acceptance of such a position creates difficulties. If the emergence of a globalised world requires that individuals and organisations are ever more enterprising, at the same time as governments within nation states are weakened, how is the former achieved without a strong form of the latter? This leads us to question the notion that currently nation states and national governments are impotent. Though accepting that the governance capabilities of nation states have changed and perhaps weakened, it can be argued that national governments are still pivotal institutions. Despite the increased confusion, turmoil and uncertainty created by the escalating geographical spread of economic activities across numerous boundaries, particularly national boundaries, nation states and national governments still remain a significant force in shaping both national economies and the world economy.[4] The aim of this chapter, therefore, will be to focus on the changing nature of the world economy, exploring whether it can be characterised in internationalisation or globalisation terms, and the relationship between this and our understanding of enterprise culture.

The Nature of the World Economy

As a process, internationalisation is understood as the increased extension of economic activities across national boundaries. Though this process is not new with some commodities having an international character for a long time, contemporary internationalisation has led to the remarkable growth of interconnections between countries, increasingly linking and integrating nations and economic actors into a range of market relationships.[5] The spread of

---

of the 'Competent' Manager" *Journal of Management Studies* (1996) 33:3, pp. 267.

3. Hirst, P & G Thompson, "Globalization and the Future of the Nation State" *Economy and Society* (1995) 24: 3, pp. 408-442.

4. Dicken, P, *Global Shift: The Internationalization of Economic Activity* (London: Paul Chapman Publishing) 2nd edn, 1992; P Hirst & G Thompson, "The Problem of 'Globalization': International Economic Relations, National Economic Management and the Formation of Trading Blocs" *Economy and Society* (1992) 21: 4, pp. 357-396; P Hirst & G Thompson, "Globalisation, Foreign Direct Investment and International Economic Governance" *Organisation* (1994) 1: 2, pp. 277-303; P Hirst & G Thompson, (1995) *op. cit.*

5. Dicken, P, (1992) *op. cit.*; P Hirst & G Thompson, (1992) *op. cit.*

such economic relationships has been achieved firstly by means of the extension of markets across national borders. This occurs through the exportation of a proportion of the output (product or service) of an organisation. Production of the product or service remains in the home country, but the company establishes agencies and builds up distribution networks abroad.

The second means by which internationalisation occurs is through foreign direct investment where companies directly invest and set up production facilities outside the confines of national boundaries.[6] According to Dicken (1992:4), national boundaries "no longer act as 'watertight' containers of the production process. Rather, they are more like sieves through which extensive leakage occurs". Though forms of foreign direct investment have been around since the 19th century, it has really only become highly significant since 1945, with the continuous emergence of new investor countries. Along with a wider geographical spread of both inward and outward investment, competition among nation states, particularly for inward investment, has intensified in recent years.[7]

In looking at the industrial policies of most nation states, it is clear that governments are actively involved in encouraging companies, large and small to export and increase levels of foreign direct investment. With regard to the latter governments actively encourage inward as well as outward investment, putting in place a range of incentives to encourage foreign companies to locate their subsidiaries within their national boundaries. The attractiveness of national locations, allied to their ability to deliver investment advantages to companies, varies greatly. Such advantages not only include cheaper labour, but also industrial policy provisions which impact on the overall cost of location and the return that can be gained from the subsidiary. Successful companies are those that can take significant advantage of such provisions.[8] Firms which operate in a range of countries having a variety of foreign direct investment interests are referred to as *multinational companies*. However a key characteristic of such companies is that despite their foreign interests they maintain a clear home base and national identity, and are subject to the 'rules of economic engagement' of their home base.

6.   Lane, C, *Industry and Society in Europe: Stability and Change in Britain, Germany and France* (Aldershot: Edward Elgar) 1995.

7.   *Ibid.*

8.   Hirst, P & G Thompson, (1994) *op. cit.*

The Internationalised Economy

The characteristics of an internationalised world economy can be summarised as follows.

- Nation states are the dominant actors within the world economy, functioning within a system of differential power relationships.

- Nations actively compete against each other in a bid to enhance their position within the world economy and to secure as large a share as possible of 'the fruits' of international trade.

- Despite increased levels of interdependence between nation states, a clear differentiation is made between the domestic sphere and the international sphere. Links between nation states are viewed as opportunities or constraints for nationally located economic actors.

- An internationalised economy is distinguished by the rise and maturation of the multinational company (MNC). Within an internationalised economy a multinational company has a clear national identity and is subject to the economic regulations of its home country.

(Dicken, 1992; Hirst & Thompson, 1992)

Considerations of the concept of globalisation are associated with the feeling that something fundamental is currently happening in the world economy. Though certainly linkages and overlaps between notions of internationalisation and globalisation can be identified, the latter is said to refer to a significant change in the nature of the linkages and interconnections that exist between national economies. However, one difficulty with trying to explore the phenomenon of globalisation is that there is no consensus among writers as to what exactly a globalised world means or constitutes. The focus and emphasis of explanations of this phenomenon range from permeable national boundaries, to the blurring of organisational boundaries and the emergence of networks, to the breakdown and blurring of internal boundaries within organisations. Still other commentators emphasise the importance of redefinitions of concepts such as time, space, cultural assumptions, and the relationship between self and others.[9] In management literature where a considerable amount of hype surrounds the notion of globalisation and a global economy, emphasis is placed on changes in production, investment and trade on an international level.[10]

However, though it is acknowledged that economic linkages between different countries are not new, it is argued that one of the most significant

---

9.   Parker, B, (1996) *op. cit.*
10. Thompson, P & D McHugh, *Work Organisations: A Critical Introduction* (London: Macmillan Business) 2nd edn, 1995.

recent developments which signals the emergence of a globalised economy is the rise of the *transnational corporation* (TNC). According to Dicken (1992), the transnational corporation is a rival to the nation state, competing for the role of dominant actor within the world economy. Transnational corporations are differentiated from multinational companies who establish branches in separate countries, by the fact that they are said to be genuinely stateless, footloose capital with no specific national identity, willing to set-up or relocate anywhere in the world in order to obtain the highest return.[11] The corporate structures of such an organisation comprise of a complicated and intricate network of parent-subsidiary relationships, with 'know-how' and knowledge being centrally located and capable of being moved across the corporation to its different subunits.[12] This contrasts with the multinational company which tends to locate in specific parts of the world and usually locates company 'know-how', manifested in activities such as research and development, in the home country. Faced with a rival, such as the transnational corporation, it is argued that nation states struggle to exert influence over the economy either nationally or internationally.

The Globalised Economy

The characteristics of a globalised economy can be summarised as follows.

- The intensification of market relationships between individuals/entities located in different national contexts, and the concomitant rise in levels of interdependence between different parts of the world, creates a situation where processes and activities are not determined at the level of the national economy.

- The speed, reach and intensity of global market forces makes public governance of economic activity exceedingly difficult. Within the context of a globalised world, nation states have ceased to be effective economic managers.

- Deregulation and innovation have led to the transformation of the global financial system. This system is characterised by 'stateless' money which seems to have eluded any kind of collective control on the part of even the most advanced nations. Capital flows in a global world appear to be oblivious to the constraints of time and space which normally impinge on activities such as production or consumption.

- The transnational corporation is a key economic actor and is the primary materialisation of a globalised economy. This organisation has no

---

11. *Ibid.*; P Hirst & G Thompson, (1992) *op. cit.*
12. Thompson, P & D McHugh, (1995) *op. cit.*

specific national identity, demonstrating an ability to locate anywhere, at anytime. The transnational corporation is the manifestation of business 'set free' from any kind of state regulation and intervention.

- Globalisation leads to the fragmentation and global dispersion of economic activities which are reintegrated by transnational corporations to create linkages between countries. This process is facilitated by new transport and communication technologies, allied to a greater homogenisation of tastes and production methods across national boundaries.

(Harvey, 1990; Hirst & Thompson, 1992, 1995;
Dicken, 1992; Lane, 1995)

Internationalisation or Globalisation?

Research demonstrates that an exploration of globalisation trends will indicate that though they do certainly exist, what we need to remember is that the emergence of entities such as the transnational corporation is currently just that, a trend as opposed to a well established reality. There are few genuine footloose transnational corporations; rather the nationally based multinational company[13] still dominates. If the world economy had genuinely moved into a period of globalisation, the transnational corporation would be a well-established entity. It would appear that patterns of interconnectedness between nation states across the world, particularly in terms of the international activities of organisations, are more local than global. Most companies which define themselves as global, or at least international, still only operate in a small number of countries or at most regionally. In fact it seems that the activities of exporting and foreign direct investment largely occur among the advanced industrial economies. Foreign direct investment is almost completely concentrated in the advanced industrial countries, i.e. the Triad of North America, the European Union and Japan, and a small number of newly industrialised economies. Thus the developing world and newly industrialised countries only contribute in a small way to this kind of international activity.[14]

---

13. It is important to note that the terms 'transnational corporation' and 'multinational company' are often used interchangeably. In much recent writing the term 'multinational company' appears to have been dropped in favour of 'transnational corporation'. However, even though the international reach of multinational companies has increased in recent years, they cannot as yet be referred to as 'stateless' corporations. Therefore for the purpose of clarity, this chapter will differentiate between the two entities and not use the terms interchangeably.
14. Hirst, P & G Thompson, (1992) *op. cit.*; P Hirst & G Thompson, (1994) *op. cit.*; P Hirst & G Thompson, *Globalization in Question* (Cambridge: Polity Press) 1996.

The non-global nature of the international activities of companies emerges if we look at the export and foreign direct investment flows from the larger industrialised nations. For example, though British companies spread foreign direct investment across a number of countries, the majority of this goes to the USA, with a very small proportion going to the developing countries. Investment in Europe by British companies has increased in recent years but the lack of significant investment in South East Asia and Africa leads commentators to conclude the British foreign direct investment does not have a truly global reach.[15] Though Germany is one of the largest exporting countries in the world the bulk of its exports and the foreign direct investment activity of its corporations tends to be directed towards developed countries. Countries such as the USA and Japan are characterised by significant levels of outward foreign direct investment, but they also have extremely low levels of inward investment, and exporting and importing activities only account for between 10 to 15 per cent of their GDP. Overall between 57 and 72 per cent of the world population receive only 8.5 per cent of global foreign direct investment.[16]

A second important characteristic of international companies is that even if they are involved in a high level of foreign direct investment, there still remains a reluctance to establish core business activity abroad. If organisations were truly transnational, we would expect to see the emergence of globally integrated production strategies where both higher and lower order corporate functions are dispersed around the globe according to an integrated business strategy. However, it would appear that there is little evidence to show that the traditional multinational structure has been usurped. Head quarters and higher level activities, such as research and development, are still largely located in the home country, and lower level activities, such as assembly work, are located abroad.[17] In addition, it would seem that organisations involved in international activities are not always eager to move their operations around from location to location on a regular basis. International businesses remain nationally embedded, being largely restricted to their home territory in terms of the location of sales, assets, affiliates, declared profits and research and development. Perhaps the question to ask is not why are organisations always threatening to relocate 'at the drop of a hat' if things aren't going their way, but why do the vast majority stay in situ, remaining for long periods of time in their home base and major sites of investment?[18]

The restricted nature of the internationalisation activities of exporting and foreign direct investment, allied to the continued existence of multina-

---

15. Lane, C, (1995) *op. cit.*
16. I*bid.*; P Hirst & G Thompson, (1992) *op. cit.*; P Hirst & G Thompson, (1996) *op. cit.*
17. Lane, C, (1995) *op. cit.*; P Dicken, (1992) *op. cit.*
18. Hirst, P & G Thompson, (1992) *op. cit.*; P Hirst & G Thompson, (1996) *op. cit.*

tional companies which still predominate over transnational corporations, leads us to question the notion that we are currently living in an era of globalisation. The scarcity of the transnational company as a truly global entity suggests that the nation state and its government is not pitched against an uncontrollable force and has not been rendered powerless. Such a conclusion is reinforced by consideration of the impact of an internationalised financial system on national economies. The emergence of internationalised capital markets, which appear to be ungovernable, has been cited as evidence of the existence of a global economy. However according to Hirst and Thompson (1992, 1996), although there has been increased internationalisation of money and capital markets, we need to be careful about the meaning we attach to this development. International financial penetration of national economies is nothing new, and levels of such penetration have been as high during other historical periods, as they have been in the 1980s and into the 1990s. The other point which they emphasise is that activity on internationalised financial markets is not irreversible, and evidence suggests that a trend towards re-regulation of financial markets during the 1990s has emerged. It may be the case that battles will continue to be fought between the governments of nation states (particularly advanced nations) and financial markets, but there is no certainty that the market will always be victorious over regulatory systems. The overall conclusion to be reached, therefore, is that today's world economy can be characterised as being highly internationalised, with nation states and their governments still making a significant contribution to its governance.

ENTERPRISE CULTURE AND INTERNATIONALISATION

Throughout the course of this book, we have placed an emphasis on the role government and governmental technologies have played in the creation of an enterprise culture. However it is important to recognise that the phenomenon of enterprise culture is not purely a political creation and that enterprise has entered into people's daily lives in a range of ways that are not directly related to policy initiatives. There are a number of other changes which have fortified the political project of enterprise culture. These include post-fordist shifts, financial pressures on government, increased levels of uncertainty and turbulence in the business world, and the internationalisation of the world economy.[19] Internationalisation not only supports the creation of an enterprise culture, but is itself also reinforced by enterprise culture technologies. The promotion of the institutional dimension of enterprise culture through policies such as privatisation and deregulation, while increasing levels of

---

19. Du Gay, P & G Salaman, "The Cult[ure] of the Customer" *Journal of Management Studies* (1992) 29:5, pp. 615-633.

competitiveness within economies (something which enterprise culture sets out to do), has also exposed domestic economies to greater external vulnerability from internationalisation processes. Thus processes of internationalisation and attempts to create an enterprise culture 'feed off' each other, with the former significantly influencing governmental activity and the way individuals and organisations are linked to the political objective of creating an enterprise culture.

As suggested above, recent analyses of transnational relationships have tended to place huge emphasis on the constraints under which national governments currently operate. In addition the belief that the nation state is in decline has led to a significant underestimation of the current role being adopted by state officials and national institutions.[20] Though certainly the options and mechanisms of economic co-ordination and regulation available to state officials and national institutions have changed, particularly given the emergence of trading blocs such as the European Union, this does not mean that nation states are powerless. Even as a nation state cedes power to something like the European Union it acquires new roles and capabilities. Within this context, increased importance has been assigned to the role of government as a regulator, facilitator and orchestrator of private individuals and organisations.[21] Though markets are increasingly international, the creation of wealth and economic prosperity are national phenomena which are intricately linked to national economic actors working together to secure key supply-side outcomes, such as growing businesses, increased productivity and enterprising activity.[22] In other words, the process of internationalisation reinforces the important role governments play in the governance of subjectivity, an activity which we have argued throughout is at the centre of attempts to create an enterprise culture.

Despite an increasingly internationalised world, it is clear that most populations are rooted and cannot easily be moved. People are not as mobile as money, goods or ideas, remaining nationalised and dependent on passports, visas, residence and labour qualifications. In such a situation, the nation state maintains the position of controller of its borders, the movement of people across them, and the activities of individuals within them.[23] As a regulator of people's lives and activities, the nation state has developed a series of techniques, procedures and means of calculation which render the population and various domains, such as the family, the economy, or individual businesses, amenable to intervention and regulation. However, such inter-

20. Campanella, M L "The Effects of Globalization and Turbulence on Policy-Making Processes" in J Drew (ed.), *Readings in International Enterprise* (London: Routledge) 1995.
21. Hirst, P & G Thompson, (1992) *op. cit.*
22. Hirst, P & G Thompson, (1992) *op. cit.*; P Hirst & G Thompson, (1996) *op. cit.*
23. *Ibid.*

vention is not direct and authoritarian; rather it is indirect, operating at a distance, linking the conduct of individuals and organisations to political objectives through a delicate network of agents and agencies.[24]

According to Miller and Rose (1990), understanding the activity of government within advanced liberal democracies requires a recognition of the increasing proliferation of government technologies which progressively attempt to act upon and instrumentalise the self-directing tendencies of individuals and organisations, with the aim of connecting them to socio-political objectives. Enterprise is particularly important in this regard as it is an issue which has become central to governments in Europe, America and the UK. As argued earlier, the creation of an enterprise culture has not meant the withdrawal of government from economic life despite the emphasis that has been placed on 'rolling back the state'. Instead, as we have seen, it has led to the development of a wide range of government technologies which endow the self-regulating abilities of individuals and businesses with increasing importance, through the regulation 'at a distance' of their economic activity.[25] The ability of the state to shape, influence and mould the activities (both personal and business) of its citizens, particularly in terms of an ethic of enterprise, is given greater prominence through the increased internationalisation of the world economy. In other words, the institutional and ethical strands of enterprise culture are operationalised through the range of governmental techniques and initiatives which are put in place to regulate and shape the endeavours of citizens, an aspect of government activity which has gained in prominence due to the impact of internationalisation on nation states.

Enterprise Culture or Cultures?

We have come to the conclusion above that, despite the fashionable emphasis placed on the notion of a global economy, the world is best understood in terms of increased internationalisation as opposed to globalisation. Our acceptance of this position signals to us the continuing importance of recognising the 'enduring distinctiveness' of national systems of economic organisation.[26] Though certainly the heightened internationalisation of today's world economy has impacted on the capabilities of the nation state, national governments can still compensate for the effects of this in various ways, one being the promotion of enterprise. However, the means by which a state promotes and nurtures enterprise both as a consequence of – and a response to – internationalisation will vary from country to country. Such differences across countries can be understood in terms of a *business system*

---

24. Miller, P & N Rose, "Governing Economic Life" *Economy and Society* (1990) 19: 1, pp.1-31.
25. *Ibid.*
26. Lane, C, *Management and Labour in Europe* (Aldershot: Edward Elgar) 1989.

which is a combination of the value orientations and general practices which characterise both the internal organisation of firms and their relationship with the external environment.[27]

Business System Components

Three components of a business system can be identified as follows.

- The nature of firms within a society including:
  - the pattern of companies' growth;
  - the dominance of large organisations within an economy;
  - the style of risk management.

- The type of market organisation that exists in an economy, in particular:
  - the relationships between competition and co-operation both within and across sectors.

- Authoritative co-ordination and control systems within companies, in particular:
  - the nature of the relationship between management and employees – is this hierarchical or one characterised by consensus?

(Whitley, 1992)

The concept of a business system recognises that there is a number of ways by which economic activity can be organised in a market economy, with no one particular pattern being inherently superior to others. In addition, it also highlights that differences in patterns of economic organisation emerge out of and are effective within, distinct institutional environments.[28]

According to Lane (1992), socio-institutional factors are now recognised as factors of production which can confer competitive advantage or disadvantage. The nature of the networks of relationships between companies and central and local governments can benefit (or harm) their business activities. Other relationships with trade associations, with organised labour, with financial institutions, with national education systems can all act as an advantage or disadvantage to a business. A national economic system can reassure a business and help it negotiate its way through difficult international markets, acting as an incentive to take greater risks, or it may discourage businesses from taking significant chances. Germany and Japan have been identified as countries which have strongly solidaristic relationships to the business world, helping companies cope with the shocks and risks of operating in

27. Lane, C, "European Business Systems: Britain and Germany Compared" in R Whitley (ed.), *European Business Systems: Firms and Markets in their National Contexts* (London: Sage) 1992.

28. Whitley, R "Societies, Firms and Markets: the Social Structuring of Business Systems" in R Whitley (ed.), (1992) *op. cit.*

an international economy.[29] Research indicates that business systems tend to be persistently distinctive in a way that other forms of national culture are not. However, it is important to recognise that changes in embedded institutional structures are possible in response to global challenges but that these usually occur and are absorbed in nationally specific ways.[30]

Discussing the issue of national distinctiveness here brings us back to the suggestion made in Chapter 1 that we treat enterprise culture:

> . . . as a historically specific set of institutionally embedded relations of government in which the forms of thought and conduct of extended populations are targeted for transformation.

> *(Bennett, 1992:26)*

We have argued earlier that the form that entrepreneurial behaviour takes is not a 'given' of human nature. Rather the enterprising behaviour of individuals/businesses is fashioned and shaped according to distinct patterns generated by a range of governmental devices and techniques. These techniques vary from one social environment to another. They are influenced by the philosophy which guides state intervention in a social context as well as the structure of the state, giving rise to the emergence of different enterprise cultural permutations. Other significant dominant institutions are the financial system and the system of education and training. The business system configuration of firm type, market organisation and authority system relies on a specific mix of these institutions which varies from country to country.[31] Thus in taking one key element of enterprise culture, i.e. the promotion of small business, in Chapter 8 we saw significant differences between the UK and Italy. Brief reference was also made to the contrast between the UK and Germany. Picking up this contrast we can again highlight how differences in approach to small business as a focus of enterprise are historically embedded.

In comparing the British approach to small business to that of Germany, similarities and differences can be identified. Like the UK, a key aim of German small business policy is to promote growing businesses. However the means by which this is done is different to the UK giving rise to a German small business sector which is characterised by large small businesses, in contrast to the micro small businesses of Britain. Germany compared to Britain has fewer self-employed *without* employees, with German firms in the size band of 2-49 employees being larger with an average employment of

---

29. Hirst, P & G Thompson, (1995) *op. cit.*
30. Thompson, G, "The Evolution of the Managed Economy in Europe" *Economy and Society* (1992) 21: 2, pp. 129-151; P Hirst & G Thompson, (1995) *op. cit.*
31. Lane, C, (1992) *op. cit.*

nine compared to six in Britain. Overall small businesses in Germany are on average larger than in the UK. Despite the fact that the number of small businesses have been growing faster in the UK throughout the 1980s and 1990s, small businesses in Germany make a larger contribution to GDP than small businesses in Britain.[32] As with the Italian contrast with Britain in Chapter 8, differences between German and British small business can be understood in terms of a very different institutional context and different cultural technologies which produce a unique cultural configuration of enterprise.

Both Britain and Germany disagree with the subsidisation of inefficient small businesses. However, one key difference between small business policies in Britain and Germany is the philosophy which underlies them. German small business policy is built around the philosophy of a social market economy with an emphasis being placed on 'help for self-help'. From this perspective government support is provided with the expectation that firms in receipt of it will continuously upgrade and meet the highest standards of competition. In contrast British small business policy is mainly concerned to remove or compensate for market imperfections.[33] Support for small business in Germany has been a constituent part of economic and social policy throughout the post-war period, unlike Britain which dates mainly from the 1980s. Because of its history of support for the small business sector Germany has not been characterised by what Lane (1995:108) defines as "the same 'small-firm' euphoria and...celebration of an enterprise culture as in Britain".

Nevertheless, despite the historical success of the German small business sector, it has been argued that the sector is beginning to show signs of 'age' appearing to lack innovation, possessing outdated organisational structures and management, and experiencing slow product development. Research suggests that a key question for many German companies is how to become entrepreneurial again, particularly within the context of an increasingly internationalised world.[34] Thus despite their different historical traditions, being 'fully enterprising' on a continuous basis is something which is of concern to both British and German companies, with policies designed to support, encourage and mould them in this endeavour. As with the Italian situation explored in Chapter 8, the contrast between Britain and Germany highlights that the activities of small business, the form of organisation which in most countries is viewed as emblematic of enterprise, is fashioned in an explicit manner which varies from context to context, giving rise to different forms of enterprise culture.

---

32. Bannock, G & H Albach, *Small Business Policy in Europe* a report for the Anglo-German Foundation (London: AGF) 1991.
33. *Ibid.*
34. Muzyka, D & H Breuninger, "Re-inventing Germany's Mittelstand" *Financial Times* (April 1997).

The 'Fully Enterprising' International Small Business

As well as impacting on the institutional and ethical dimensions of enterprise culture, the process of internationalisation also impacts on its growth dimension. Small business policies embody all three dimensions with a view to shaping and moulding the entrepreneurial activity of small business owners. Increasingly small companies are encouraged to involve themselves in international ventures as a means of growing the business. The increased internationalisation of the world economy means that small businesses cannot afford to ignore what is going on outside their own national boundaries. In addition, even if a small business trades solely on the domestic market and is not actively involved in international business, it will be involved in international competition either through involvement in subcontracting relationships or by directly competing against imports.[35]

Studies of the international activities of companies tend to focus on large organisations, with little attention being paid to the small business. However increasingly it is recognised that the potential to participate in international activities is not restricted to the large organisation. Small and medium-sized companies in Germany have a long history of participation in international markets, particularly through export activities, holding a 70-90 per cent share of world markets in the 1990s. For the first time in 1995, small business in America sent more exports abroad than large organisations.[36] In addition to exporting, small firms are increasingly involving themselves in foreign direct investment. According to Parker (1996), in 1992 small firm foreign direct investment activities accounted for US$43 billion or 7.5 per cent of foreign investments made by developed European countries. Similarly in Japan small firms accounted for US$40 billion or 15 per cent of foreign investments, with the figure being US$15 billion or 3 per cent in America. It would seem that nearly 28 per cent of American SMEs and 60 per cent of Japanese SMEs are involved in some form of direct investment abroad.

Conventional analyses of the internationalisation activities of firms tend to adopt a stage-model approach, presenting the internationalisation of companies as an evolutionary process. An example of this is Johanson and Wiedersheim-Paul's (1993) model based on a study of Swedish companies, which outlines four unique stages which firms pass through when undergoing the internationalisation process. These are:

- no regular export activities;
- export via independent representatives (agents);
- the setting up of a sales subsidiary abroad;

35. Holmlund, M & S Kock, "Relationships and the Internationalisation of Finnish Small and Medium-sized Companies" *International Small Business Journal* (1998) 16: 4, pp. 46-63.
36. Muzyka, D & H Breuninger, (1997) *op. cit.*; B Parker, (1996) *op. cit.*

• the setting up of a foreign production/manufacturing facility.

The Uppsala model presents internationalisation as an incremental process which relies on the slow build-up and integration of knowledge regarding foreign market characteristics, as well as a willingness to use firm resources in international markets. This model also suggests that companies will first enter those markets that are closest to the home market in terms of language, culture, business practice and industrial development. The aim of such an approach is to lower the risks and improve information flows between the company and the target market.[37] These approaches to understanding how companies internationalise have been heavily criticised, with a more recent criticism emerging from the identification of small firms referred to alternatively as 'Global Start-Ups, High Technology Start-Ups or International New Ventures. Such small firms are defined as those businesses which very quickly develop international operations, largely by exporting, after start-up.[38]

The growing prevalence of international activity on the part of small firms and the emphasis that is placed on it by government support agencies presents new organisational challenges for these businesses, particularly in terms of management. Significant success on an international scale requires the implementation of a highly complex and flexible management strategy, an area in which many small firms are weak. As with networking discussed in the previous chapter, government initiatives, which encourage the internationalisation of the small firm, contribute to the development and evolution of the entrepreneurial management discourse. Enterprising attributes, such as risk-taking, daring, creativity and flexibility, are required in abundance if a small firm is to successfully negotiate its way through international markets. Internationalising the activities of small firms also requires the development of additional management skills such as sensitivity to different cultures contributing to an ability to do business cross culturally. A major reason for failure on international markets on the part of small businesses is managerial behaviour.

The emergence of a highly internationalised world economy has contributed to the development of enterprise technologies which encourage small firms to internationalise their activities either through exporting or foreign direct investment. These technologies have the dimensions of enterprise culture 'written into' them and contribute to the materialisation of enterprise culture and the entrepreneurial management discourse connected to it. The form such technologies will take and the enterprise culture which they give rise to will vary across national contexts. However, as with networking discussed in Chapter 10, the emergence of enterprise initiatives and strategies

---

37. Gurau, C & A Ranchhod, "The 'Born Global' Firms in the UK Biotechnology Sector" *The British Academy of Management Conference* (Manchester) 1999.
38. *Ibid.*

which encourage internationalisation, indicate the fluidity and mobility of the procedures, disciplines and routines which contribute to the production of enterprise culture.

SUMMARY OF KEY IDEAS

- Currently it is fashionable to argue that we are living in a globalised world characterised by national borderlessness and emasculated national government.

- Research indicates however that though the world economy is currently highly internationalised, it is not yet globalised.

- The hyper-internationalisation of the world economy has not emasculated the nation state but has changed the mechanisms of economic co-ordination and regulation available to state officials and national institutions.

- Within this context, increased importance has been assigned to the role of government as a regulator of private individuals and organisations. Internationalisation strengthens the important role governments play in the governance of subjectivity, an activity at the centre of attempts to create an enterprise culture.

- The ability of the state to shape and fashion the activities of individuals and businesses in terms of an ethic of enterprise is reinforced by the increased internationalisation of the world economy. However the means by which a state promotes enterprise will vary from country to country.

- Different national contexts give rise to different cultural technologies which produce different cultural configurations of enterprise culture.

- Government initiatives which promote internationalisation contribute to the production and evolution of the entrepreneurial management discourse, particularly through the development of a management mindset which is sensitive to other cultures.

CHAPTER 12

The Future of Enterprise and Entrepreneurial Management

The neo-liberal homo economicus is both a reactivation and a radical inversion of the economic agent as conceived by the liberalism of Smith, Hume or Ferguson. The reactivation consists in positing a fundamental human faculty of choice...But the great departure here from eighteenth-century precedent is that, whereas homo economicus originally meant that subject the springs of whose activity must remain forever untouchable by government, the . . . neo-liberal homo economicus is manipulable man, man who is perpetually responsive to modifications in his environment.

(Gordon, 1991:43)

THE REALITY OF ENTERPRISE CULTURE

This book began by questioning two contemporary suggestions regarding the phenomenon of enterprise culture. Firstly, it queried the notion that enterprise culture has had no impact on economic life. In doing this, it challenged the proposition that enterprise culture has only acted as an ideological justification for a pre-given social context of extensive economic restructuring. Secondly, it contests the idea that we are now living in a post enterprise culture era. Starting from the position that a market order will not succeed unless there exists the sorts of individuals who can be trusted to behave in a way that the market order requires, this book calls into question the idea that enterprise culture has had no independent, concrete effect on the reality of economic life, by arguing that a notion of government should be incorporated into our understanding of enterprise culture. Government here can be understood as an ensemble of rationalities and technologies or representations and material practices. Rationalities or representations provide a way of discussing an issue as well a means for producing a certain kind of knowledge about that issue. They refer to changing vocabularies which give collective meaning to the standards and principles that describe the objectives of government. Technologies or material practices are the means by which the rationalities of government are made operable at the level of businesses and individuals.[1] They are a range of practices which are drawn upon to intervene and act upon individuals, processes and organisations (large and small, public and private) with a view to transforming them to achieve certain ends such as an enterprise economy. These practices or technologies do not just reflect a pre-given social world they actively fashion and mould the social reality and devise new ways for individuals to operate in the economy.[2] Thus, from this perspective, we have sought to demonstrate that the government objective of creating an enterprise culture is achieved through the establishment and implementation of a set of:

> . . . practices that affects the type of world we live in, the type of social reality we inhabit, the way in which we understand the choices open to business undertakings and individuals, the way in which we manage and organize activities and processes of diverse types, and the way in which we administer the lives of others and ourselves.

> (Miller, 1994:1)

Understanding enterprise culture in terms of a set of social and institutional practices, highlights how enterprise initiatives and policies can be conceptualised as devices which aim to act in a transformative manner upon individuals, their activities, and the organisations in which they are located. It also draws attention to the way in which the economic realm is created and recreated by the continually changing practices that provide us with a knowledge of it. The purpose of the technologies of enterprise culture is to give a material reality to the abstract images of enterprise, at the levels of organisations (large and small), departments and divisions within these organisations and individuals.[3] The creation and maintenance of an enterprise culture can be understood as a central and constitutive component of what Miller and Rose (1990) refer to as the government of economic life. Within contemporary liberal democracies the government of economic life refers to the means by which governments seek to mould and shape the conduct and behaviour of individuals through action at a distance.

---

1. Miller, P & T O'Leary, "Governing the calculable person" in A G Hopwood & P Miller (eds), *Accounting as social and institutional Practice* (Cambridge: Cambridge University Press) 1994; P Du Gay, G Salaman & B Rees, "The Conduct of Management and the Management of Conduct: Contemporary Managerial Discourse and the Constitution of the 'Competent' Manager', *Journal of Management Studies* (1996) 33: 3, pp. 263-282.
2. Du Gay, P, *Consumption and Identity at Work* (London: Sage) 1996.
3. Miller, P, "Accounting as Social and Institutional Practice: An Introduction" in A G Hopwood & P Miller (eds), (1994) *op. cit.*

The Enterprising Society and the Enterprising Individual

A key aim of government is the establishment of a reciprocal relationship between individuals, organisations and the state. Enterprise culture is a key means by which such reciprocity is established, contributing to the setting up of relays between entities located in different parts of the economy. Notions of enterprise present an image of a certain way of behaving and acting both in a personal and business context. The project of establishing an enterprise culture entails the ongoing development and implementation of a range of technologies which give life to abstract representations of enterprise. The key strands of enterprise culture discussed at length throughout the course of this book, i.e. an institutional strand which privileges the private sector commercial enterprise, and an ethical strand which promotes an ethic of enterprise can be understood as representations or rationalities of enterprise. These are given a material reality and linked to each other through a range of enterprise technologies including Privatisation, Entrepreneurial Governance and small business policies such as the Enterprise Allowance/Business Start-Up Scheme.

A key aim of such technologies is the application of an enterprise form to a range of organisations and individuals including hospitals, universities, government departments, voluntary organisations, businesses and individuals in their everyday existence.[4] However, the way in which enterprise manifests itself through these governmental techniques can be varied and uncertain, particularly in regard "to their consequences and the forms of action they make possible on the part of both government and the governed".[5] Nevertheless, despite the uncertainty and variability surrounding these governmental techniques, they do share a range of characteristics such as an emphasis on markets, contracts and non-bureaucratic forms of organisation.

The establishment of contract-like relations both within and between organisations as well between individuals and organisations, requires that an entity (organisation or individual) assumes active responsibility and is accountable for the efficient and dynamic running of a particular sphere of activity. In assuming such responsibility, they are expected to conduct themselves according to an ethic of enterprise, i.e. demonstrate initiative, daring, independence and self-reliance.[6] Acting in an enterprising manner within the context of an enterprising form of organisation is not something which can be taken for granted. Individuals and organisations must continually strive to

---

4.   Miller, P & N Rose, "Production, Identity and Democracy" *Theory and Society* (1995) 24, pp. 427-467.

5.   Burchell, G, "Liberal Government and the Techniques of the Self" in A Barry, T Osborne & N Rose (eds), *Foucault and Political Reason* (London: UCL Press) 1996, p. 29.

6.   *Ibid.*; P Du Gay, G Salaman & B Rees, (1996) *op. cit.*

be enterprising, with continual encouragement given to ensure that they are 'fully enterprising'. Enterprise technologies play a highly significant role in ensuring that a 'fully enterprising' status is continually sought after.

The Small Business in Enterprise Culture

In Chapter 6 we suggested that one fundamental attribute of enterprise culture is the shaping of the identity of individuals in terms of the small business owner, allied to the promotion of the small firm as the form of private sector organisation which is particularly nurturing of enterprise and entrepreneurship. A large number of small business initiatives and policies were implemented with the express aim of increasing the birth rate of small firms. Such enterprise technologies have aimed to shape and mould the formation of the small business and its owner. In particular small business owners have been encouraged to grow their business as a means of being 'fully enterprising'. High failure rates among small business start-ups have tended to move the policy support agenda towards growth companies. However, recent research has argued for a realignment of small business support towards new enterprises, thereby giving start-ups as much encouragement as growth firms.[7]

Despite arguments for a renewed emphasis on the start-up small business, allied to an increased recognition that staying small is a legitimate and valuable option for the small business, there is still a tendency to suggest as David Rae (1999:84) does, that "entrepreneurial behaviour is, fundamentally, about growing the business". In thinking about the future of small business and how enterprise technologies aim to shape the identity of individuals in terms of the small business, the growth strand of enterprise culture continues to illustrate a paradox between small and large. Thus, while large businesses are encouraged to introduce a small business ethic and small business management within their boundaries, small businesses are actively nurtured, through a range of enterprise technologies, to strive to become large organisations. In addition the 1990s have been characterised by:

> . . . the most extravagant take-over boom of all time. Last year (1997) the total changing hands in the global corporate reshuffle topped $2,400 billion or nearly £1,500 billion. Oil giant Exxon heads the pack with the largest successful bid, valued at £48 billion, for Mobil, bringing together organisations with 123,000 employees.
>
> (Buckingham & Cowe, 1999)

---

7. Gavron, R, M Cowling, G Holtham & A Westhall, *The Entrepreneurial Society* (London: Institute for Public Policy Research) 1998.

Other major takeovers include the takeover of Guinness by Grand Metro-
politan for a cost of £10 billion creating a hugely powerful, highly internationalised spirits and foods empire. Increasingly companies are merging with
their direct rivals creating a range of giant corporations. These include Daimler
Benz the German motor manufacturer with the American company Chrysler,
British Aerospace and GEC Marconi, Vodafone and Airtouch, BP and Amoco
and the pharmaceutical companies Zeneca and Astra.[8] This continuous 'urge
to merge' allied to the emphasis that is placed on the growing small business
despite the fact that the majority of small firms stay small, leads us to question the suggestion that the small firm (even if a member of a network such as
an industrial district) is the organisational unit of the future. Though certainly the creation of an enterprise culture in countries such as the UK has led
to the renaissance of the small business sector, it would appear that in material as well as abstract terms, a co-existence and interplay of large and small
is likely to continue into the future.

The Future of Enterprise and Entrepreneurial Management

A key suggestion arising out of the conceptualisation of enterprise culture
presented in this book, is that the creation and production of this phenomenon through the implementation of a range of enterprise technologies, has
led to the emergence of an entrepreneurial management discourse. The development of entrepreneurial management can be linked to the various dimensions of enterprise culture. Firstly, the institutional dimension which privileges the private sector organisation has contributed to a privileging of the
manager and management activities. In particular within the context of the
flexible private sector organisation, the role of management is significantly
enhanced. Throughout the 1980s in the UK, concern was expressed about
the state of British management and management education. It was argued
that attempts should be made to 'professionalise' British management, while
at the same time inculcating it with an enterprising value system.[9] The latter
is associated with the ethical dimension of enterprise culture which insists on
the need to manage in an active and entrepreneurial manner, with an open-
ness to using initiative, taking risks and involving oneself in daring activities. As Du Gay *et al.* (1996) argue, at the end of the 20th century managers
may be more important to the success of an organisation, but these managers
are not just expected to perform a range of discrete tasks, rather they are
supposed to possess and actively utilise a range of enterprising attributes
when managing.

The conventional approach taken to management and entrepreneurship is

---

8.   Buckingham, L & R Cowe, "Merger Mania – Coming to a Company Near You"
     The Guardian (January 1999).

to treat them as mutually exclusive entities. This approach very often translates into what Watson (1995) refers to as an 'evolutionist straitjacket' where it is suggested that at different stages of the development of a business, different skills and traits are required. Thus a business requires entrepreneurial skills at start-up and when it expands, and then requires management skills at its development stage. The suggestion is that businesses as they advance make a transition from an entrepreneurial phase to a management phase. In contrast what we have been suggesting is that the relationship between entrepreneurship and management should be understood as one of co-existence. Businesses and the individuals who work within them are encouraged to display a range of 'enterprising' qualities, such as self-reliance, a daring spirit, a risk-taking and proactive orientation, conceptual flexibility, and self-confidence, a range of characteristics which should be inherent to their management activity.

What is the future of this entrepreneurial management discourse? As with enterprise culture in general, the entrepreneurial management which it gave rise to is not just a passing fad. A continuing legacy of the creation of an enterprise culture in the 1980s is the notion of self-improvement. This has not only affected the UK but also plays a role in other Western societies. A notion of self-improvement implies that we are all entrepreneurs of our own lives, that we should be continuously employed in a process of self-advancement, involving ourselves in the preservation, reproduction and reconstruction of our own human capital.[10] A notion of continuous self-improvement deriving out of the ethic of enterprise has also entered into management, where managers are encouraged to become more autonomous, accountable selves. The future success of organisations appears to be increasingly based on managers' abilities to nurture their own personal (enterprising) attributes and those of their staff as the following management advertisements suggest.

---

9. Reed, M & P Anthony, "Professionalizing Management and Managing Professionalization: British Management in the 1980s" *Journal of Management Studies* (1992) 29: 5, pp. 591-613; P Du Gay, G Salaman & B Rees, (1996) *op. cit.*

10. Gordon, C, "Governmental Rationality: An Introduction" in G Burchell, C Gordon & P Miller (eds), *The Foucault Effect* (Hertfordshire: Harvester Wheatsheaf) 1991.

Contemporary Management Advertisements

Create an immediate impact
The number one company in its market, our client – a household name – is committed to excellence across all aspects of its business operations...To succeed in this highly commercial organisation you will need to call upon your proven management and motivational skills. In addition, you will have the determination to achieve outstanding results and have high personal expectations. This is an excellent opportunity for an individual seeking the scope and freedom to make their mark and provide imaginative solutions in a demanding environment.

Tackle the challenges of growth
Tenacious, resourceful and imaginative, your strength of character will have been developed in a hard working role within a distributed service business. A persuasive communicator, sensitive to culture, you are adept at juggling numerous issues whilst maintaining a clear set of priorities. Travel within the UK can be extensive.

(Watson & Harris, 1999:7-9)

In adopting the approach to the phenomenon of enterprise culture which is being suggested here, it is important to highlight that the development of an extensive range of technologies through which abstract notions of enterprise, entrepreneurship and entrepreneurial management are instrumentalised, is continually contested and constantly changing as the architects of enterprise adopt new practices.[11] As Miller and Rose (1990) argue, enterprise technologies very often produce unintended consequences, are utilised by individuals for their own ends, or do not have the resources attached to them to ensure successful implementation. Nevertheless, the impact these technologies have and the way in which they embed themselves in individuals and organisations should not be underestimated. Recognition that the shaping and moulding of individuals, managers and businesses in an enterprising manner is "not a hermetically sealed, unitary, and static"[12] process that can easily be stopped, signals to us that the suggestion that we abruptly entered into a post enterprise culture era with the demise of Margaret Thatcher in the early-1990s is misguided. The creation of an enterprise culture has led to a redefinition of the relationship between the public and private sectors, revitalised the small business sector and granted ontological priority to the entrepreneur. The governance and mobilisation of the subjectivity of individuals (both managers

---

11. Du Gay, P, G Salaman & B Rees, (1996) *op. cit.* Thrift, N, "Capitalism's Cultural Turn" in L Ray & A Sayer (eds), *Culture and Economy After the Cultural Turn* (London: Sage) 1999.
12. Thrift, N, (1999) *op. cit.*

and employees in a range of organisations) through notions of self-improvement, self-reliance and independence has been central to attempts to create an enterprise culture. Re-imagining or redefining the culture and practices of any organisation and the way individuals work within it in enterprise terms implies that that organisation and those individuals assume a new enterprise identity which cannot easily be "rolled back".[13]

---

13. Du Gay, P & G Salaman, "The Cult[ure] of the Customer" *Journal of Management Studies* (1992) 29: 5, pp. 615-633.

Bibliography

Abercrombie, N. 1991: 'The Privilege of the Producer'. In R. Keat & N. Abercrombie (eds.) *Enterprise Culture*. London: Routledge.

Allen, S. & Truman, C. 1993: 'Women and men entrepreneurs: Life strategies, business strategies'. In S. Allen & C. Truman (eds.), *Women in Business: Perspectives on women entrepreneurs*. London: Routledge 1993.

Armington, C. & Odel, M. 1982: 'Small Business - How Many Jobs?' in *The Brookings Review,* Winter, pp. 14-17.

Bach, S. & Winchester, D. 1994: 'Opting Out of Pay Devolution? The Prospects for Local Pay Bargaining in UK Public Services', *British Journal of Industrial Relations,* 32: 2, pp. 263-282.

Badaracco, J.L. 1988: 'Changing Forms of the Corporation', in J.R. Meyer & J.M. Gustafson (eds.), *The U.S. Business Corporation: An Institution in Transition.* Cambridge MA; Ballinger.

Bannock, G. & Albach, H. 1991: *Small Business Policy in Europe.* Report for the Anglo-German Foundation. London: AGF.

Bauman, Z. 1995: *Life in Fragments.* Oxford: Blackwell Publishers.

Bennett, T. 1992: 'Putting Policy into Cultural Studies'. In L. Crossberg, C. Nelson, P. Treichler (eds.), *Cultural Studies.* London: Routledge.

Bennett, T. 1992a: 'Useful Culture', *Cultural Studies,* 6: 3, pp. 395-408.

Bennett, T. 1998: *Culture: A Reformer's Science.* London: Sage.

Binns, J. & Kirkham, J. 1997: 'Do Personal Business Advisors Add Value'. Paper presented at the ISBA National Small Firms Policy & Research Conference, Belfast.

Birch, D. 1981: 'Who creates jobs?' in *The Public Interest,* 65, pp. 3-14.

Blackburst, C. 1998: 'At the Court of King Richard'. *Management Today,* April, pp. 39-44.

Blackburn, R., Curran, J. & Woods, A. 1992: 'Exploring Enterprise Cultures: Small service sector enterprise owners and their views'. In M. Robertson, E. Chell & C. Mason (eds.), *Towards the Twenty-First Century: The Challenge for Small Business.* Cheshire: Nadamal Books.

Bosanquet, N. & Salisbury, C. 1998: 'The Practice'. In I. Loudon, J. Horder & C. Webster (eds.) *General Practice Under the National Health Service 1948-1997.* London: Clarendon Press.

Bridge, S., O'Neill K. & Cromie, S. 1998: *Understanding Enterprise, Entrepreneurship and Small Business.* London: Macmillan Business.

Bright, M. & Wintour, P. 1998: 'I'm going to teach them my three R's', *The Observer,* 29 November.

Brusco, S. 1982: 'The Emilian model: productive decentralisation and social integration', *Cambridge Journal of Economics,* 6, pp. 167-184.

Brusco, S. 1986: 'Small firms and industrial districts: The experience of Italy'. In D. Keeble & E. Weaver (eds.) *New firms and regional development in Europe.* London: Croom Helm.

Buckingham, L. & Cowe, R. 1999: 'Merger mania - coming to a company near you', *The Guardian,* January.

Burchell, G. 1996: 'Liberal government and techniques of the self'. In A. Barry, T. Osborne & N. Rose (eds.) *Foucault and Political Reason.* London: UCL Press.

Burrows, R. 1991: 'The discourse of the enterprise culture and the restructuring of Britain: A polemical contribution'. In J. Curran & R. Blackburn (eds.) *Paths of Enterprise: The Future of Small Business.* London: Routledge.

Burrows, R. 1991a: 'Introduction: entrepreneurship, petty capitalism and the restructuring of Britain'. In R. Burrows (ed.) *Deciphering the Enterprise Culture.* London: Routledge.

Burrows, R. & Curran, J. 1991: 'Not Such a Small Business: Reflections on the Rhetoric, the Reality and the Future of the Enterprise Culture'. In M. Cross & G. Payne (eds.) *Work and Enterprise Culture.* Basingstoke: The Falmer Press.

Burrows, R. & Ford, J. 1998: 'Self-Employment and Home Ownership After the Enterprise Culture', *Work, Employment and Society,* 12: 1, pp. 97-119.

Burton, J. 1983: *Picking Losers....?* London: Institute of Economic Affairs.

Callon, M. 1999: 'Actor-network theory-the market test'. In J. Law & J. Hassard (eds.), *Actor Network Theory and after.* Oxford: Blackwell Publishers.

Campanella, M.L. 1995: 'The effects of globalization and turbulence on policy-making processes'. In J. Drew (ed.), *Readings in International Enterprise.* London: Routledge.

Campbell, M. & Daly, M. 1992: 'Self-employment: into the 1990s', *Employment Gazette,* June, pp. 269-291.

Carey, B. 1997: 'Riding the Celtic tiger comes easily to IDA's magnet for industrial investors', *The Sunday Business Post,* 9 March.

Carland, J.W., Hoy, F., Boulton, W.R. & Carland, J.A. 1984: 'Differentiating Entrepreneurs from Small Business Owners: A Conceptualization', *Academy of Management Review,* 9: 2, pp. 354-359.

Carr, P. 1995: Book review on *Privatization and Popular Capitalism* (1994) by P. Saunders & C. Harris. In *Sociology,* 29: 4, pp. 755-756.

Carr, P. 1996: 'Reconceptualising Enterprise Culture'. *The Conference of the British Sociological Association,* University of Reading.

Carr, P. 1996a 'Reconceptualising Enterprise Culture'. Unpublished PhD thesis, Trinity College, Dublin.

Carr, P. 1998: 'The Cultural Production of Enterprise: Understanding Selectivity as Cultural Policy'. *Economic and Social Review,* 29: 2: pp. 27-49

Castells, M. 1996: *The Rise of the Network Society.* Oxford: Blackwell Publishers.

Caulkin, S. 1999: 'Work: a glass ceiling made of lead', *The Observer,* 3 January.

Chandler, A. 1990: 'The Enduring Logic of Industrial Success', *Harvard Business Review,* March-April, pp. 130-140.

Chia, R. 1996: 'Teaching Paradigm Shifting in Management Education: University Business Schools and the Entrepreneurial Imagination', *Journal of Management Studies,* 33: 4, pp. 409-428.

Clarke, J. & Newman, J. 1993: 'The Right to Manage: A Second Managerial Revolution?', *Cultural Studies,* 7: 3, pp. 427-441.

Clarke, J. & Newman, J. 1997: *The Managerial State.* London: Sage.

Cohen, A.P. 1992: 'The personal right to identity: a polemic on the self in the enterprise culture'. In P. Heelas & P. Morris (eds.), *The Values of the Enterprise Culture.* London: Routledge.

Cohen, S.S. & Zysman, J. 1987: *Manufacturing Matters: The Myth of the Post-Industrial Economy.* Basic Books: New York.

Collinson, D. & Hearn, J. 1994: 'Naming Men as Men: Implications for Work Organization and Management', *Gender, Work and Organization,* 1: 1, pp. 2-22.

Collinson, D. & Hearn, J. 1996: 'Breaking the Silence: On Men, Masculinities and Managements'. In D. Collinson & J. Hearn (eds.) *Men as Managers, Managers as Men.* London: Sage.

Cromie, S. & Hayes, J. 1988: 'Towards a typology of female entrepreneurs', *The Sociological Review,* 36: 1, pp. 87-109.

Culliton Report: 1992: *A Time for Change: Industrial Policy for the 1990s.* Dublin: Stationery Office.

Cunningham, J.B. & Lischeron, J. 1991: 'Defining Entrepreneurship', *Journal of Small Business Management,* 25: 1, pp. 45-61.

Curran, J. 1997: 'The Role of the Small Firm in the UK Economy', unpublished paper.

Daly, M. 1991: 'The 1980s - A Decade of Growth in Enterprise', *Employment Gazette,* March, pp. 109-134.

Daly, M. & McCann, A. 1992: 'How many small firms?', *Employment Gazette,* February, pp. 47-51.

Davies, A. & Kirkpatrick, I. 1995: 'Performance indicators, bureaucratic control and the decline of professional autonomy: the case of academic librarians'. In I. Kirkpatrick & M. Martinez Lucio (eds.)*The Politics of Quality in the Public Sector.* London: Routledge.

Davis, S.J., Haltiwanger, J. & Schuh, S. 1993: 'Small Business and Job Creation: Dissecting the Myth and Reassessing the Facts', Working Paper No. 4492, Boston, National Bureau of Economic Research.

Deakins, D. 1996: *Entrepreneurship and Small Firms.* Berkshire: McGraw-Hill.

Deakins, D. 1999: *Entrepreneurship and Small Firms,* Second Edition. Berkshire: McGraw-Hill.

Deal, T. & Kennedy, A. 1982: *Corporate Cultures: The Rites and Rituals of Corporate Life.* New York: Addison-Wesley.

Dean, M. 1992: 'A genealogy of the government of poverty', *Economy and Society,* 21: 3, pp. 215-247.

Dean, M. 1994: *Critical and Effective Histories: Foucault's Methods and historical Sociology.* London: Routledge.

Dean, M. 1995: 'Governing the unemployed self in an active society', *Economy and Society,* 24: 4, pp. 559-583.

Dean, M. 1996: 'Foucault, government and the enfolding of authority'. In A. Barry, T. Osborne & N. Rose, *Foucault and Political Reason: Liberalism, neo-liberalism and rationalities of government.* London: UCL Press.

Department of Industry and Commerce, 1990: *Review of Industrial Performance 1990.* Dublin: Stationery Office.

Dicken, P, 1992: *Global Shift: the internationalization of economic activity,* second edition. London: Paul Chapman Publishing.

Drucker, P. 1985: *Innovation and Entrepreneurship.* London: William Heinemann.

Drudy, P.J. 1995: 'From Protectionism to Enterprise: A Review of Irish Industrial Policy'. In A. Burke (ed.) *Enterprise and the Irish Economy.* Dublin: Oaktree Press.

Dubois, P. 1996: 'Economic Sociology and Institutionalist Economics in France: A Trend to Convergence', *Work, Employment and Society,* 10: 2, pp. 361-376.

Du Gay, P. 1991: 'Enterprise Culture and the Ideology of Excellence'. *New Formations,* 13, pp. 45-61

Du Gay, P. 1993: 'Entrepreneurial Management in the Public Sector', *Work, Employment and Society,* 7: 4, pp. 643-648.

Du Gay, P. & Salaman, G. 1992: 'The Cult[ure] of the Customer', *Journal of Management Studies,* 29: 5, pp. 615-633.

Du Gay, P. 1996: *Consumption and Identity at Work.* London: Sage.

Du Gay, P. 1996a: 'Making Up Managers: Enterprise and the Ethos of Bureaucracy'. In S. Clegg & G. Palmer (eds.), *The Politics of Management Knowledge.* London: Sage.

Du Gay, P., Salaman, G., & Rees, B. 1996: 'The Conduct of Management and the Management of Conduct: Contemporary Managerial Discourse and the Constitution of the "Competent" Manager', *Journal of Management Studies,* 33: 3, pp. 263-282.

Du Gay, P. 1997: 'Organizing Identity: Making Up People at Work'. In P. Du

Gay (ed.) *Production of Culture/Cultures of Production.* London: Sage.

Dumez, H. & Jeunemaitre, A. 1994: 'Privatization in France: 1983-1993'. In V. Wright (ed.) *Privatization in Western Europe: Pressures, Problems and Paradoxes.* London: Pinter Publishers.

Featherstone, M. 1995: *Undoing Culture.* London: Sage.

Flynn, N. 1994: 'Control, Commitment and Contracts'. In J. Clarke, A. Cochrane & E. McLaughlin (eds.) *Managing Social Policy.* London: Sage.

Forfas 1996: *Shaping Our Future.* Dublin: Stationery Office.

Foucault, M. 1982: 'The Subject and Powers'. In H. Dreyfus and P. Rabinow, *Michel Foucault: Beyond Structuralism and Hermeneutics.* Chicago: The University of Chicago Press.

Foucault, M. 1988: 'Technologies of the Self'. In L.H. Martin, H. Gutman & P.H. Hutton (eds.), *Technologies of the Self: A Seminar with Michel Foucault.* London: Tavistock Publications.

Foucault, M. 1991: 'Governmentality'. In G. Burchell, C. Gordon and P. Miller (eds.) *The Foucault Effect: Studies in Governmentality.* London: Harvester Wheatsheaf.

Freel, M.S. 1997: 'Towards an Evolutionary Theory of Small Firm Growth'. Paper presented at the ISBA National Small Firms Policy & Research Conference, Belfast.

Fuller, L. & Smith, V. 1991: 'Consumers' Reports: Management by Customers in a Changing Economy', *Work, Employment and Society,* 5: 1, pp. 1-16.

Gamble, A. 1994: *The Free Economy and the Strong State.* Second Edition. London: The Macmillan Press.

Gamble, A. 1996: *Hayek: The Iron Cage of Liberty.* Cambridge: Polity Press.

Gavron, R., Cowling, M., Holtham, G., & Westall, A. 1998: *The Entrepreneurial Society.* London: Institute for Public Policy Research.

Gerth,H.H. & Wright Mills, C. 1948 & 1970: *From Max Weber.* London: Routledge.

Gibb, A. 1987: 'Enterprise Culture - Its Meaning and Implications for Education and Training'. *Journal of European Industrial Training,* 11: 2, pp. 3-38.

Gibb, A. 1996: 'Entrepreneurship and Small Business Management: Can We Afford to Neglect Them in the Twenty-first Century Business School?'. *British Journal of Management,* 7, pp. 309-321.

Giddens, A. 1991: *The Consequences of Modernity.* Cambridge: Polity Press.

Goffee, R. & Scase, R. 1983: 'Business ownership and women's subordination: a preliminary study of female proprietors', *The Sociological Review,* 31: 1, pp. 625-648.

Goffee, R. & Scase, R. 1985: *Women in Charge.* London: Allen & Unwin.

Gordon, C. 1987: 'The Soul of the Citizen: Max Weber and Michel Foucault on Rationality and Government'. In S. Lash & S. Whimster (eds.), *Max Weber, Rationality and Modernity.* London: Allen & Unwin.

Gordon, C. 1991: 'Governmental rationality: an introduction'. In G. Burchell, C. Gordon & P. Miller (eds.) *The Foucault Effect*. Hertfordshire: Harvester Wheatsheaf.

Goss, D. 1991: *Small Business and Society*. London: Routledge.

Grandori, A. & Soda, G. 1995: 'Inter-firm Networks: Antecedents, Mechanisms and Forms', *Organization Studies,* 16: 2, pp. 183-214.

Granovetter, M. 1985: 'Economic Action and Social Structure: The Problem of Embeddedness', *American Journal of Sociology,* 91: 3, pp. 181-510.

Gray, C. 1998: *Enterprise and Culture*. London: Routledge.

Green, S. 1995: 'Organisational Culture, Strategic Change and Symbolism'. In B. Leavy and J.S. Walsh (eds.) *Strategy and General Management*. Dublin: Oak Tree Press.

Greenwood, J. & Wilson, D. 1989: *Public Administration in Britain Today*. London: Unwin Hyman.

Grint, K. & Case, P. 1998: 'The Violent Rhetoric of Re-Engineering: Management Consultancy on the Offensive', *Journal of Management Studies,* 35: 5, pp. 557-577.

Guest, D., 1990: 'Human Resource Management and The American Dream', *Journal of Management Studies,* 27: 4, pp. 377-397.

Gurau, C. & Ranchhod, A. 1999: 'The "Born Global" Firms in the UK Biotechnology Sector', *The British Academy of Management Conference,* Manchester.

Habermas, J. 1976: *Legitimation Crisis*. London: Heinemann.

Hacking, I. 1986: 'Making Up People'. In T.C. Heller, M. Sosna & D.E. Wellbery (eds.) *Reconstructing Individualism*. California: Stanford University Press.

Hakim, C. 1988: 'Self-Employment in Britain: Recent Trends and Current Issues', *Work, Employment & Society,* 2: 4, pp. 421-450.

Hakim, C. 1989: 'Identifying Fast-Growth Small Firms', *Employment Gazette,* 9: 1, pp. 29-41.

Hakim, C. 1989/90: 'Workforce restructuring in Europe in the 1980s' in *The International Journal of Comparative Labour Law and Industrial Relations,* 5: 4, pp. 167-203.

Halford, S. & Savage, M. 1995: 'The Bureaucratic Career: Demise or Adaptation?'. In T. Butler & M. Savage (eds.) *Social Change and the Middle Classes*. London: UCL Press.

Halford, S. & Savage, M. 1995: 'Restructuring Organisations, Changing People: Gender and Restructuring in Banking and Local Government', *Work, Employment and Society,* 9: 1, pp. 97-122.

Hall, S. 1988: *The Hard Road to Renewal*. London: Verso.

Hall, S. 1997: 'The Work of Representation'. In S. Hall (ed.), *Representation: Cultural Representations and Signifying Practices*. London: Sage.

Halsey, A.H. 1988: 'A Sociologist's View of Thatcherism'. In R. Skidelsky (ed.), *Thatcherism.* Oxford: Basil Blackwell.

Hanlon, G. 1998: 'Professionalism as Enterprise: Service Class Politics and the Redefinition of Professionalism', *Sociology,* 32: 1, pp. 43-63.

Harris, M. 1998: 'Rethinking the Virtual Organisation'. In P. Jackson & J. M. Van der Wielen (eds.) *Teleworking: International Perspectives.* London: Routledge.

Harrison, B. & Kelley, M.R. 1993: 'Outsourcing and the Search for Flexibility', *Work, Employment and Society,* 7: 2, pp. 213-235.

Harvey, D. 1990: *The Condition of Postmodernity.* Oxford: Basil Blackwell.

Hebdige, D. 1979: *Subculture: the meaning of style.* London: Routledge.

Heelas, P. 1991: 'Reforming the Self: Enterprise and the Characteris of Thatcherism'. In R. Keat & N. Abercrombie (eds.) *Enterprise Culture.* London: Routledge.

Hennis, W. 1983: 'Max Weber's Central Question', *Economy and Society,* 12: 2, pp. 135-80.

Hill, S. 1991: 'How do you manage a flexible firm? The Total Quality model', *Work, Employment and Society,* 5: 3, pp. 397-415.

Hirst, P. & Thompson, G. 1992: 'The problem of 'globalization': international economic relations, national economic management and the formation of trading blocs', *Economy and Society,* 21: 4, pp. 357-396.

Hirst, P. & Thompson, G. 1994: 'Globalisation, foreign direct investment and international economic governance', *Organisation,* 1: 2, pp. 277-303.

Hirst, P. & Thompson, G. 1995: 'Globalization and the future of the nation state', *Economy and Society,* 24: 3, pp. 408-442.

Hirst, P. & Thompson, G. 1996: *Globalization in Question.* Cambridge: Polity Press.

Holmlund, M. & Kock, S. 1998: 'Relationships and the Internationalisation of Finnish Small and Medium-sized Companies', *International Small Business Journal,* 16: 4, pp. 46-63.

Howard, R. 1990: 'Can Small Business Help Countries Compete?', *Harvard Business Review,* November-December, pp. 88-103.

Industrial Policy, 1984: *Government White Paper.* Dublin: Stationery Office.

Industrial Policy, 1993: *Employment Through Enterprise: The Response of the Government to the Moriarty Task Force on the Implementation of the Culliton Report.* Dublin: Stationery Office.

Invernizzi, B. & Revelli, R. 1993: 'Small firms and the Italian economy: structural changes and evidence of turbulence'. In Z.J. Acs & D.B. Audretsch (eds.), *Small Firms and Entrepreneurship.* Cambridge MA: Cambridge University Press.

Jacques, E. 1990: 'In Praise of Hierarchy', *Harvard Business Review,* Jan-Feb.

Jessop, B. 1994: 'The transition to post-Fordism and the Schumpeterian workfare state'. In R. Burrows & B. Loader (eds.) *Towards a Post-Fordist*

Welfare State? London: Routledge.

Johnson, S. 1990: 'Small Firms Policy: An Agenda for the 1990s'. Paper presented to the National Small Firms Policy and Research Conference, Harrogate.

Johnson, S. & Storey, D.J. 1993: 'Male and female entrepreneurs and their businesses: A comparative study'. In S. Allen & C. Truman (eds.), *Women in Business: Perspectives on Women Entrepreneurs.* London: Routledge.

Kanter, R.M. 1989: *When Giants Learn to Dance: Mastering the Challenges of Strategy, Management and Careers in the 1990s.* New York: Simon & Schuster.

Kanter, R.M. 1991: 'The Future of Bureaucracy and Hierarchy in Organizational Theory: A Report from the Field'. In P. Bourdieu & J.S. Coleman (eds.) *Social Theory for a Changing Society.* Colorado: Westview Press.

Keat, R. 1991: 'Introduction'. In R. Keat and N. Abercrombie (eds.), *Enterprise Culture.* London: Routledge.

Kelly, A. 1991: 'The enterprise culture and the welfare state: restructuring the management of health and personal social services'. In R. Burrows (ed.) *Deciphering the Enterprise Culture.* London: Routledge.

Kerfoot, D. & Knights, D. 1993: 'Management, Masculinity and Manipulation: From Paternalism to Corporate Strategy in Financial Services in Britain', *Journal of Management Studies,* 30: 4, pp. 659-677.

Kinsella, R., Clarke, W., Storey, D.J., Mulvenna, D. & Coyne, D. 1994: *Fast-Growth Small Firms: An Irish Perspective.* Dublin: Irish Management Institute.

Kirkpatrick, I. & Martinez Lucio, M. 1995: 'The use of 'quality' in the British government's reform of the public sector'. In I. Kirkpatrick & M. Martinez Lucio (eds.) *The Politics of Quality in the Public Sector.* London: Routledge.

Koper, G. 1993: 'Women entrepreneurs and the granting of business credit'. In S. Allen & C. Truman (eds.), *Women in Business: Perspectives on women entrepreneurs.* London: Routledge.

Lane, C. 1989: *Management and Labour in Europe.* Aldershot: Edward Elgar.

Lane, C. 1992: 'Industrial structure and performance: common challenges - diverse experiences'. In J. Bailey (ed.) *Social Europe.* Essex: Longman Group UK Ltd.

Lane, C. 1992a: 'European Business Systems: Britain and Germany Compared'. In R. Whitley (ed.), *European Business Systems: Firms and Markets in their National Contexts.* London: Sage.

Lane, C. 1995: *Industry and Society in Europe: Stability and Change in Britain, Germany and France.* Aldershot: Edward Elgar.

Lawton, A. & Rose, A. 1992: *Organisation and Management in the Public Sector.* London: Pitman Publishing.

Lean, J., Down, S. & Sadler-Smith, E. 1997: 'An Examination of the Developing Role of PBAs Within Business Link'. Paper presented at the ISBA

National Small Firms Policy & Research Conference, Belfast.

Legge, K. 1989: 'Human resource management: a critical analysis'. In J. Storey (ed.), *New Perspectives in Human Resource Management.* London: Routledge.

Leonard, M. 1999: 'New Europeans', *The Guardian,* 4 September.

Loscocco, K.A., Robinson, J., Hall, R.H. & Allen, J.K. 1991: 'Gender and Small Business Success: An Inquiry into Women's Relative Disadvantage', *Social Forces,* 70: 1, pp. 65-85.

Lynch, K. 1992: 'Education and the Paid Labour Market', *Irish Education Studies,* 11, pp. 13-33.

MacDonald, R. & Coffield, F. 1991: *Risky Business? Youth and the Enterprise Culture.* London: The Falmer Press.

Marquand, D. 1988: 'The Paradoxes of Thatcherism'. In R. Skidelsky (ed.) *Thatcherism.* Oxford: Basil Blackwell.

Marquand, D. 1992: 'The enterprise culture: old wine in new bottles?' In P. Heelas & P. Morris (eds.), *The Values of the Enterprise Culture.* London: Routledge.

Marsden, D. & Richardson, R. 1994: 'Performing for Pay? The Effects of "Merit Pay" on Motivation in a Public Service', *British Journal of Industrial Relations,* 32: 2, pp. 243-261.

Martin, J. & Frost, P. 1996: 'The Organizational Culture War Games: A Struggle for Intellectual Dominance'. In Clegg, S., Hardy, C. & Nord, W. (eds.) *Handbook of Organization Studies.* London: Sage.

Marx, K. & Engels, F. (1888) 1985: *The Communist Manifesto.* London: Penguin Classics.

McGuigan, J. 1996: *Culture and the Public Sphere.* London: Routledge.

McKechnie, S.A., Ennew, C.T. & Read, L.T. 1998: 'The Nature of the Banking Relationship: A Comparison of the Experiences of Male and Female Small Business Owners', *International Small Business Journal,* 16: 3, pp. 39-55.

McLoughlin, R.J. 1972: 'The Industrial Development Process: An Overall view', *Administration,* 20: 1, pp. 27-38.

McNay, L. 1994: *Foucault: A Critical Introduction.* Cambridge: Polity Press.

Miller, P. 1998: 'The Margins of Accounting'. In M. Callon (ed.), *The Laws of the Markets.* Oxford: Blackwell Publishers.

Miller, P. 1994: 'Accounting as social and institutional practice: an introduction'. In A.G. Hopwood & P. Miller (eds.), *Accounting as social and institutional practice.* Cambridge: Cambridge University Press.

Miller, P. & O'Leary, T. 1994: 'Governing the calculable person'. In A.G. Hopwood & P. Miller (eds.), op. cit.

Miller, P. & Rose, N. 1990: 'Governing economic life', *Economy and Society,* 19: 1, pp. 1-31.

Miller, P. & Rose, N. 1995: 'Production, identity and democracy', *Theory and Society,* 24, pp. 427-467.

Mitchell, J. 1990: 'Britain: Privatisation as Myth?'. In J. Richardson (ed.) *Privatisation and Deregulation in Canada and Britain.* Aldershot: Dartmouth Publishing.

Morgan, G. 1997: *Images of Organisations.* California: Sage.

Moriarty Task Force Report, 1992. Dublin: Stationery Office.

Morris, P. 1991: 'Freeing the Spirit of Enterprise: The Genesis and Development of the Concept of Enterprise Culture'. In R.Keat and N. Abercrombie (eds.), *Enterprise Culture.* London: Routledge.

Mulcahy, A. 1997: 'Irish Indigenous SME's Co-operating to Compete: A Short Run or Long Run Phenomenon', Unpublished dissertation, Department of Management and Marketing, University College Cork.

Mulholland, K. 1996: 'Entrepreneurialism, Masculinities and the Self-Made Man'. In D. Collinson & J. Hearn (eds.), *Men as Managers, Managers as Men.* London: Sage.

Murphy, C. 1993: 'IDA is Dead, Long Live IDA', *The Sunday Tribune,* 18 July.

Muzyka, D. & Breuninger, H. 1997: 'Reinventing Germany's Mittelstand', *Financial Times,* April.

NESC, 1984: *The Role of the Financial System in Financing the Traded Sectors.* Dublin: NESC Report, No. 76.

Newman, J. & Clarke, J. 1994: 'Going about Our Business? The Managerialization of Public Services'. In J. Clarke, A. Cochrane & E. McLaughlin (eds.) *Managing Social Policy.* London: Sage.

Nixon, S. 1997: 'Exhibiting Masculinity'. In S. Hall (ed.), *Representation: Cultural Representations and Signifying Practices.* London: Sage.

Nohria, N. 1992: 'Is a Network Perspective a Useful Way of Studying Organizations?'. In N. Nohria & R.G. Eccles (eds.), *Networks and Organizations: Structure, Form and Action.* Boston: Harvard Business School Press.

Offe, C. 1984: 'Ungovernability: On the Renaissance of Conservative Theories of Crisis'. In J. Habermas (ed.) *Observations on the Spiritual Situation of the Age.* Cambridge: MIT Press.

Osborne, D. & Gaebler, T. 1992: *Reinventing Government.* Reading MA: Addison-Wesley.

Palmer, I. & Dunford, R. 1996: 'Interrogating Reframing: Evaluating Metaphor-based Analyses of Organizations'. In S. Clegg & G. Palmer (eds.) *The Politics of Management Knowledge.* London: Sage.

Parker, B. 1996: 'Evolution and Revolution: from International Business to Globalization'. In S.R. Clegg, C. Hardy & W.R. Nord (eds.), *Handbook of Organization Studies.* London: Sage.

Perrow, C. 1992: 'Small-Firm Networks'. In N. Nohria & R.G. Eccles (eds.), *Networks and Organizations: Structure, Form and Action.* Boston: Harvard Business School Press.

Peters, T. & Waterman, R.H. 1982: *In Search of Excellence.* New York: Harper

& Row.

Peters, T. 1987: *Thriving on Chaos.* Basingstoke: Macmillan.

Peters, T. 1992: *Liberation Management.* Basingstoke: Macmillan.

Philp, N.E., 1998: 'The Export Propensity of the Very Small Enterprise (VSE), *International Small Business Journal,* 16: 4, pp. 79-93.

Pierson, C. 1996: *The Modern State.* London: Routledge.

Pitt, D. 1990: 'An essentially contestable organisation; British Telecom and the privatisation debate', in J. J. Richardson (ed.) *Privatisation and Deregulation in Canada and Britain.* Aldershot: Dartmouth Publishing Company.

Pollitt, C. 1993: *Managerialism and the Public Services,* Second Edition. Oxford: Blackwell Publishers.

Powell, W.W. 1990: 'Neither Market nor Hierarchy: Network Forms of Organization', *Research in Organizational Behavior,* 12, pp. 295-336.

Pratt, A. 1990: 'Enterprise Culture: Rhetoric or Reality - The Case of Small Firms and Rural Localities'. In P. Lowe et al (eds.), *Petit Capitalism in Rural Areas: East-West Perspecives.* London: David Fulton.

Pyke, F. 1988: 'Co-Operative Practices Among Small and Medium-Sized Establishments', *Work, Employment and Society,* 2: 3, pp. 352-365.

Rae, D. 1999: *The Entrepreneurial Spirit.* Dublin: Blackhall Publishing.

Ray, C. A. 1986: 'Corporate Culture: The Last Frontier of Control?'. *Journal of Management Studies,* 23: 3, pp. 287-297

Rainnie, A. 1985: 'Small firms, big problems: the political economy of small businesses'. *Capital and Class,* 25, pp. 140-168.

Rainnie, A. 1991: 'Small firms: between the enterprise culture and 'New Times''. In R. Burrows (ed.) *Deciphering the Enterprise Culture.* London: Routledge.

Rainnie, A. 1991: 'Just-In-Time, Sub-Contracting and the Small Firm', *Work, Employment and Society,* 5: 3, pp. 353-375.

Reed, M. & Anthony, P. 1992: 'Professionalizing Management and Managing Professionalization: British Management in the 1980s', *Journal of Management Studies,* 29: 5, pp. 591-613.

Reed, M. 1995: 'Managing quality and organizational politics: TQM as a governmental technology'. In I. Kirkpatrick & M. Martinez Lucio (eds.) *The Politics of Quality in the Public Sector.* London: Routledge.

Reed, R. 1996: 'Entrepreneurialism and Paternalism in Australian Management: A Gender Critique of the "Self-Made" Man'. In D. Collinson & J. Hearn (eds.), *Men as Managers, Managers as Men.* London: Sage.

Rees, T. 1992: *Women and the Labour Market.* London: Routledge.

Richardson, J. 1994: 'The politics and practice of privatization in Britain'. In V. Wright (ed.) *Privatization in Western Europe: Pressures, Problems and Paradoxes.* London: Pinter Publishers.

Ritchie, J. 1991: 'Enterprise cultures: a frame analysis'. In R. Burrows (ed.) *Deciphering the Enterprise Culture.* London: Routledge.

Rosa, P., Hamilton, D., Carter, S. & Burns, H. 1994: 'The Impact of Gender on Small Business Management: Preliminary Findings of a British Study', *International Small Business Journal,* 12: 3, pp. 25-32.

Rose, N. 1989: *Governing the Soul: The Shaping of the Private Self.* London: Routledge.

Rose, N. 1992: 'Governing the enterprising self'. In P. Heelas & P. Morris (eds.) *The Values of the Enterprise Culture: The Moral Debate.* London: Routledge.

Rose, N. & Miller, P. 1992: 'Political power beyond the State: problematics of government', *British Journal of Sociology,* 43: 2, pp. 173-205.

Rose, N. 1993: 'Government, authority and expertise in advanced liberalism', *Economy and Society,* 22: 3, pp. 283-299.

Rose, N. 1996: 'Governing "advanced" liberal democracies', in A. Barry, T. Osborne & N. Rose (eds.), *Foucault and Political Reason: Liberalism, Neo-liberalism and Rationalities of Government.* London: UCL Press.

Rossman, M.L. 1990: *The International Businesswoman of the 1990s: A Guide to Success in the Global Marketplace.* New York: Basic Books.

Rustin, M. 1994: 'Unfinished Business: FromThatcherite Modernisation to Incomplete Modernity'. In M. Perryman (ed.) *From Altered States: Postmodernism, Politics, Culture.* London: Lawrence & Wishart.

Salaman, G. 1997: 'Culturing Production'. In P. Du Gay (ed.) *Production of Culture/Cultures of Production.* London: Sage.

Samson, C. 1994: 'The Three Faces of Privatisation'. *Sociology,* 28: 1, pp.79-97.

Samuels, J.M. & Morrish, P.A. 1984: 'An Analysis of Concentration'. In C. Levicki (ed.), *Small Business: Theory and Policy.* Beckenham: Croom Helm.

Saunders, P. & Harris, C. 1994: *Privatization and Popular Capitalism.* Buckingham: Open University Press.

Schumpeter, J.A. (1943) 1976: *Capitalism, Socialism and Democracy,* fifth edition. London: Allen & Unwin.

Sengenberger, W. & Pyke F. 1992: 'Industrial districts and local economic regeneration: Research and policy issues'. In F. Pyke & W. Sengenberger (eds.), *Industrial Districts and Local Economic Regeneration.* Geneva: International Institute for Labour Studies.

Smith Ring, P. & Van de Ven, A.H. 1992: 'Structuring Cooperative Relationships Between Organizations', *Strategic Management Journal,* 13, pp. 483-498.

Spekman, R.E., Forbes, T.M., Isabella, L.A. & MacAvoy, T.C. 1998: 'Alliance Management: A View From the Past and a Look to the Future', *Journal of Management Studies,* 35: 6, pp. 747-772.

Stephens, M. 1989: 'She's the boss', *Employment Gazette,* October, pp. 529-533.

Storey, D.J. 1993: 'Should We Abandon Support to Start-Up Businesses?'.

In F. Chittenden, M. Robertson & D. Watkins (eds.) *Small Firms: Recession and Recovery.* London: Paul Chapman Publishing.

Storey, D.J. 1994: *Understanding the Small Business Sector.* London: Routledge.

Storey, D.J. & Johnson, 1987: *Job Generation and Labour Market Change.* London: Macmillan Press.

Storey, D.J. & Johnson, S. 1987a: *Are Small Firms the Answer to Unemployment.* London: Employment Institute.

Storey, J. 1992: 'Human resource management in the public sector'. In G. Salaman, S. Cameron, H. Hamblin, P. Iles, C. Mabey & K. Thompson (eds.) *Human Resource Strategies.* London: Sage.

Sweeney, P. 1990: *The Politics of Public Enterprise and Privatisation.* Dublin: Tomar Publishing Ltd.

Szarka, J. 1989: 'Networking and Small Firms', *International Small Business Journal,* 8: 2, pp. 10-22.

Task Force on Small Business 1994, Dublin: Stationery Office.

Taylor, G. 1993: 'In Search of the Elusive Entrepreneur'. *Irish Political Studies,* Vol. 8, pp. 89-103.

Telesis Consultancy Group, 1982: *A Review of Industrial Policy,* National Economic and Social Council Report No. 64. Dublin: NESC.

The Sunday Business Post, February 1997.

Thompson, A. 1995: 'Customizing the public for health care: What's in a label?'. In I. Kirkpatrick & M. Martinez Lucio (eds.) *The Politics of Quality in the Public Sector.* London: Routledge.

Thompson, G. 1990: *The Political Economy of the New Right.* London: Pinter Publishers.

Thompson, G. 1992: 'The evolution of the managed economy in Europe', *Economy and Society,* 21: 2, pp. 129-151.

Thompson, P. & McHugh, D. 1995: *Work Organisations: A Critical Introduction,* second edition. London: Macmillan Business.

Thrift, N. 1999: 'Capitalism's Cultural Turn'. In L. Ray & A. Sayer (eds.), *Culture and Economy After the Cultural Turn.* London: Sage.

Trigilia, C. 1992: 'Italian industrial districts: Neither myth nor interlude'. In F. Pyke & W. Sengenberger (eds.), *Industrial Districts and Local Economic Regeneration.* Geneva: International Institute for Labour Studies.

Veljanovski, C. 1987: *Selling the State: Privatisation in Britain.* London: Weidenfeld and Nicolson.

Vickers, J. & Yarrow, G. 1988: *Privatization: An Economic Analysis.* London: MIT Press.

Wallerstein, I. 1990: 'Culture as the Ideological Battleground of the Modern World-System'. In M. Featherstone (ed.) *Global Culture.* London: Sage.

Walsh, K. 1994: 'Citizens, charters and contracts'. In R. Keat, N. Whiteley & N. Abercrombie (eds.) *The Authority of the Consumer.* London: Routledge.

Watson, J. & Everett, J. 1999: 'Small Business Failure Rates: Choice of Definition and Industry Effects', *International Small Business Journal,* 17:
2, pp. 31-45.

Watson, T. 1995: 'Entrepreneurship and Professional Management: A Fatal
Distinction', *International Small Business Journal,* 13: 2, pp. 34-46.

Watson, T. & Harris, P. 1999: *The Emergent Manager.* London: Sage.

Weiss, L. 1988: *Creating Capitalism: The State and Small Business Since
1945.* Oxford: Basil Blackwell.

Westhead, P. & Storey, D. 1996: 'Management Training and Small Firm Performance: Why is the Link So Weak?', *International Small Business
Journal,* 14: 4, pp. 13-24.

Whitley, R. 1992: 'Societies, Firms and Markets: The Social Structuring of
Business Systems'. In R. Whitley (ed.), *European Business Systems:
Firms and Markets in their National Contexts.* London: Sage.

Wickham, P. 1998: *Strategic Entrepreneurship.* London: Pitman Publishing.

Wigley, J. & Lipman, C. 1992: *The Enterprise Economy.* London: The
Macmillan Press.

Willmott, H. 1993: 'Strength is Ignorance; Slavery is Freedom: Managing
Culture in Modern Organizations'. *Journal of Management Studies,* 30:
4, pp. 515-552.

Wood, S.J. 1989: 'New Wave Management?'. *Work, Employment & Society,*
3: 4, pp. 379-402.

Wright, V. 1994: 'Industrial privatization in Western Europe: pressures, problems and

paradoxes'. In V. Wright (ed.) *Privatization in Western Europe: Pressures,
Problems and Paradoxes.* London: Pinter Publishers.

Zbaracki, M.J. 1998: 'The Rhetoric and Reality of Total Quality Management', *Administrative Science Quarterly,* 43, pp. 602-636.

Index